EVER FAITHFUL

A 365-Day Devotional

DAVID JEREMIAH

THOMAS NELSON

Since 1798

January

*Therefore know that the LORD your God, He
is God, the faithful God who keeps covenant
and mercy for a thousand generations with those
who love Him and keep His commandments.*

DEUTERONOMY 7:9

HE WATCHES

The eyes of the LORD are in every place, keeping watch on the evil and the good.

PROVERBS 15:3

As we welcome a new year, Proverbs 15 is a very helpful chapter to turn to. Every verse is applicable to our daily life. It begins with the ever-relevant advice: "A soft answer turns away wrath." Verse 2 counsels us to speak wisely about the state of our lives and the world. Verse 3 reminds us that the Lord observes all our actions and reactions. His eyes are always open, watching both the good and the evil.

Those who don't know the Lord never pause to think that God is observing them like bees in a glass hive, aware of all they say, think, do, and plan. Those of us who *do* know and love Him are grateful we have someone watching over us.

In 1926, George and Ira Gershwin wrote a popular song entitled "Someone to Watch over Me." How wonderful to know we have someone watching over us every moment of the year. As Psalm 145:20 says, "The LORD watches over all who love him" (NIV). Great is His faithfulness to us!

SUCCESS—GOD'S WAY

*"I have glorified You on the earth. I have finished
the work which You have given Me to do."*

JOHN 17:4

*S*uccess," said General George S. Patton, "is how high you bounce when you hit bottom." That's not a bad definition, but here's a better one: Success is faithfully tackling and accomplishing the work God gives us day by day. In biblical terms, success has nothing to do with wealth, position, power, respect, or awards. God promises to grant us success in life, but He views success as finishing the work He has assigned us. Colossians 4:17 says, "Say to Archippus, 'Take heed to the ministry which you have received in the Lord, that you may fulfill it.'"

The Bible tells us to persevere in obedience: "Be careful to obey all the law my servant Moses gave you . . . that you may be successful wherever you go. Keep this Book . . . meditate on it day and night, so that you may be careful to do everything written in it. Then you will be prosperous and successful" (Joshua 1:7–8 NIV).

Don't worry about failure; just be faithful in your Christian walk and work. That's SUCCESS in capital letters.

TRUE TO THE WORD

"And you shall know the truth, and the truth shall make you free."
JOHN 8:32

hristians are often questioned about their faith. It happened in the first century as well as in our day, which is why the apostle Peter encouraged believers to "be ready to give a defense to everyone who asks you for a reason for the hope that is in you" (1 Peter 3:15). But what if you aren't sure? What if you don't know an answer to a question? You will never go wrong by simply saying what the Word says—the living *and* written Word of God.

Jesus called Himself "the truth" (John 14:6) and "He who is true" (Revelation 3:7). Therefore, saying what Jesus said is to say what is true. A Christian will never go wrong by agreeing with Jesus. But Jesus also called God's Word "the truth." He knew that the psalmist had written, "The entirety of Your word is truth" (Psalm 119:160), and he borrowed those words in His prayer to the Father: "Sanctify them by Your truth. Your word is truth" (John 17:17). So Jesus called Himself the truth and He called the Word of God the truth. Jesus was the human embodiment of the eternal truth of God.

If you want to speak the truth, quoting Jesus and the Bible is the best place to begin. If what we say departs from those two sources, we have departed from the truth.

SOMETHING TO LOOK FORWARD TO

Behold, He is coming with the clouds, and every eye will see Him, even they who pierced Him.

REVELATION 1:7

*W*hat are you looking forward to? An upcoming trip? The end of a medical treatment? A visit with your children? A new car? The birth of a child?

A sense of anticipation is vital for mental health, and that's why the Bible ends with the book of Revelation. Without Revelation, the Bible would have no ending. Or rather, it would end with the book of Jude, which is a wonderful book about contending for the faith. But it's not a book that heralds God's future. It doesn't leave us with descriptions of the new heavens and new earth. It doesn't end with the city whose builder and maker is God.

In times like these, the swift return of Christ fuels our anticipation of coming events—and we're living in days when we need all the reassurance we can find. Peter said, "Therefore, beloved, looking forward to these things, be diligent" (2 Peter 3:14).

Don't live in the past, and don't become so bogged down with present burdens that you forget your future glory. Things are going to get better—much better! Jesus is coming! Let's look forward to that day!

LIFTING UP CHRIST

"And I, if I am lifted up from the earth, will draw all peoples to Myself."
JOHN 12:32

reachers stand on platforms; flags are raised to the top of poles; signs are put high up on billboards. Raising something high makes it visible to more people and gives it a sense of importance. That's why God told Moses to make a serpent out of bronze, set it on a pole, and raise it up so the Israelites could see it. God had punished their sin by allowing serpents into their camp, and Moses' bronze serpent became a source of deliverance for them when they gazed on it and believed (Numbers 21:4–9).

Knowing the Jews would grasp the metaphor immediately, Jesus said that He would be "lifted up" and become a source of salvation to all who looked to Him (John 3:14–15; 12:32). By "lifted up," He was referring to the Roman cross that lay ahead of Him. His words were prophetic—His death on a cross has drawn millions to Him for two thousand years. We continue to lift up Christ today in the Lord's Supper, "[proclaiming] the Lord's death till He comes" (1 Corinthians 11:26). We also lift Him up as we praise Him for His blessings in our lives.

Our lives should continually point the world to Jesus Christ—lifting Him up for all to see and be saved.

BRAGGING RIGHTS

"But let him who glories glory in this, that he understands and knows Me, that I am the LORD, exercising lovingkindness, judgment, and righteousness in the earth."

JEREMIAH 9:24

s Christians, we have bragging rights. We have something to boast about. We have something to be proud of, to be thankful for, and to glory in. We may never be music superstars or cultural icons. Fame and fortune may not come our way. But we are sons and daughters of God, and we can boast of our relationship with Jesus Christ.

The New Living Translation renders Jeremiah 9:23–24 like this: "Don't let the wise boast in their wisdom, or the powerful boast in their power, or the rich boast in their riches. But those who wish to boast should boast in this alone: that they truly know me and understand that I am the LORD."

The apostle Paul said something similar in Galatians 6:14: "But God forbid that I should boast except in the cross of our Lord Jesus Christ."

Lasting inner satisfaction doesn't come from the externals of life—education, wealth, and power. It comes from a personal relationship with God through Jesus Christ, and with the kind of wonderful lifestyle we develop as He reforms, remolds, and renovates our lives for His glory.

Boast today—of Him!

Be Still

"In returning and rest you shall be saved; in quietness
and confidence shall be your strength."
Isaiah 30:15

Psychologists are warning we're losing some basic skills of life by our reliance on mobile devices. People no longer add or subtract; they use the calculators on their phones. We no longer type or use keyboards; we punch icons with our thumbs. We don't worry about memorizing anything; our devices have become our brains. We don't even think as much because we plug in our earphones and listen to podcasts and music.

Those may be valid concerns, but they pale beside the danger of losing the basic skill of walking with God. For all our electronics, nothing can replace the simple art of meditation and prayer, of faith and trust, of quietness and confidence. As we contemplate God's law and manifest His holiness, we preserve the character of His creation. We prevent the deterioration of human society, and we preserve our culture from moral collapse.

No matter how modern our world, the time-tested habits of prayer, meditation, faith, trust, and obedience will never be replaced. The twenty-first century needs salt and light as much as the first century did; perhaps even more. So, keep your phone, but unplug it long enough to be still and know that He is God.

STRENGTH TRAINING

But David strengthened himself in the LORD his God.

1 SAMUEL 30:6

*I*f you feel weary or weak, think of these Bible verses on the subject of strength. Choose one to commit to memory, and ask God to use it to impart strength to your fainting heart.

"Your sandals shall be iron and bronze; as your days, so shall your strength be" (Deuteronomy 33:25). "Seek the LORD and His strength; seek His face evermore!" (1 Chronicles 16:11). "Do not sorrow, for the joy of the LORD is your strength" (Nehemiah 8:10). "The LORD is the strength of my life. . . . Wait on the LORD; be of good courage, and He shall strengthen your heart" (Psalm 27:1, 14). "The LORD will give strength to His people; the LORD will bless His people with peace" (Psalm 29:11). "My flesh and my heart fail; but God is the strength of my heart and my portion forever" (Psalm 73:26). "Be strengthened with might through His Spirit in the inner man" (Ephesians 3:16). "I can do all things through Christ who strengthens me" (Philippians 4:13).

When our strength is exhausted, His is undiminished. The supply of His strength will equal the length of your days, and you can lean on His words and fortify yourself in His strength today.

The Gift of Time

See then that you walk circumspectly, not as fools but as
wise, redeeming the time, because the days are evil.
EPHESIANS 5:15–16

lmost everything in life is "stoppable." Even gravity can be suspended temporarily. But one part of life cannot be stopped by us. And that is TIME. Right now, as you read these words, time is marching on. But it doesn't march without a purpose. Time marches toward the consummation of God's redemptive plan for planet Earth and its inhabitants.

The apostle Paul didn't advise the Ephesians to redeem the time just so they would be busy. It was because he knew that the kingdom of darkness is always at work to stop the advancement of God's kingdom. His words are a reminder that Satan never stops working *against* God and that we should never stop working *for* God. But there is another reason: stewardship. Like everything we have—life, breath, material goods, salvation, abilities—time is a gift from God. Our responsibility as stewards (managers) of God is to use time in the way the Owner of time wants it used.

Consider today: The next twenty-four hours belong to God. They have been given to you as a gift. Be sure to use this day in a conscious manner, consistent with God's desires.

A TRUE FRIEND

A man of too many friends comes to ruin, but there
is a friend who sticks closer than a brother.

PROVERBS 18:24 NASB

*S*ocial media has redefined the concept of a "friend." In the early days of the most prominent social media platform, people accumulated "friends" by the hundreds. Often those "friends" were people they barely knew—an acquaintance of an actual friend or a long-lost childhood playmate. Yet they were called "friends." Participants soon realized what psychologists have said: no one can manage more than a half dozen actual friendships.

True friendships take time, part of which is spent recovering from the disappointments that come with all human relationships. Maybe that's why Solomon wrote that having lots of friends is dangerous but having "a friend who sticks closer than a brother" is a good thing. Note, "friend" (singular), not "friends." It's rare to find a friend who is there through thick and thin *and* who will encourage us in our walk with Christ. That is, a friend like Jesus, who was a friend to His disciples (John 15:14–15).

First, invest in your friendship with Jesus. Second, if you have a friend like Jesus, invest in that friendship as well. The best way to find such a friend is to be that kind of friend yourself.

A MERRY HEART

A merry heart makes a cheerful countenance, but
by sorrow of the heart the spirit is broken.

PROVERBS 15:13

fter Richard Norris was badly disfigured by a gunshot wound in 1997, he remained hidden at his parents' home for years. They covered the mirrors to keep him from glimpsing his face. But a team of doctors changed that by performing a "face transplant." Using medical advancements, the physicians gave Richard a new countenance. In 2014, his transformational story was featured in a major magazine.

While Richard's story is unusually dramatic, there's a sense in which we all need a new countenance. Study the faces of people you meet every day. Steal a quick glance at your own face as you pass a mirror or reflective window. How stressed and grim we look! Our emotions inexorably flash through the forty-three muscles in our face, and we communicate our feelings through our eyes, our brows, and the set of our mouths. One smile can light up a room; one frown can darken a day.

The Bible tells us a merry heart makes a cheerful countenance. Rejoice in the Lord today, and let the joy of Jesus shine through.

ONE LIGHT AT A TIME

For you were once darkness, but now you are light
in the Lord. Walk as children of light.

EPHESIANS 5:8

*I*magine walking into a pitch-dark room—no windows, no lamps, no shadows, no light of any kind. You light a single candle and hold it over your head. When your eyes adjust, you can see a bit of what's in the room. Now imagine that same room with five people with candles—the overall light is brighter. Then imagine ten people with candles, then twenty-five, then fifty. At some point the darkness is overcome by the light.

Think of that room as this spiritually dark world (Colossians 1:13). Being born into this world is like walking into that dark room. Your candle is lit when you receive and believe the Gospel. Even a tiny bit of light dispels some of the darkness. Then you share the Gospel—the candles of others are lit—and more and more darkness is driven out. Every time the Gospel is shared, Satan's kingdom of darkness is threatened. When the Gospel is embraced, Satan's influence and dominion (1 John 5:19) is weakened.

Paul wrote that we were once darkness but are now light "in the Lord." Our responsibility is to invade Satan's kingdom with the light of the glory of God.

HOPE IN THE LORD

For the Lord Himself will descend from heaven with a shout, with the voice of an archangel, and with the trumpet of God. And the dead in Christ will rise first.

1 THESSALONIANS 4:16

Anyone standing by the graveside of a departed loved one or friend considers the question that arises: What do I believe about this event called death? Even knowledgeable Christians have to defend themselves against waves of sadness and longing by remembering the promises of Jesus Christ concerning faith and eternal life. Those promises—promises based on the Resurrection—give the Christian renewed hope that is sometimes clouded by grief.

Job asked the same question: "If a man dies, shall he live again?" (Job 14:14). And Jesus answered, straight to the point: "He who believes in Me, though he may die, he shall live" (John 11:25). But the new, first-century believers living in far-flung places didn't have Jesus' words at hand, so they were often concerned about death. Paul wrote to the church in Thessalonica to assure them that when Jesus appears, "the dead in Christ will rise first" (1 Thessalonians 4:16).

Christ was the firstfruits from the grave; we are the harvest to follow (1 Corinthians 15:20). The grave of those who die in Christ is a place of hope.

INSEPARABLE

"Have I not commanded you? Be strong and of good courage; do not be afraid, nor be dismayed, for the LORD *your God is with you wherever you go."*

JOSHUA 1:9

s Adam and Eve looked back to the Garden of Eden, their physical removal from the garden was a visual reminder of their break in their relationship with God. Despite their dismal circumstances, God had a different ending in mind. He did not forsake His creation.

God's continued affection for us is revealed through His presence. He heard Jonah's prayer from the belly of the fish. He sustained David as he waited to become king while being ruthlessly pursued by King Saul. And He positioned Queen Esther to save His people from annihilation.

The God of the Garden became the God of Gethsemane, sacrificing everything for our salvation. Jesus does not run or recoil from our weakness, pain, or brokenness. He took our sin upon Himself and beckons us to come to Him. Even in the midst of our darkest days, God is with us. Nothing can separate us from Him and His love. We are inseparable!

THE TIME OF LIFE

"Is anything too hard for the LORD? At the appointed time I will return to you, according to the time of life, and Sarah shall have a son."
GENESIS 18:14

t the beginning of the twentieth century, women began wearing wristwatches, but not men. World War I changed that, for it's hard to use a pocket watch in a battle zone. Now, a hundred years later, our wristwatches have become small computers giving us total access to all our electronic needs.

Still, for the Christian, our best sense of timing isn't found on our wrists but on our knees. In Genesis 18, the Lord appeared to Abraham, promising a son to be heir of God's covenant. This wasn't something God intended to do immediately, but "at the appointed time." Who set the time? The Lord! He had His own schedule; the timetable was His; and things happened according to His agenda. To Abraham and Sarah, they were so old that Sarah laughed at it. But the Lord's clock never missed a beat. He had His appointed times.

Perhaps you're looking at your wristwatch, wondering why God isn't moving more quickly. But He knows what He's doing. Stop looking at your wrist, fall on your knees, and trust Him for His perfect sense of timing.

POVERTY AND PEOPLE

Your life should be free from the love of money. Be satisfied with what you have . . . The Lord is my helper; I will not be afraid. What can man do to me?

HEBREWS 13:5–6 HCSB

It seems there is no lack of things to worry about these days. Too often fear is not far from our hearts. Two particular things frequently trouble us—money and people. Many of our fears are bound up in those two commodities. Do you ever worry about *running out of* money? What about *running into* people?

Notice how Hebrews 13:5–6 covers both of those concerns. These verses tell us that because of the Lord's ever-present care, we shouldn't waste our time worrying about either one. We shouldn't covet money, for God will provide. We shouldn't fear men, for God will protect.

Read it again from the New King James Version: "Let your conduct be without covetousness; be content with such things as you have. For He Himself has said, 'I will never leave you nor forsake you.' So we may boldly say: 'The LORD is my helper; I will not fear. What can man do to me?'"

The Lord is our helper. Trust Him to provide and to protect.

January 17

PRAISING GOD FOR MIRACLES

My help comes from the LORD, who made heaven and earth.
PSALM 121:2

Among the stories connected to the memory of Francis of Assisi is this one: One day Francis gathered his friends at a remote monastery in central Italy. When he asked them about their journeys, each brother had an exciting tale to report. One had been riding his mule across a narrow bridge that spanned a deep gorge. When the mule bolted, the man was nearly thrown into the ravine. He praised God he hadn't been killed.

Another brother had nearly drowned fording a river, but he said, "God in His grace provided a tree that had fallen across the water. I was able to grasp a branch and pull myself to safety." Other brothers expressed similar stories of God's protection. Then someone asked Francis about his trip. "I experienced the greatest miracle of all," said the famous friar. "I had a smooth, pleasant, and uneventful journey."

We should always remember to praise God for His miracles in whatever form they come. He blesses, heals, rescues, delivers, helps, and uplifts more times every day than we can count. We should always be saying, "Thank You, Lord!"

SATAN'S GOAL

But stretch out Your hand now, and touch [Job's] bone and
his flesh, and he will surely curse You to Your face!

JOB 2:5

What is best known about Job is that Satan attacked the man, his children, and his livelihood. Job and his wife survived; everything else was gone. What is less well-known is *why* Job was the target of Satan's attack. And therein lies the key to understanding spiritual warfare.

Job was a righteous man who "feared God and shunned evil" (Job 1:1). Satan targeted Job because he wanted to prove to God that righteous people will curse God when they are in difficulty. Satan wanted to get Job to change his attitude about God. He wanted Job to take his wife's advice and "curse God" (Job 2:9) because of what God allowed to happen. God had confidence in Job, however, and it was well-founded. Job didn't curse God. Instead he set out on a quest to understand what God was doing in his life. Satan's goal in spiritual warfare is not just to hurt us. His goal is to persuade us, because of our pain, to "curse God" and to stop believing in the goodness of God.

If you are hurting today, remember Job's story. Don't let your circumstances change your faith in God. Instead, resist the devil and submit to God's plan (James 4:7).

EXCEPTION TO THE RULE

The first of all the commandments is: "Hear, O Israel, the LORD our God, the LORD is one. And you shall love the LORD your God with all your heart, with all your soul, with all your mind, and with all your strength."
MARK 12:29–30

Carl J. Printz, Norway's consul to Canada during World War II, lived a long life and left a deep legacy. When he was ninety-nine years old, Printz was interviewed on television. The journalist asked, "Give us the rule you have followed during your long and useful life, the rule which has most influenced your life and molded your character." Printz replied, "I would mention one definite rule—one must be temperate in all things." But he paused and added, "Perhaps I should say temperate in all things except one—fulfilling the commandment to love God with all your heart, soul, and mind and your neighbor as yourself. These are the only things we can rightly do with excess."

He's right. The Bible tells us to offer ourselves as living sacrifices to the Lord and to serve Him with passionate zeal. We can't love God too much, but we can love Him better. Rather than being conformed to the world, let's be transformed by the renewing of our minds. Let's be temperate in all things this year—except in loving God with all that's within us.

A FIRM FOUNDATION

Your wife shall be like a fruitful vine in the very heart of your house, your children like olive plants all around your table. Behold, thus shall the man be blessed who fears the LORD.

PSALM 128:3–4

The question is often asked, "Why do bad things happen to good people?" A corollary is, "Why do godly parents sometimes have ungodly children?" When parents do their best to fear the Lord and raise their children with admonition and nurture in Him, and children still go astray, it can be a heartbreaking experience.

The Bible doesn't promise that godly parents will never have ungodly children any more than it promises that a godly Christian will never sin. The Old Testament covenant promised the Israelites that the starting place for success in life begins with fearing the Lord (Deuteronomy 28:1–14; Proverbs 1:7; 9:10). We should never think that *not* fearing the Lord is the path to blessing. If we want to create a godly family, we should begin by fearing the Lord (Psalm 128:1), lest we labor in vain (Psalm 127:1). That is the only direction the Bible offers, even when things don't go as prayed for.

Never waver from your lifelong commitment to honor the Lord. Your firm foundation is the fear of the Lord.

WHATEVER YOU DO

And whatever you do, do it heartily, as to the Lord and not to men.
COLOSSIANS 3:23

*O*ne of the thorniest issues to arise in the first-century Christian church came from that hotbed of controversies, Corinth. Because Corinth was a seat of pagan worship and idolatry, much of the meat that found its way into the local markets was meat that was left over from pagan sacrificial and worship rituals. And the question arose: Should Christians eat meat that had been sacrificed to idols?

Long story short (1 Corinthians 10:14–32), Paul said not to participate in pagan feasts; but once the meat was removed from the pagan temple and sold in the market, its religious taint was lost and it was acceptable to eat. But more importantly, he said that each Christian's conscience was the final arbiter, and no one should criticize another for his or her decision. Some may choose to eat; others may choose not to. Then Paul said the most important thing: "Therefore, whether you eat or drink, *or whatever you do*, do all to the glory of God" (verse 31, italics added). *Everything* in life is to be done with a view toward pleasing God.

Whatever you have planned to do today, consider how it might be done heartily for the Lord in a way that glorifies Him.

DELIGHT IN THE LORD

Make me walk in the path of Your commandments, for I delight in it.
PSALM 119:35

*W*e don't often hear it said, "God happy you!" But it would be entirely appropriate. "God bless you!" could accurately be translated, "May God grant you happiness, joy, favor, and spiritual prosperity!" The so-called Beatitudes of Jesus (Matthew 5:2–11) are normally rendered, "Blessed are those who . . ." but could just as easily be translated, "Happy are those who . . ."

"Blessed is" or "Blessed are" was a common Old Testament expression, one of the most well-known being from Psalm 1: "Blessed is the man who" avoids the way of the ungodly. Instead, "his delight is in the law of the LORD, and in His law he meditates day and night" (verses 1–2). Finding delight, prosperity, favor, and happiness by walking according to God's statutes is an underlying theme of both the Old (Joshua 1:7–8; Psalm 119) and New Testaments (2 Timothy 3:16; 2 Peter 1:4).

Rather than seeking happiness in the temporary things of this world, let your daily delight be in the Word of God: "The grass withers, the flower fades, but the word of our God stands forever" (Isaiah 40:8). The things that offer a momentary source of delight cannot compare with true, eternal joy.

OUR ADVOCATE

And they stoned Stephen as he was calling on God and saying, "Lord Jesus, receive my spirit."
ACTS 7:59

*I*n the fullest version (1563 edition) of his work (*Foxe's Book of Martyrs*), John Foxe chronicled, in more than twenty-three hundred pages, the lives of Christians who were persecuted, and often martyred, in England and Scotland during the sixteenth-century Protestant Reformation.

Though it is true that many faithful ones lost their lives, something else is true: God defended each one who died in true faith. Which raises a question: If God defended them, why did they die? Which begs an answer to this question: What does it mean to be defended by God? The story of Stephen in Acts 7 gives insight. When Stephen stood firm for Christ in the face of Jewish persecution in Jerusalem, he was stoned. But just before the stones began to fly, he had a vision of Jesus in heaven, standing at the right hand of God, waiting to receive Stephen's spirit. Normally, Jesus is pictured *seated* at the right hand of God (Ephesians 1:20; Hebrews 8:1). But Jesus stood in honor of Stephen's courage and commitment.

There is something more important than life, and that is *eternal* life. God defends the eternal life of all who, in true faith, stand for Him.

CAUSE AND EFFECT

"A good man out of the good treasure of his heart brings forth good things, and an evil man out of the evil treasure brings forth evil things."

MATTHEW 12:35

There is a predictable principle at work in life—you get what you put into it. You can't plant carrots and expect to harvest watermelon. You can't fill your piggy bank with pennies and expect a hundred-dollar bill to emerge. You may wish for results to magically appear, but the cause-and-effect principle remains.

Of course, there are exceptions. When a child puts his newly pulled tooth under his pillow, a coin appears in its place—as long as his parents don't forget. But the most important exception is Christ's gift to us. We surrender our sin and failure to God, and He replaces it with the flawless righteousness of Christ. God's commitment to us includes an eternal home and purpose for today. He delights in transforming us to bring forth good treasure. We become His lights, impacting and encouraging the people around us.

Submit yourself and your efforts to Him, and you will gain more than you could ever give.

Burdened

For the love of Christ compels us, because we judge thus: that if One died for all, then all died; and He died for all, that those who live should live no longer for themselves, but for Him who died for them and rose again.
2 Corinthians 5:14–15

*J*ournalists often use the word *burden* in their headlines. They talk about tax burdens and the burden of health care, the burden of student debt, and how to ease the burden of our overcrowded prison system. The word *burden* comes from an old term for *load* or *weight*.

The Bible tells us to cast our burdens on the Lord (Psalm 55:22). But there's one burden God wants to cast on us—the burden to evangelize the world. Dr. Lee Roberson once said, "Some Christians have never had a real burden for souls. When they were saved, they had a temporary desire to see others converted. There was a brief concern for their families; then this concern was gone." In his book *Touching Heaven*, Roberson suggests rekindling a burden for souls by getting a new glimpse of our Savior dying for us, reading our Bibles to see what God says about hell, praying for sinners by name, and learning how to share the Gospel.[1]

Evangelizing begins when the love of Christ compels us to share the Gospel. It begins with a burden for the lost.

PILGRIM'S PROGRESS

These all died in faith, not having received the promises, but having seen them afar off were assured of them, embraced them and confessed that they were strangers and pilgrims on the earth.

HEBREWS 11:13

What's your favorite road trip? The Pacific Coast Highway is one of America's best drives. As is the forested Blue Ridge Parkway. Even old Route 66 has its charms. In Germany, try Route 500 through the Black Forest. Travelers in England enjoy trekking through the Cotswolds. There's a carefree feeling to spending a day on the road, finding overnight accommodations, and continuing the excursion the next day.

But there's no place like home.

As Christians, we are journeying through this world. It isn't our home, and our citizenship is in another land. Through Christ we hold a heavenly passport. When we become too attached to earthly possessions, it diminishes our sense of pilgrimage. When we become too distraught by earthly distresses, we lose the reality of being wayfaring strangers. As travelers, we're just passing through. It's a wonderful world full of sights to see and services to perform. God has a mission for us here. But there's no place like Home.

HUNGRY?

"Blessed are those who hunger and thirst for righteousness, for they shall be filled."
MATTHEW 5:6

One morning, in the fall of 2014, a homeowner in Rockland, Massachusetts, was awakened at 1:30 a.m. by sounds in his kitchen. After calling the police, he went to investigate himself. An intruder was cooking corn on the cob. The two men got into a scuffle, but police officers arrived in time to arrest the thief before anyone was hurt. What happened to the corn wasn't reported.

Everyone knows what it's like to be hungry. We have stomach pains, feel weak and famished, and crave our favorite foods. But how is our spiritual appetite? Do we ever feel spiritual hunger pains? Jesus told us we should be hungry and thirsty every day—that we should crave righteousness. But this might not come naturally; it's an acquired taste.

Like a child learning to like a new food, let's begin tasting what God desires for us. Turn away from sin; give up spiritual junk food. Start reading your Bible more, living it out, and practicing the Spirit-filled life. Soon you'll notice if you miss a day of conscious fellowship with the Lord. That's when you'll discover that a good spiritual appetite is a blessing.

God's Idea

*"It is not good that man should be alone; I will
make him a helper comparable to him."*

Genesis 2:18

he family is God's idea. In fact, it's His primary idea.
Civil government and the church also came from the
mind of God; but long before He created those institutions, God
thought of the family. In the very beginning, He looked at Adam
and said, "It is not good that man should be alone." He brought a
woman to him, and family life began.

Since the family is God's idea, it operates best when it follows
His patterns and operates under His lordship. Until Christ is the
center of our homes, all our attempts to improve our families will
end in frustration. Unless the Lord builds the home, we labor in
vain in building it.

Even in the easiest of times and best of circumstances, it's
hard to build a Christian home; but any attempt apart from the
lordship of Christ is doomed to failure. God loves you and wants to
be the Lord of all your moments, days, attitudes, and habits. When
He is Lord, it changes the atmospherics of the family. Problems
may not disappear overnight; but when Christ dwells under your
roof, He brings hope to the home and healing to the heart.

Forgotten, but Not Forgotten

Yet the chief butler did not remember Joseph, but forgot him.
GENESIS 40:23

After spending years in slavery and prison, Joseph finally found a possible way of escape—through the help of Pharaoh's butler, whose dream he had wisely interpreted. But the butler forgot him, and Joseph's hopes again faded. Still, he waited on the Lord. He had no choice; but no other choice could have been better for him. Taking the long view, God was planning a coming day when Joseph would be released, exalted, and mightily used to change human history.

Though forgotten by the butler, Joseph was not forgotten by the Lord.

John Piper wrote, "To wait! That means to pause and soberly consider our own inadequacy and the Lord's all-sufficiency and to seek counsel and help from the Lord. . . . The folly of not waiting for God is that we forfeit the blessing of having God work for us. The evil of not waiting for God is that we oppose God's will to exalt Himself in mercy. God aims to exalt Himself by working for those who wait for Him."[2]

Wait on the LORD; be of good courage, and He shall strengthen your heart. (Psalm 27:14)

INTERCESSION

Now I beg you, brethren, through the Lord Jesus Christ, and through the love of the Spirit, that you strive together with me in prayers to God for me.

ROMANS 15:30

In the sentencing phase of a trial, the judge will often allow individuals to address the court to influence the judge's decision about the sentence. Some are there to ask for a harsh sentence. But others are there out of love. They understand the need for justice, but they also are there to ask for mercy and fairness.

Those are complicated situations, but unconditional love will always try to intercede. Think of Jesus on the cross. He was totally innocent, His killers totally guilty. Yet, out of love for His enemies, He interceded; He asked God to forgive them. But intercession is about more than forgiveness. It is about asking God to do what we can't. Paul asked the Roman church to pray "through the love of the Spirit" for his protection when he traveled to Jerusalem. The church in Rome couldn't protect Paul themselves, but out of love they prayed that God would protect the great apostle.

There are many ways to express love to others. Perhaps the most sacrificial way is to pray for God to bless, protect, and provide for those we love.

A Picture of Sin

Take note, you have sinned against the LORD;
and be sure your sin will find you out.

Numbers 32:23

A man in Palm Beach County, Florida, was arrested for theft, and he unwittingly provided the evidence. He might have gotten away with it except he posted selfies of himself with the loot on his Instagram page. Officials searched his house and found a quarter-million dollars' worth of stolen plunder. As they filled out the arrest warrant, they asked the man his occupation. He replied, "Thief."

It's strange when we're proud of the things we should be ashamed of—and ashamed of the things we should boast about. The Bible tells us to boast in the Lord, but to avoid the appearance of evil. Even as fully forgiven, born-again Christians, we can become proud of some evil habit in our lives. And, sad to say, we can be ashamed of serving Jesus. That's a terrible condition.

Although we enjoy God's grace here on earth, we need to remember He is just in all His dealings with us, and we should never take His grace for granted. Listen instead to 2 Corinthians 7:1: "Therefore, having these promises, beloved, let us cleanse ourselves from all filthiness of the flesh and spirit, perfecting holiness in the fear of God."

February

*Oh, love the L*ORD*, all you His saints!*
*For the L*ORD *preserves the faithful,*
And fully repays the proud person.

PSALM 31:23

Praying for Unity

These all continued with one accord in prayer and supplication, with the women and Mary the mother of Jesus, and with His brothers.

Acts 1:14

here was a time when there was only one Christian church. It was the church in Jerusalem, and immediately after Christ's ascension, it appears to have had 120 members (Acts 1:15). By contrast, today there are more than 40,000 Christian denominations in the world.

The most striking difference between the first church and today's worldwide church is that they were all of "one accord in prayer" (Acts 1:14). Jesus had told them to wait in Jerusalem for the gift of the Holy Spirit, so that was likely the focus of their prayer (Acts 1:4). But after the Spirit came at Pentecost, their unity in prayer continued as they chose a replacement for Judas Iscariot and chose men to assist the apostles in serving the church (Acts 1:24–25; 6:1–6). Jesus had made unity among His followers a matter for His own prayer (John 17:20–21).

It is to be expected that human beings, even Christians, will differ in their ideas. But the goal of unity through prayer is always the highest priority. If there is "one body and one Spirit" (and there is—Ephesians 4:4), unity should be the result.

THE GIFT OF WORK

And out of the ground the LORD *God made every tree
grow that is pleasant to the sight and good for food.*

GENESIS 2:9

here is a stark difference between Genesis 2 and Genesis 3—but there is also an underlying and uniting theme. The difference is in how man was to procure what he needed to live on and provide for himself and his family. In Genesis 2, before sin entered the world, mankind was given a lush, abundant environment in which to live. Everything man needed was there for the taking. But in Genesis 3, after man's sin, man would be forced to work by "the sweat of [his] face" to coax out of the ground what he needed (verse 19).

But here's what unites the two different situations: God's provision was present in both. In Eden, God provided abundantly from an earth devoid of sin. Outside of Eden, the earth was still God's provision, but it was changed. A cursed earth (Genesis 3:17) would yield its resources only by the hardest of labor. Yet the ability to secure what was needed was the gift of God in both eras.

The work you do today may be difficult and tiring, but we should still thank God for it because it is His gift to us—the ability to provide for our needs. Thank Him today for that gift and pray for the ability to work "as to the Lord" (Colossians 3:23).

WHY WE WORK

For by grace you have been saved through faith, and that not of
yourselves; it is the gift of God, not of works, lest anyone should boast.
EPHESIANS 2:8–9

ot all employers are happy with a generation of young
employees who were raised receiving "participation
trophies" for being on an athletic team. Older generations were
taught that showing up and doing one's best was normal—a
responsibility not deserving of a trophy.

There is a parallel in the Christian life. There are things
expected of us as Christians. But we do not receive the "prize"
of salvation for doing those works. Scripture makes abundantly
clear that we are saved "by grace . . . through faith," not by works.
Young athletes can take pride in the trophies they win for hard-
fought victories. But if we were awarded the prize of salvation
for our works, our pride would be a problem. There is only one
"work" that has ever earned salvation—the death of Christ out of
obedience to the Father. But His death did not earn *His* salvation;
He didn't need to be saved. Instead, His death earned salvation
for us. And our works are an imitation of His—our gratitude for
His obedience.

Work hard for Christ! But work for the right reason—as a
"Thank You" for the gift you have received by faith.

WHAT IS POSSIBLE?

Jesus said to him, "If you can believe, all things
are possible to him who believes."

MARK 9:23

here is a part of the body of Christ that has adopted a slogan from the secular self-help movement: "If you can conceive it and believe it, you can achieve it!" If you can conceive of yourself as an astronaut or a star player in the NBA, and believe it with all your heart, are you likely to achieve such a goal? The answer for most adults is no.

What's good about the "name it and claim it" school is that it encourages us not to limit ourselves or God. What's wrong with this approach is that it misapplies the words of Jesus. For example, a corollary of Jesus' words in Mark 9:23 is that "all things are possible for [God]"—words Jesus spoke on the night of His arrest in the Garden of Gethsemane (Mark 14:36). Jesus believed it was possible for Him not to go to the cross, and He also believed it was possible for God to keep Him from that suffering. Yet He went to the cross anyway.

Our beliefs and possibilities have to be in line with the will of God. That's how Jesus lived His life and how He taught His disciples to live (John 5:30). When our lives are lived in obedience to God's will, nothing is impossible. Dream big—but dream biblically!

WILLING TO BE WILLING

"If anyone wills to do His will, he shall know concerning the doctrine, whether it is from God or whether I speak on My own authority."
JOHN 7:17

he book *Revive Us Again* includes the story of Ruth Sundquist, a Moody Bible Institute student in the 1940s who was attending a missionary conference at nearby Moody Memorial Church. The speaker challenged the students to come forward and offer themselves for missionary service, but Ruth didn't feel willing to go forward. The speaker then said, "If you aren't willing to go, ask the Lord to make you willing to go." Still Ruth hesitated. Then he said, "If you aren't willing to do that, ask Him to make you willing to be willing to pray that prayer."

Ruth said, "That's about where I had to start!"[1]

The Lord has a calling on our lives, and we'll discover His will as we trust and obey Him without reservation. Sometimes it's hard to say, "I'm willing." But perhaps, like Ruth Sundquist, you can start by saying, "Lord, I'm willing for You to make me willing to be willing."

Open your life to the fullness of God's plan for you—be willing to be willing.

WISE SPEECH

The heart of the righteous studies how to answer, but the mouth of the wicked pours forth evil.

PROVERBS 15:28

ccording to *A Dictionary of American Proverbs,* there are lots of variations to the rule "Think before you speak." One version says, "Think before you leap." Another says, "Think more and talk less." Another says, "Think twice and say nothing." And yet another says, "You can think what you like, but don't say it." [2]

However it's put, this is biblical advice. It's easy to open our mouths and let the words fly. We're living in a day when people talk without using the filters of wisdom. But wise people study how to answer. One of the best ways of doing this is to pray before speaking. This is what Nehemiah did. "Then the king said to me, 'What do you request?' So I prayed to the God of heaven. And I said to the king . . ." (Nehemiah 2:4–5).

Every child of God can develop a reputation for giving good advice. We can be people to whom others come for counsel. By God's grace, we can be respected for our quiet wisdom. But only if we learn to think—and to pray—before we speak.

LORD OF YOUR LIFE

*I know how to be abased, and I know how to abound.
Everywhere and in all things I have learned both to be full
and to be hungry, both to abound and to suffer need.*

PHILIPPIANS 4:12

ord is one of those words used so frequently in Christian conversation that it runs the risk of being used too casually. The Greek word, *kurios*, can be translated "master, owner," or "authority." However it is rendered, *lord* suggests the one who is in charge, the one whose word is the final authority. If the same person who is lord is also compassionate, loving, purposeful, and good, you have a combination that allows for total trust and contentment.

Paul had to learn this in his life: "I have learned . . ." (Philippians 4:12). But he didn't know it at the moment of his conversion, when Jesus said, "For I will show [Paul] how many things he must suffer for My name's sake" (Acts 9:16). Paul was sent out to suffer! And suffer he did (2 Corinthians 6, 11). But he learned to be at peace in his circumstances when he combined *Lord* with *loving*. If a loving master sent him into a difficult circumstance, Paul could be okay with that.

If you know Jesus as Lord, learn to trust His direction and plan for your life—day by day.

SPIRITUAL MENTOR

Now Joshua the son of Nun was full of the spirit of
wisdom, for Moses had laid his hands on him.

DEUTERONOMY 34:9

reg Rubar, a waiter at an Italian restaurant in Houston, served a particular couple many times over eight years. One day they left him an unusual tip—fifty $100 bills. Greg tried to return the money, but the two customers told him to take it and buy himself a car. It turned out they knew Greg had recently lost his car in a flood, and they wanted to help him in gratitude for his years of serving them.

If customers and acquaintances can be generous in expressing gratitude, shouldn't we seize every opportunity to thank those who have meant the most to us? That certainly includes our spiritual mentors. Someone prayed for you before you were saved. Someone—perhaps several—were instrumental in leading you to Christ. Someone taught you the Bible. Someone showed you how to pray. Someone guided you into personal ministry and taught you to serve.

Joshua was full of wisdom because Moses had laid his hands on him. Who has laid their hands on you? Have you ever thanked them for their influence? You don't have to buy them a car. Just a word of thanksgiving will do.

February 9

LITTLE CHILDREN

Then little children were brought to Him that He might put His hands on them and pray.

MATTHEW 19:13

very church should rejoice in life's mile markers, starting with birth, as we dedicate our children to the Lord. This is a biblical practice. In the Old Testament, Hannah brought her boy, Samuel, to the temple. There she dedicated him to the Lord, saying, "For this child I prayed, and the LORD has granted me my petition. . . . I also have lent him to the LORD; as long as he lives he shall be lent to the LORD" (1 Samuel 1:27–28).

In the New Testament, Joseph and Mary did the same. In Luke 2:22–32, they brought Jesus to the temple in Jerusalem to consecrate Him to the Lord.

When our Lord grew up and began His ministry, He was eager to bless the youngsters brought to Him. People even brought their infants and newborns to Jesus. "And He took them up in His arms, laid His hands on them, and blessed them" (Mark 10:16).

When we bring our children before the Lord in church and dedicate them to Him, we're doing the same. It's an important celebration; for how greatly our children need Jesus, even from birth!

WHO AM I?

What is man that You are mindful of him . . . ? For
You have made him a little lower than the angels, and
You have crowned him with glory and honor.

PSALM 8:4–5

here are only two ways we humans can posture ourselves. Either we're bent over like a question mark, or
we're straight as an exclamation point. It depends on our view
of God. Our lives only have meaning within the context of a
Creator. His life, love, holiness, and ultimate ends—these are the
things that give us hope and purpose. Reject God, and the answer
to "Who am I?" doesn't even require a single word. A simple
question mark will do. Without Him, we feel we're nothing but
momentary sparks that flicker in meaninglessness and die into
nothingness. There are no answers, only question marks.

When our view of God is true and biblical, we're as upright
as an exclamation point. We're made in God's image for His purposes, recipients of His peace and perpetual life through Jesus
Christ, who loved us and died for us. We stand firm with hope
and purpose.

We're only able to understand who we are when we understand the Creator. The secularized culture yields despair, but
our faith produces joy as we exclaim with Psalm 8: "O LORD, our
Lord, how excellent is Your name in all the earth!" (verse 9).

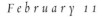

February 11

THE GOD WHO MADE US

O LORD, *our Lord, how excellent is Your name in all the earth!*
PSALM 8:9

*S*cientists are learning more and more about the lives of animals. Primates have been found to use tools, fish have demonstrated memory, and dogs have been trained to detect and point out human cancers. But there is no record of any members of the animal kingdom contemplating their origin or expressing appreciation for their existence and the blessings of nature.

Self-awareness and understanding separates man from the animal kingdoms. Even the psalmist, when contemplating the wonders of man's place in God's creation, noted that God created "the beasts of the field, the birds of the air, and the fish of the sea"—but makes no mention of those animals' understanding that fact (Psalm 8:7–8). Only humans are created in the image of God, with the intellectual capacity designed by God (Genesis 1:26–27). And our intellectual thought processes allow us to know that Someone beyond ourselves is responsible for our creation and sustenance.

Take time to read and meditate on Psalm 8, David's song of praise to the God who created him and us! Marvel with him at the works of God.

CHRIST IN US

For He shall grow up before Him as a tender plant, and as a root out of dry ground. He has no form or comeliness; and when we see Him, there is no beauty that we should desire Him.

ISAIAH 53:2

f you had lived in first-century Israel and crossed paths with Jesus in a market (before He became well-known), you would not have given Him a second glance. Outwardly, there was little or nothing about Jesus' external appearance that would have commended Him (Isaiah 53:2).

That wasn't true of all of Israel's kings. First Samuel 16:18 says that David, son of Jesse of Bethlehem, was a "fine-looking man" (NIV). The Hebrew word for "fine-looking" is the same word translated "beauty" when describing in Isaiah 53:2 what Jesus the Messiah lacked. David was fine-looking, but Jesus, apparently, was not. That's a comfort, because it indicates that external attributes are not the point. You can be beautiful, handsome, or plain in the world's sight, and God can use you all the same. Why? Because it is Christ *in us* that matters (Galatians 2:20).

Our self-worth comes from how we reflect Christ, not how we are reflected in the mirror. Our appearance should enhance the image of Christ as an appropriate frame enhances a priceless painting.

PRAY FOR PEACE

Pray for the peace of Jerusalem: "May they prosper who love you."
PSALM 122:6

hree times each year the men of Israel journeyed to Jerusalem to celebrate three feasts: Passover, Pentecost, and Tabernacles (Deuteronomy 16:16; Acts 2:1, 9–11). Most scholars believe the fifteen "Songs of Ascents"—Psalms 120–134—were sung by the pilgrims as they ascended to Jerusalem. Psalm 122 exhorts the faithful in Israel to "pray for the peace of Jerusalem." Jerusalem was the heart of Israel—the site of the temple, the center of Jewish worship. All the descendants of Abraham knew that Jerusalem, the place where God dwelt, was God's city of peace.

Should we continue to pray for the peace of Jerusalem today? For a host of reasons, yes! Perhaps the best reason is the same reason the ancient Israelites prayed for Jerusalem: They were descendants of Israel, bound by the covenants of God to His holy city. The New Testament teaches that those who have faith in God's salvation plans, whether Jew or Gentile, "are sons of Abraham" (Galatians 3:7). Jerusalem, the most embattled city on earth, is still very much in God's plans.

Pray for the peace of God's city and God's chosen people, who remain "the apple of His eye" (Zechariah 2:8).

LOVE IS . . .

*In this is love, not that we loved God, but that He loved us
and sent His Son to be the propitiation for our sins. Beloved,
if God so loved us, we also ought to love one another.*

1 JOHN 4:10–11

ove is an emotion that's hard to describe. It's an emotional longing for another person and a deep satisfaction when that love is reciprocated. It suffers intense anguish when it isn't.

Love is an attitude that operates more deeply than feelings.

Love is a supernatural virtue instilled in us by God. "The fruit of the Spirit is love . . ." (Galatians 5:22).

Love is an action. It manifests itself in selfless service. When we love others, we do things for them. "Whoever has this world's goods, and sees his brother in need, and shuts up his heart from him, how does the love of God abide in him?" (1 John 3:17).

Love is a choice. We can determine in our hearts to love even the unlovely. This comprehensive, inclusive quality of love can only be experienced by opening our lives to Calvary. When we receive God's love through Jesus Christ, it flows through us to others.

Just as God chose to love us, we must choose to love others, "for love is of God" (1 John 4:7). Today and every day, put love into practice.

PRECIOUS IN HIS SIGHT

My frame was not hidden from You, when I was made in secret,
and skillfully wrought in the lowest parts of the earth.
PSALM 139:15

onozygotic (identical) twins result when one fertilized egg divides to form two separate but "identical" embryos. Fraternal (dizygotic) twins are as different as any two siblings. But even in the case of identical twins, they are not totally identical—different fingerprints being an example. Several hundred genetic differences can occur in identical twins that may eventually manifest themselves in slight, but noticeable, ways.

In short, every human being is unique—including you! You are the only version of you God has ever made. The biblical writers understood and expressed this using prescientific language. David knew that he was "fearfully and wonderfully made" in his mother's womb (Psalm 139:13–14). Job knew that God had "shaped [him] and made [him]," and "molded [him] like clay" (Job 10:8–9 NIV). The knowledge that the God of the universe has known and loved us from the moment of conception puts to flight any of Satan's strategies to suggest that we are unloved or of no value.

Never doubt that you are unique and precious in God's sight. Just as He watches over the sparrow (Luke 12:6), He watches over you.

BAPTISM

"I believe that Jesus Christ is the Son of God." So he commanded
the chariot to stand still. And both Philip and the eunuch
went down into the water, and he baptized him.

ACTS 8:37–38

Just before Jesus returned to heaven, He told His disciples to preach His message to all the nations, "baptizing them in the name of the Father and of the Son and of the Holy Spirit" (Matthew 28:19). A few weeks later, thousands of people heard Peter's sermon about Jesus on the Day of Pentecost, and "those who gladly received his word were baptized" (Acts 2:41). When Philip took the Gospel to Samaria, many responded; "both men and women were baptized" (Acts 8:12). When he explained the Gospel to the Ethiopian eunuch, the man said, "What hinders me from being baptized?" (Acts 8:36). When Saul of Tarsus was saved, he was baptized as a public demonstration of his private decision (Acts 9:18). Throughout the book of Acts, the new Christians gave public testimony of their faith through the act of baptism.

In the New Testament, baptism isn't taken lightly. It provides an opportunity for Christians to testify to their faith before family, friends, and the world. It gives the Church an opportunity to celebrate the news of sinners being saved.

Have you been baptized? If not, why not?

THE GREAT ENCOURAGER

*"And the glory which You gave Me I have given them, that they may
be one just as We are one . . . and that the world may know that
You have sent Me, and have loved them as You have loved Me."*
JOHN 17:22–23

very parent has had the privilege of being a source of
encouragement to a discouraged child. When children's lives are going well, they seem to fuel themselves with
renewed energy. But when life hits a roadblock, they need someone to draw them close. And parents usually get the call.

That is true not just for our sons and daughters, but it was
true for the Son of God as well. There were times when Jesus
was appreciated and sought after—when feeding the multitudes
or making a triumphant entry into Jerusalem (Matthew 14; 21).
But there were other times when He heard jeers instead of cheers.
In those situations Jesus turned to His Father, the one Person
He knew would understand and confirm for Him that there was
purpose in His troubles. When Jesus' arrest was imminent, He
poured out His heart to the Father (John 17). Right before it happened, He was still praying (Matthew 26).

If you are experiencing more discouragement than encouragement today, do what Jesus did: turn to the Father, who loves
you.

A Stolen Bible

Blessed are those whose lawless deeds are
forgiven, and whose sins are covered.

Romans 4:7

*R*amona grew up in a troubled home. Her mother was a Christian, but her father was an abusive alcoholic. As a young adult, Ramona made many unwise choices, married multiple times, and descended into drug and alcohol abuse. One night at the Pagoda Hotel in Hawaii, she saw a Gideon Bible in one of the drawers, and she took it home with her. About two years later, she started reading it. "After reading it a while," she said, "it was like the words on the pages came to life and opened my eyes. God cleansed me of the anger and resentfulness. He set me free." Her life changed so dramatically that she forgave her father, cared for him in his latter days, and had the joy of leading him to Christ before his death.[3]

The grace of God is a shaft of light that can penetrate any darkness, illumine any heart, and brighten any life. God's arms are open to receive us always—regardless of where we've been or what we've done.

How blessed we are to find and receive the forgiveness of God!

Spirit Power

"But you shall receive power when the Holy Spirit has come upon you; and you shall be witnesses to Me in Jerusalem, and in all Judea and Samaria, and to the end of the earth."

Acts 1:8

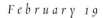enerally, the theory of causation seeks to explain the connection between one event (the cause) and another (the effect). There are causes and effects throughout life—even in the Christian life.

A clear cause and effect is seen in Acts 2. The effect was that the apostles of Christ suddenly began carrying out Christ's Great Commission to preach the Gospel and to teach and baptize new believers. And the cause? The descent of the Holy Spirit to fill the apostles. Before ascending into heaven, Christ connected the spiritual cause with the practical effect: "You shall receive power when the Holy Spirit has come . . . ; and you shall be witnesses to Me" (Acts 1:8). Before Pentecost, the disciples had been fearful and intimidated. After Pentecost, they were powerful witnesses. The cause of this transforming effect was the Holy Spirit.

Is it any wonder that Paul admonished the church in Ephesus to be filled with the Holy Spirit (Ephesians 5:18)? Create a clean vessel (1 John 1:9) for the Spirit to fill on a daily basis.

ACCORDING TO YOUR WORD

I am afflicted very much; revive me, O LORD, according to Your word.

PSALM 119:107

distinguished professor at an evangelical seminary was invited to speak to an adult Sunday school class at a large, mainstream church. When he began his lesson, he noticed none of the class members had a Bible. He asked if there were any Bibles available that could be used during the class. An extensive search was made, and finally, in a storage closet, a box of unused Bibles was discovered. Once this key tool for spiritual growth was distributed to the class, the professor proceeded to teach.

It has been said that a valid measure of a Christian's spiritual growth is the amount of dust that has settled on his Bible. The Bible is considered food for the follower of Christ—the daily source of nourishment, counsel, inspiration, correction, and hope (2 Timothy 3:16). The Word of God can do what no other book can: penetrate deeply into our hearts and souls and reveal our "thoughts and intents" (Hebrews 4:12). It can do that because it is "living and powerful," empowered by the Spirit who inspired it (2 Peter 1:21).

Don't let your Bible be hidden or dusty. Let God revive you according to His Word.

BY FAITH

By his faith [Noah] . . . condemned the world and became
heir of the righteousness that comes by faith.
HEBREWS 11:7 NIV

Since its founding in the 1770s, America was known as a Christian nation. Many pilgrims were Christians seeking religious freedom, many founding fathers were Christian, and many foundational documents expressed biblical principles. But beginning in the mid-twentieth century, America began to be known as a post-Christian nation as God was moved further toward the edge of public influence.

Is it harder to live as a Christian in a post-Christian nation than in a Christian one? Some would say so. But in truth, it doesn't matter where we live. The biblical requirement for faithfulness as the way to please God is the same. The need to remain faithful never changes. Noah proved it is possible to live in a corrupt culture and still please God. His "holy fear" (holy reverence) of God caused him to stand firm in faithfulness in spite of getting no support from the culture in which he lived.

You may feel unsupported in your nation, your home, your workplace—but you can remain faithful to the One who is always faithful to you (2 Timothy 2:13).

NARROW-MINDED?

I charge you therefore before God and the Lord Jesus Christ, who will judge the living and the dead at His appearing and His kingdom.

2 TIMOTHY 4:1

*S*ome say biblical Christianity is too narrow. If it is true (and it is), then it is indeed narrow compared with modern sensibilities. It helps to remind ourselves of what the Bible teaches about Jesus Christ, to make sure we remain committed to a biblical faith.

For instance, the Bible says that Jesus Christ will sit as judge of all humanity one day in the future (Romans 2:16; 2 Timothy 4:1). *Do you believe this?* Jesus Himself said that He is the way, the truth, and the life—that no one comes to the Father except through Him (John 14:6). *Do you believe this?* The Bible says that one day every knee will bow and every tongue confess that Jesus Christ is Lord (Philippians 2:10–11). *Do you believe this?* Jesus said that everyone who does not believe in Him stands condemned already (John 3:18). *Do you believe this?* But the Bible also says there is no condemnation for those who are in Christ Jesus (Romans 8:1). *Do you believe this?*

The law of gravity is narrow, but it is also true. The best response to truth is to believe and rejoice in its blessing.

THE RIGHT LOT

*"Therefore whoever hears these sayings of Mine, and does them, I
will liken him to a wise man who built his house on the rock."*
MATTHEW 7:24

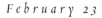ewspapers recorded the story of a Missouri couple who
built their 5,300-square-foot home in a gated community in Florida. The three-story house had five bedrooms, three
floors, beautiful verandas, and it was bordered with palm trees.
The only problem: the contractor built the house on the wrong
lot. The builder is tracing the mistake to an error in a land survey,
but is assuring all concerned that a fair settlement will be made
to this couple.

In building your life, make sure to construct it on the right
lot. Build your life on the Lord Jesus Christ and on the foundation
of obedience to His Word. The Bible is a firm foundation for our
faith, and Jesus is a cornerstone that will never collapse. When we
hear His sayings and do them, we are likewise people being built
up into a holy temple for His glory (see Ephesians 2:21).

While we don't want to think of the Bible as simply a list of
dos and don'ts, we do respect it as the foundation and authority
for life itself. By revering, reading, and obeying it, we can keep
ourselves from . . . lots of problems.

LOVE IN ACTION

For God so loved the world that He gave His only begotten Son, that whoever believes in Him should not perish but have everlasting life.

JOHN 3:16

irst John 4:8 says, "God is love." And John 3:16 says, "He gave." God's loving nature was the reason for more than just giving—He created, He redeems, He provides, He forgives, He restores, and more. Yet almost everything God does can be put under the heading of giving.

Everything we have comes from God and comes to us because He has given. As David noted in his prayer, "For all things *come* from You, and of Your own *we have given You*" (1 Chronicles 29:14, italics added). David's response to God's giving was to give back to Him as an act of worship. In fact, the apostle Paul said that giving (to others) is a test of the sincerity of our love (2 Corinthians 8:8). And what example of giving did he cite? The fact that though He was rich, for our sakes Christ became poor that we might become spiritually rich (2 Corinthians 8:9).

What do we have to give to God and others that demonstrates our love? Think of time, talent, and treasure. All we have comes from God and belongs to Him. We are only stewards who give to demonstrate His love through our hands. Put your love into action today!

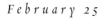

February 25

TIED TO THE ROCK

The LORD God is my strength; He will make my feet like
deer's feet, and He will make me walk on my high hills.
HABAKKUK 3:19

Ever done any rock climbing or seen pictures of climbers clinging to the sheer sides of enormous cliffs? It can be a terrifying sight, but a recent book on the sport offers some advice: "The fear of heights and high places is a natural human fear. That fear keeps you alive. Sometimes a fear of heights comes from ignorance of your safety system. If you're afraid, check your knots, your belay anchor (which ties you to the rock), and don't look down. You can build up a tolerance for heights by climbing higher each time you go."[4]

That's great advice for all of us. It's natural to suffer pangs of fear as we go through life, and that fear can be healthy and keep us alert. But sometimes we live in fear because we're ignorant of our safety system in Christ. We need to check our knots and anchors, make sure we're tied to the Rock, and learn to look up rather than down as we climb higher from day to day.

THE CHURCH

Husbands, love your wives, just as Christ also loved
the church and gave Himself for her.

EPHESIANS 5:25

When Jesus returned to heaven, He left behind one institution to continue His Gospel work—His Church. He didn't establish a university, a hospital, or an orphanage. He just left His Church. Other wonderful ministries have sprung out of His Church—like universities, missions organizations, and hospitals. But at the core of it all is His special group of people, the local church. This is where life happens. This is where babies are dedicated, where baptisms are witnessed, and where marriages are established.

Many Christians still pledge their wedding vows in the chapels and sanctuaries of our church buildings. Even when the wedding is elsewhere, the local church plays an important role in providing a spiritual foundation for the couple as they begin their marriage. Couples need spiritual underpinnings to their homes. They need a local church, and one day their children will also be strengthened and nourished by the local church.

Paul wrote this great passage about marriage to the local church at Ephesus. He knew that was where the teaching would take root—within the context of a church. To strengthen your family, get involved in a God-honoring and Bible-teaching church in your community.

LOVE

Greater love has no one than this, than to lay down one's life for his friends.
JOHN 15:13

*I*t was the English poet Elizabeth Barrett Browning who began one of her most famous poems with this line: "How do I love thee? Let me count the ways." She went on to enumerate the various ways her love could be measured and described. And her last line comes close to a biblical thought: "I love thee with the breath, smiles, tears, of all my life; and, if God choose, I shall but love thee better after death."

Saying that her love would only be perfected in heaven comes close to the idea Jesus shared with His disciples: "Greater love has no one than this, than to lay down one's life for his friends." Love may be perfected in heaven, but the pinnacle of love on earth is to deny oneself and prefer the needs of others over one's own—even to the point of laying down one's life, as Jesus would demonstrate only a few hours after stating these words. It would be wrong to think Jesus was talking only about literal death. There are many ways to die to oneself in the pursuit of loving and serving others while living.

Paul said the greatest virtue of all is love (1 Corinthians 13:13), and Jesus said the best way to demonstrate it is by dying to self while living for others.

BREAK THE CYCLE

Therefore comfort one another with these words.

I THESSALONIANS 4:18

orry and discomfort can create a downward cycle of emotions. You receive some bad news—the death of a loved one, perhaps. In your discouraged state you find yourself unable to respond to additional troubling events, weakening you further. And the downward cycle continues until hope and relief are interjected by yourself or another.

The apostle Paul found the Thessalonian Christians in a troubled state of mind. They were deeply worried about never seeing their loved ones again who had died before Christ's return. They were afraid that Christ had already returned and they had missed His appearing. Paul wrote to them words with which they could comfort one another. The subject of his words? The Rapture of the Church—the appearing of Christ in the heavens to gather His followers to Himself just before the seven-year Tribulation on earth. Taking the sting out of death would go a long way toward relieving any other earthly trouble.

Are you troubled? Don't let the downward cycle begin. Comfort yourself with the truth of the any-moment appearing of Christ to gather you to Himself and take you to heaven. That blessed truth is enough to overcome any earthly trial.

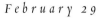

THE FOURTH WATCH

Now about the fourth watch of the night He came to them,
walking on the sea, and would have passed them by.

MARK 6:48

Once after a busy day, Jesus hurried His disciples onto a boat and sent them across the lake while He retreated to a hillside spot for prayer and solitude. A storm descended, and for hours the disciples strained at their oars in the raging darkness. Jesus didn't show up to help them until shortly before sunrise. Why did He wait so long?

We don't know all the reasons for the delay, but we recognize the frustration they felt. Sometimes the Lord doesn't seem to show up as quickly as we'd like. Yet our times are in His hands, and He is always perfectly on time. Perhaps the apparent delays are His way of developing our faith, patience, perseverance, prayer habits, endurance, and courage. Sometimes it's for testimony's sake or to allow circumstances to align correctly.

If you're impatient today for the Lord to answer your prayers and relieve your burden, remember the disciples on Galilee's lake and our Lord's words to them: "Be of good cheer! It is I; do not be afraid" (Mark 6:50). Trust His timing and wait patiently on Him.

MARCH

God is faithful, by whom you were called into the
fellowship of His Son, Jesus Christ our Lord.

1 CORINTHIANS 1:9

DISPELLING DARKNESS

*If we say that we have fellowship with Him, and walk
in darkness, we lie and do not practice the truth.*

1 JOHN 1:6

*D*arkness and light are consistent themes in the Bible. In fact, the biblical story opens with "darkness . . . on the face of the deep" (Genesis 1:2). The entire planet was totally dark! The very first thing God created was light (Genesis 1:3–5). This was consistent with His nature: "God is light and in Him is no darkness at all" (1 John 1:5).

While physical light remained, the world was plunged into spiritual darkness when Adam and Eve sinned. Since then God has been reintroducing spiritual light into the world, anticipating the coming day when the world will be illuminated by the glory of God—when "the Lamb is its light" (Revelation 21:23). The brightest light came when Christ entered the world (John 1:5–9): "I am the light of the world" (John 8:12; 9:5). But it did not dim when He returned to heaven. Instead, He passed the light to His followers: "*You* are [now] the light of the world. . . . Let your light so shine before men, that they may see your good works and glorify your Father in heaven" (Matthew 5:14–16; italics added).

Every Christlike word and deed from you dispels an equal amount of darkness. Let Christ shine through you today.

A CONTRITE HEART

The sacrifices of God are a broken spirit, a broken and a
contrite heart—these, O God, You will not despise.

PSALM 51:17

t is not uncommon for a student who is hoping to be successful in a specific subject area to retain the services of a tutor. While the role of a tutor is important, it is a temporary assignment. The tutor's mission is to move a student to a new level of understanding on a specific course of study. When Paul said that the Mosaic Law was "our tutor to bring us to Christ" (Galatians 3:24), he illustrated the law's temporary status. We can even see glimpses of the changing status of the law in the Old Testament.

In spite of the central place of animal sacrifices, by the time of King David, we find him writing that God does not desire sacrifices (Psalm 40:6–8). The focus was moving from external sacrifice to internal sacrifice: "the sacrifices of God are a broken spirit, a broken and a contrite heart" (Psalm 51:17). We find Jesus helping the Pharisees make that shift in Matthew 23:23—moving from the letter to the spirit of the law. Now that Christ has come, when we sin, God desires that we act as living sacrifices with broken and repentant hearts (Romans 12:1), confessing (agreeing with God about) our sins, that we may find His forgiveness (1 John 1:9).

If you have sins to confess, let them spill out of a broken heart before God. The sacrifice of Christ means our only sacrifice is humble confession.

Be an Encourager

*Then Jonathan, Saul's son, arose and went to David in
the woods and strengthened his hand in God.*

I Samuel 23:16

To *encourage* means to *in-courage*, that is, to instill fresh
courage into someone who is faltering. God calls us to be
spiritual encouragers to those who are spiritually fading. We're to
build up those facing great challenges. Throughout Scripture, we
see this in action.

Moses told the Israelites, "Joshua the son of Nun, who stands
before you, he shall go in there. Encourage him" (Deuteronomy
1:38). King Hezekiah "gave encouragement to all the Levites who
taught the good knowledge of the Lord" (2 Chronicles 30:22).
Because Barnabas so uplifted those around him, the early church
named him "Son of Encouragement" (Acts 4:36).

Life is hard, and living for Christ has its own challenges. Our
Christian labor is often wearying. One of Satan's greatest weapons is discouragement, and we need to learn to draw from the
encouragement of the Scriptures. But we also need to encourage
one another. Your pastor, your church leaders, your teachers,
your husband or wife, or perhaps your children need someone to
strengthen them, to instill them with fresh courage.

Who can you encourage today?

Persist in Being Positive

Do all things without complaining.

PHILIPPIANS 2:14

ccording to a news item, a man in California had a pet parrot with a lovely British accent, but somehow the bird escaped and went missing for four years. Finally, the owner and bird were reunited, but there's an odd twist in the tale. The parrot now speaks Spanish. No one knows where the bird went during his sabbatical, but he came back with a whole new vocabulary, jabbering away with words like: *gracias, amigo,* and *por favor.*

Life has its odd twists and ruffled feathers; but as we grow in Christ, our vocabulary changes. As we mature in Christ, we do less complaining and more thanking. We learn to look at things through the lens of God's providence and to thank Him for His overruling grace. The apostle Paul said, "Rejoice always, pray without ceasing, in everything give thanks; for this is the will of God in Christ Jesus for you" (1 Thessalonians 5:16–18).

Our lips are the barometer of the heart, and His praise should be continually in our mouths. Today, try to restrain the complaining spirit; in everything give thanks.

DIVINE PROTECTION

*What then shall we say to these things? If God
is for us, who can be against us?*

ROMANS 8:31

ometimes it helps to have an insight from Greek grammar to get the fullest meaning of a New Testament text.
There are several kinds of conditional sentences in Greek, one
being "if . . . then." This kind, by its grammatical form, con-
veys that the premise ("if") is understood to be true. This is the
form that occurs in Romans 8:31, which could be translated this
way: "If God is for us—*and He definitely is for us*—who can be
against us?"

This verse occurs in one of the most powerful passages in
all of Paul's letters: Romans 8:28–39. Paul has said that God uses
everything in life (verse 28) to contribute to His purpose of conforming us to the image of His Son (verse 29). Given that fact,
"What then shall we say to these things? If God *is* for us—*and
He definitely is for us as I have just said in verses 28–30*—who *can
be* against us?" This is the greatest form of spiritual security the
Christian can have, both temporally and eternally.

Your ultimate defense against Satan is God Himself. Nothing
can separate you from His love in Christ (verse 39). Your protection is assured. God's promises are the shield of your faith and
helmet of your salvation (Ephesians 6:16–17).

A COMMUNITY OF ENCOURAGERS

Rejoice with those who rejoice, and weep with those who weep.

ROMANS 12:15

he Hebrew culture had a unique way of referring to "everything": identify two opposite poles and let them represent everything in between (Psalm 139:8–12). There are traces of that figure of speech in Romans 12:15, where Paul writes about our need to identify with and encourage each other. The two opposite extremes are when someone weeps and when he rejoices. The implication is, "those two and all the times in between."

If we are honest, we might say it is easier to "weep with those who weep" than to "rejoice with those who rejoice." Another person's pain or hardship evokes empathy and compassion in us. We ourselves have suffered, and we know what the other person is going through. Rejoicing in another's success is more challenging. Perhaps we have experienced no equal successes or joys and find ourselves envious, even jealous, of another's good fortune. Paul doesn't place one need above the other; they are equally our responsibility.

You will meet someone today who is at either end of the emotional spectrum or somewhere in between. Ask God for grace to identify with that person—especially to applaud that individual in his or her success.

CHASTENING

"As many as I love, I rebuke and chasten."
REVELATION 3:19

s you read the Gospels, notice that some of Jesus' sharpest rebukes were directed to those He loved the most. He told Peter, "Get behind Me, Satan!" (Matthew 16:23). To Martha He said, "Martha, Martha, you are worried and troubled about many things. But one thing is needed, and Mary has chosen that good part" (Luke 10:41–42). He told His disciples, "Why are you fearful, O you of little faith?" (Matthew 8:26). In Luke 9:55, Jesus turned and rebuked James and John, telling them, "You do not know what manner of spirit you are of."

Jesus never rebukes us to tear us down but to build us up. When He reproves us, it's to prove His love. Sometimes He uses our conscience to rebuke us. Sometimes it's a sermon, book, or article. Occasionally He will send another person to admonish us. As you read the Bible, sometimes a verse will strike you with conviction.

Don't shrug off the chastening word. As many as He loves, He rebukes and chastens. But correction is always out of love and designed to help us, to make us pleasing to Him and more effective in our service for the kingdom.

UNIVERSAL PRAISE

Blessing and honor and glory and power be to Him who sits on the throne.
REVELATION 5:13

hen we praise the Lord, we're joining the saints of Scripture and the hymnists of history in lifting up our worship to Him who sits on the throne. We're joining the hosts in heaven now gathered by the crystal river. We're sharing in the natural praise that arises from creation as the birds sing, the winds howl, and the thunders rumble across the sky. The whole universe is designed to praise the Lord.

A nineteenth-century English divine prayed:

> We join, O God, in the blessed strain Thy holy children sang of old, when, filled full of gladness and Divine glory, they all met to sing Thy praise, to praise Thee as a God of glory, and to magnify Thy mighty name. We too would call upon all things to praise Thee, and join the song poured forth unto Thee by the sweet birds and the flowers, and by all Thy works in nature.

From first to last, Revelation brims and overflows with worship. It isn't a book of perplexity but of praise. If worship will be universal during the Millennium and eternal state, let's get a head start on it today!

HIGH AND LIFTED UP

*In the year that King Uzziah died, I saw the Lord sitting on a throne,
high and lifted up, and the train of His robe filled the temple.*
ISAIAH 6:1

ometimes after a calamitous event, a well-meaning person will say, "Not to worry. God is still on His throne, and everything will be all right." That is definitely true, and such statements affirm our belief in the sovereignty and providence of God in all things. But the word *still* poses a bit of a problem.

When we say something is "still" true, it suggests the possibility that one day it might *not* be true. It suggests that we have looked into heaven to see if something terrible occurred because God was momentarily away from His throne. Relieved, we say, "No—God is still on the throne, so we know this event was part of His plan." By definition, God would not be God if He was not on the throne of God. Indeed, God can never *not* be God; God can never *not* be on His throne. That's why Paul could write verses like Romans 8:28: Even when bad things happen, we know they are within God's sovereign plan to conform us to Christ's image.

Praise God today that He has always been on His throne and always will be.

PRACTICE ENCOURAGEMENT

Therefore comfort each other and edify one
another, just as you also are doing.
I THESSALONIANS 5:11

aul wanted the Thessalonians to give one another the gift of encouragement. He encouraged them in 1 Thessalonians 5 to remember the suddenness of our Lord's return. Since Jesus will come like a thief in the night (verse 2), we're to be prepared, "putting on the breastplate of faith and love, and . . . the hope of salvation (verse 8). And since God has a great future for us, "whether we wake or sleep, we should live together with Him" (verse 10). We should therefore encourage each other to look up with hopefulness (verse 11). We should honor those who labor among us, living with peace and patience toward all (verses 12–14).

What a great chapter Paul wrote in 1 Thessalonians!

When we're conscious of the imminent return of Christ, we're filled with hope; and that helps us offer Scripture-based encouragement to others. When we encourage someone else with such scriptural truth, he or she will in turn encourage others. Our attitudes are passed on down the line.

Jesus is coming soon! "Therefore comfort each other and edify one another, just as you also are doing."

March 11

FAILURE ISN'T FINAL

For a righteous man may fall seven times and rise
again, but the wicked shall fall by calamity.
PROVERBS 24:16

he Bible is filled with heroes, but only one man was perfect—the Lord Jesus. All the other saints in the biblical record made mistakes, took detours, lost their way, faltered, failed, wandered, and sinned. Abraham lied about Sarah. Noah got drunk. Moses lost his temper. Naomi traveled to Moab. David created scandals. Elijah fell into depression. Jonah ran away. Peter denied Christ. James and John squabbled about who was greatest. Even Paul admitted, "For what I will to do, that I do not practice; but what I hate, that I do" (Romans 7:15).

We mustn't tolerate spiritual failure in our lives. We shouldn't sin so that grace may abound (see Romans 6:1). But on the other hand, when we mess up, we shouldn't give up. Even when we wander, God is there. We have a merciful God. He knows how to draw us back, and He helps us to repent and grow from the experience. The Bible says, "If we are faithless, He remains faithful; He cannot deny Himself" (2 Timothy 2:13).

If you've fallen down, let Jesus help you rise back up, for failure isn't final.

God's Promises

For all the promises of God in Him are Yes, and in
Him Amen, to the glory of God through us.

2 Corinthians 1:20

When people talk about politicians, especially during heated races before elections, a frequently heard complaint is that politicians make promises they can't keep. Politicians can promise change, but only Congress can legislate change. Not keeping a promise one *can* keep is bad; making a promise one *can't* keep may be even worse. But that's true for all of us, not just politicians. "Better not to vow than to vow and not pay," Solomon wrote (Ecclesiastes 5:5).

God is different on both accounts. He is *capable* of making any promise and keeping it—a reflection of His omnipotence (power). But He is *incapable* of making a promise and not keeping it—a reflection of His never-changing character. God's words are always true and always trustworthy (Psalm 19:7–9). When God says something or makes a promise—about forgiveness, eternal life, grace and mercy, His love, His provision for our needs—those words are trustworthy.

That is why the proverb says to trust in the Lord with *all* your heart. In times of trouble, trust in the promises of God—He will keep every promise He has ever made.

SPIRITUAL TRAINING

Before I was afflicted I went astray, but now I keep Your word.
PSALM 119:67

he primary New Testament Greek word for "training" or
"instruction" is *paideia*. It is based on the verb *paideuo*,
which is based on the primitive Greek word *pais*—"a child, boy,
or servant." Therefore, as its base meaning, *paideia* means child
training. Because Christians needed training in righteousness
(2 Timothy 3:16), *paideia* entered the New Testament epistles to
refer to the way God trains and disciplines us as His children
(Hebrews 12:5).

Every parent knows that children come into the world with a
will of their own. The parent's job is to train children in the way
they should go so when they are older they will not depart from it
(Proverbs 22:6). Sometimes that training is uncomfortable, even
painful. When we are born again by the Spirit through faith in
Christ, a similar task begins: God trains the Christian toward the
goal of being conformed to the image of Christ (Romans 8:29).
And yes, sometimes training can be uncomfortable, even painful.
But there is always a reason and a goal.

Allow God to use life's pain to create deeper faith and greater
maturity in you. God uses everything in your life for your good
and His glory—even hard things (Romans 8:28).

As Time Draws Near

And do this, knowing the time, that now it is high time to awake out
of sleep; for now our salvation is nearer than when we first believed.

ROMANS 13:11

The morning headlines hit us with alarm as we realize we're drawing closer to the season of our Lord's return. One of our great comforts is what the Bible says about the Lord shielding His people in times like these.

- Psalm 17 says we are hidden under the shadow of His wings.
- Psalm 27 says we are hidden in the shelter of His tabernacle.
- Psalm 32 says that God is our hiding place.
- Isaiah 49 says we are hidden in the shadow of His hand.
- And Colossians 3 says our lives are hidden with Christ in God.

When you read a frightening headline, remind yourself that you are hidden in the hollow of His hand, and He will keep you from the coming Day of Judgment. He will preserve your going out and your coming in from this time forth and forever. He will preserve your soul. That frees us from fear, allowing us to preach the Word with boldness and to experience His peace and joy as time draws near.

VIEW LIFE PROVIDENTIALLY

Concerning this [thorn] I pleaded with the Lord
three times that it might depart from me.

2 CORINTHIANS 12:8

One of the most profound insights the apostle Paul experienced may have been the result of some people who were making life difficult for him. There were false apostles at Corinth who sought to discredit Paul's ministry. Some scholars believe these were the "thorn in the flesh" Paul asked God to remove from him (2 Corinthians 12:7–8). He was in danger of pride over the divine revelations he had received (12:1–7). The "false apostles" (11:13–15) attacking him may have been God's method to keep Paul humble.

Whether Paul's thorn was people or circumstances, the situation caused Paul to realize that, in his weakness, Christ was his sufficiency (12:9–10). And who doesn't need to gain that insight and be reminded of it over and over? The truth is, God often does His deepest work in us through the people and circumstances in our life. Instead of resisting or rebelling against people and problems, we might want to pray, "Lord, show me what I can learn and how I can grow in You."

View life providentially. Let God use every person and problem to continue conforming you to the image of Christ (Romans 8:28–29).

Be Anxious for Nothing

Be anxious for nothing, but in everything by prayer and supplication,
with thanksgiving, let your requests be made known to God; and
the peace of God . . . will guard your hearts and minds.

Philippians 4:6–7

What's the most popular verse in the Bible? Some time back, the retailer Amazon released a list of the most popular passages from its most popular books, and the most commonly highlighted portion of the Bible was Philippians 4:6–7. Readers of e-Bibles underlined that passage more often than any other in Scripture.

When we look around at our anxious world and our fretful lives, we can understand why people are drawn to the promises of Philippians 4. But notice the context of the passage. The Lord tells us here to rejoice in Him (verse 4); to be gentle in our dealings with others (verse 5a); to remember how near He is to us (verse 5b); to pray earnestly about our concerns (verse 6a); to count our blessings with thankfulness (verse 6b); and to focus our minds on what is true, noble, just, pure, lovely, and praiseworthy (verse 8).

What a wonderful description of the life of faith! When we trust the Lord like this, we don't have to fret about the small details of life. We can rely on God with issues both big and small.

PATRICK'S TROUBLES

*. . . always carrying about in the body the dying of the Lord Jesus,
that the life of Jesus also may be manifested in our body.*

2 CORINTHIANS 4:10

oday is the day that the patron saint of Ireland, Saint
Patrick, is honored. A native of Britain, he was captured
in the late fourth century AD by Irish pirates at age sixteen and
enslaved for six years in Ireland. During that time he committed
himself to Christianity. He escaped and returned to his family in
Britain, where, a few years later, he had a vision of the Irish calling
him to return and minister to them.

Rather than resenting his years as a slave to the Irish, Patrick
used his time as a shepherd to contemplate what it meant to know
Christ, what it meant to know God's forgiveness. He left Britain
as an unconverted teenager but returned as a believer in Christ.
Without those six years of suffering, who knows how different
Patrick's life might have been? And who knows how many Irish
might never have heard the Gospel through Patrick's ministry in
Ireland in the fifth century?

Times of trouble in life, be they brief or extended, require a
change in perspective. Instead of asking, "Why is this happening
to me?" we must ask, "What is God doing in my life? What does
He want me to learn in this situation?"

SAVED TO SERVE

*For you, brethren, have been called to liberty; only do not use liberty
as an opportunity for the flesh, but through love serve one another.*

GALATIANS 5:13

Children think that the absence of rules means the absence of restraint—and not just physical children; spiritual children often think that too. Paul dedicated part of his letter to the Galatians, teaching that "liberty"—freedom from the law—is not a license for the unbridled appetites of the flesh. Rather, the energy formerly spent obeying the law is now to be redirected to serving others.

Jesus told His disciples that He did not come into the world to be served but to serve and to give His life for others (Mark 10:45). Indeed, He said that greatness is determined by the humility of service. Two of Isaiah's most powerful images are that of the nation of Israel as a servant to the Gentiles (Isaiah 49:3), then of the Messiah as the Suffering Servant for both Jews and Gentiles alike (Isaiah 53:11). If Christ came to honor God by serving the will of God, we who go by His name must do the same.

Look for an opportunity today to serve someone in your life. Serve that one as Christ would serve—sacrificially and unconditionally.

OUR KINSMAN-REDEEMER

Christ has redeemed us from the curse of the law, having become a curse for us (for it is written, "Cursed is everyone who hangs on a tree").
GALATIANS 3:13

*I*srael had statutes that provided for stability in society: regulation of debt, slavery, poverty, the transfer of property, and the preservation of families and clans. The story of Ruth is an example. When she found herself a young widow, one of her former husband's relatives—Boaz, known as a kinsman-redeemer—stepped in to marry her and purchase her former father-in-law's property.

When people found themselves in unfortunate circumstances, God provided a means for their care and redemption—a way to be delivered from trouble through the extended family. That provision is fully manifested in the New Testament. Christians are adopted into God's family (Romans 8:15–16), a family in which Jesus Christ is the firstborn Son (verse 29), and we are coheirs with Him of all God's promises (verse 17). When we found ourselves in trouble—guilty of sin—God sent His firstborn Son to redeem us and incorporate us into God's family. Jesus Christ is our Kinsman-Redeemer.

Thank God today that, though you were once an orphan and an outcast, you have been purchased by Christ's blood and made an heir of God.

STEADFAST FAITH

Therefore, my beloved brethren, be steadfast, immovable, always abounding in the work of the Lord, knowing that your labor is not in vain in the Lord.

1 CORINTHIANS 15:58

Three years of growing faith and hope among His followers were dashed on the shoals of despair when Jesus was apprehended and killed. Typical of the despair felt by those in Jerusalem were two despondent followers of Christ who left Jerusalem to walk to the village of Emmaus. On the way, they encountered a stranger who seemed to know nothing of the past days' events in Jerusalem. Yet he rebuked them for their despondency, for not recognizing the meaning of the death of the Nazarene. And then He revealed to them that He was the Christ, raised from the dead. "So [the two] rose up that very hour and returned to Jerusalem . . . and they told about the things that had happened on the road" (Luke 24:33, 35).

When the two disciples saw that Jesus had been given new life, they received new life as well. Such is the power of the Resurrection; such is the meaning of Easter!

If you grow despondent in the face of life's circumstances, remember the Resurrection—proof that God's power is sufficient to resurrect your faith.

TIMING IS EVERYTHING

To everything there is a season, a time for every purpose under heaven.
ECCLESIASTES 3:1

hink about the timing necessary to keep our solar system stable. Every 24 hours the earth spins on its axis. Every 365.26 days the earth orbits the sun. The moon orbits the earth every 27.3 days. In premodern days, the certainty of those numbers formed the basis of calendars, agriculture, navigation, and more. While calculations today may be easier with computers, those calculations still depend on the timing of the solar system.

The psalmist David didn't know what we know about the cosmos, but he knew that God was responsible for it. He was amazed at the "heavens" and "the moon and the stars, which [God had] ordained" (Psalm 8:3). In the face of such majesty, he wondered how God could be concerned about a mere human like himself. But the same God who times the movement of the planets also times the days of our lives (Psalm 139:16). With that confidence, the apostle Paul could be at peace when he realized that the end of his life was near (2 Timothy 4:6).

If you trust that the sun will rise on time tomorrow morning, trust the God who keeps it on schedule—and ordains the timing of your life as well.

SIGNS OF EASTER

"A wicked and adulterous generation seeks after a sign, and no sign shall be given to it except the sign of the prophet Jonah."

MATTHEW 16:4

merica begins showing signs of Easter earlier and earlier every year. Plastic eggs for sale by the millions, chocolate eggs and bunny rabbits in every store, pastel-colored Easter baskets and bundles of plastic green "grass" to fill them—the world's signs of Easter can't be missed. But today's signs of Easter are a far cry from the signs that proved the reality of the very first Easter morning.

Jesus told His detractors who had asked Him for a miraculous sign that they would see only one sign—the sign of Jonah, who spent three days in the belly of a great fish before being rescued from death. On the third day after Jesus' own death, He came out of the grave to give the world a sign it cannot deny. For a man to predict His own death and resurrection was something only God could do. The Gospel writers give us many proofs of His resurrection: sightings by witnesses, nail-scarred hands, a stone rolled away, and more. Truly, Jesus was—is—alive!

As you prepare to celebrate Easter this year, give thanks to God that your faith is not in vain—that Christ was raised for you (1 Corinthians 15:14).

March 23

RESURRECTED SAVIOR

Jesus answered and said to them, "Destroy this
temple, and in three days I will raise it up."
JOHN 2:19

*H*ow would knowing the outcome of a difficult situation change your outlook while going through it? Jesus
knew He was going to die in Jerusalem, but He also knew He was
going to be raised from the dead. He believed the Messianic Psalms
applied to Him: "For You will not leave my soul in Sheol, nor will
You allow Your Holy One to see corruption" (Psalm 16:10).

Did that lessen the anguish of the moments before His death?
No, He was human, and He grieved the pain and suffering He
was about to endure (Luke 22:44). But His faith in His Father's
plan and protection was greater than His anticipation of suffering.
He was wholly submitted to the Father's will (Luke 22:42). Jesus
knew nothing could separate Him from God's love, and we have
been given the same promise (Romans 8:35–39). And we have
also been given the same promise of resurrection Jesus was given
(1 Corinthians 15:12–19; 1 Thessalonians 4:16). And we are to
comfort one another with these promises (1 Thessalonians 4:18).

Easter is the time when we remember the Savior's resurrection, which makes our own resurrection sure. Comfort yourself
with these words today.

Peace Be with You

Then, the same day at evening, being the first day of the week, when the doors were shut where the disciples were assembled, for fear of the Jews, Jesus came and stood in the midst, and said to them, "Peace be with you."

John 20:19

When a mother and child become separated at the mall, the parent is filled with anxiety over the lost child. Then the mom sees a security guard approaching, holding the hand of the child, and anxiety is turned to joy and peace. The transition happens in a moment—what was missing has been found.

On the third day after Jesus' crucifixion, His disciples and followers were filled with anxiety. They huddled together behind locked doors for fear that the people who put Jesus to death would be coming next for them (John 20:19). The anxiety of some was heightened even further when they went to visit the tomb where Jesus lay, only to discover that His body was missing. Not only was He dead; His body had been stolen! But then Jesus made Himself known to Mary Magdalene at the Garden tomb. Peace replaced anxiety as she returned to tell the others that Jesus was alive.

We serve a living Savior, not a dead one. When your fear or anxiety level is high, let the presence of the resurrected Jesus give you peace.

March 25

HONOR

"Those who honor Me I will honor, and those who despise Me shall be lightly esteemed."
1 SAMUEL 2:30

aris was in the grip of a heat wave during the 1924 Summer Olympics, and the Colombes Stadium was like a frying pan. For runner Eric Liddell, heat was the least of his concerns. His best event—the 100 meter—had been scheduled for a Sunday. He withdrew because he didn't want to run on the Lord's Day. He set his sights on the 400-meter race instead, which was held on Saturday. In the dressing room before the event, the masseur handed him a folded paper. It contained a quotation from 1 Samuel 2:30: "Those who honor Me I will honor." Inspired by those words, Eric Liddell broke the existing world record and won the gold medal.

God honors those who honor Him and put their trust in Him. Honoring ourselves is a thankless task, and hoping to be honored by others is prideful. When we acknowledge Jesus Christ as Lord and seek to worship and glorify Him in all we say and do, He has a way of blessing us, using us, providing for us, and establishing our reputation before others.

CLOUDED VISION

Finally, all of you be of one mind, having compassion for one another; love as brothers, be tenderhearted, be courteous.

1 PETER 3:8

he story is told of a woman who could look out her kitchen window and see her neighbor's laundry drying on the line. But the woman continually complained to her husband about how dingy the neighbor's laundry looked: "Doesn't she know how to get her clothes clean?" But one day she announced, "Finally—our neighbor has learned to do her laundry! I wonder what has changed?" Her husband said, "It may be because I washed the outside of that window yesterday."

Sometimes, our own impaired vision causes us to see faults in others. It reminds us of what Jesus said about removing the beam in our own eye before trying to remove a speck from someone else's eye. And of how Paul wrote that we should focus more on the needs of others rather than our own needs. Jesus had the ability to see people as they really were—and His clear spiritual sight moved Him to compassion toward them (Matthew 9:36). We need to see the world around us through the eyes of Christ.

As we wash the windows of our hearts, we will more clearly see the needs of others and show compassion on them.

March 27

THE PERFECT ENDING

*But we see Jesus, who was made a little lower than the angels,
for the suffering of death crowned with glory and honor, that
He, by the grace of God, might taste death for everyone.*

HEBREWS 2:9

hen we dislike the ending of a book or movie, we try to imagine a better one: what we think should have happened. The wonder and goodness of creation was broken when Adam disobeyed God. We feel the burden of this brokenness and separation from God. Thankfully, the Creator did not end the story there.

Just as a producer determines the last scene of a movie and a writer carefully crafts the final sentence of a book, God mercifully provided what we desire and desperately need: a Savior. We cannot save ourselves. Only God, who is powerful enough to create the world out of nothing and to give us life, could find the perfect solution to our brokenness and separation from Him: Jesus.

Jesus is God's final answer to the dilemma we face. He is God in the flesh, and the book of Hebrews elaborates on why Jesus is all we need. He is superior to every human leader, prophet, and priest. He offers us Himself along with forgiveness, life, and meaning.

UNENDING PRAISE

Praise the LORD! Oh, give thanks to the LORD, for He is good!
For His mercy endures forever. Who can utter the mighty
acts of the LORD? Who can declare all His praise?

PSALM 106:1–2

hen the Bible directs us to give thanks to the Lord, it reminds us of the importance of extolling His goodness to us. As sinners saved by grace, we have much to praise Him for! The benefits of living a praise-filled life are too numerous to mention, but know this: changing your focus from "me to Thee" will radically change your perspective in life.

Psalm 106:2 says, "Who can declare all His praise?" Think about it—who, indeed, can declare all His praise? Our praises should be unending! Don't limit your worship of the Lord to an hour on Sunday. Keep a song in your heart throughout your day. Begin first thing each morning. Scottish preacher Duncan Campbell resolved to bless the Lord at all times, starting with his morning devotions. According to his biographer, Campbell rose each morning as the farmers harnessed their horses to the plows. He was convicted by their work ethic and determined to be as diligent with his spiritual harvest as they were with their crops.

When we start the day praising the Lord, it keeps a song in our hearts throughout our waking hours. As we offer our praise and worship to the Lord, He dries our tears and banishes our fears. Remember that the Lord is good—be thankful to Him and bless His name (Psalm 100).

March 29

THE MOTHER OF JOHN MARK

So, when [Peter] had considered this, he came to the house
of Mary, the mother of John whose surname was Mark,
where many were gathered together praying.

ACTS 12:12

eing called by our names is a sign of inclusion, a sign
that we are "known." But when Luke, the writer of
Acts, mentioned a significant woman by name, he had to explain
who she was because she was not well-known: "Mary, the mother
of John whose surname was Mark." Most people would have
been familiar with Mark, the cousin of Barnabas and missionary assistant to Barnabas and Paul. But very few knew Mark's
mother's name.

Mary was not a leader, that we know of. But she used what
she had to serve the Jerusalem church. She apparently had a large
house—vestibule, courtyard, and possibly two stories of living
area—and a servant. Her house could be the one referred to as a
meeting place in Acts 1:12–14; it was definitely a meeting place in
Acts 12:12–17. It was the place where the church gathered to pray
for Peter when he was imprisoned in Jerusalem.

You may not have a large house and servants, but everybody
has something to use—including the abilities and spiritual gift(s)
God has given you. Ask God to show you how to use *for* Him
what you have *from* Him.

GOD'S JUSTICE

Surely God will never do wickedly, nor will the Almighty pervert justice.

One of the most unfair parables Jesus told—unfair to the natural mind—concerned a landowner who hired men throughout the day to work in his vineyard. They all stopped work at the same time and were paid the same wage. The last men hired were paid the same as the first men hired—and the first men hired grumbled about the unfairness of everyone being paid the same amount even though not everyone worked the same amount (Matthew 20:1–16). The landowner replied, "What's unfair about me doing with my money what I will?"

Jesus' parable was directed toward the religious leaders, who thought it unfair that latecomers to the kingdom of heaven should receive the full measure of grace and kingdom standing as those who had devoted their life to God. Jesus' point is that God's actions are a blend of justice, grace, and mercy, all balanced by His perfect purposes. God is never unfair, but He is always just, gracious, and merciful. Faith comes when we trust Him to blend those elements perfectly in every situation.

God is the landowner, and we are the workers. It is His right to do as He will with what is His.

SAY YES TO CHRIST

For the grace of God that brings salvation has appeared to all men, teaching us that, denying ungodliness and worldly lusts, we should live soberly, righteously, and godly in the present age.

TITUS 2:11–12

The same grace that brings us salvation gives strength to live biblically in this age. We need grace-based living, but that can only happen as we focus our thoughts on God's Word and live it out. A study by the Evangelical Alliance found that many Christians struggle with making time for prayer and Bible study. Sixty percent of those born before 1960 said they read their Bibles daily; only 31 percent of younger Christians did the same.[1]

As Christians, we're to live a different lifestyle from the world by loving God and loving others. As we grow in grace, we should understand God's Word more, respect others, care for the poor, tend to the widows, and keep ourselves unspotted by the world. Pastor Tony Evans wrote, "Grace-based Christians obey because it's their delight. . . . To grace-based Christians, the spiritual life is the lifting of a burden."[2]

The same grace that helps us say yes to Christ helps us say no to the world.

April

But the fruit of the Spirit is love, joy,
peace, longsuffering, kindness, goodness,
faithfulness, gentleness, self-control.

Galatians 5:22–23

April 1

BEWARE THE THORNS

Now he who received seed among the thorns is he who hears
the word, and the cares of this world and the deceitfulness
of riches choke the word, and he becomes unfruitful.

MATTHEW 13:22

The Japanese name is *kuzu*; the Americanized name is
kudzu. And if you live in America's Deep South, you
know it well. It is a fast-growing, invasive vine introduced to
America in 1876. Farmers were originally paid by the government
to plant the vine to prevent soil erosion. It also adds nitrogen to
the soil and is palatable to grazing animals. So, what's not to like
about kudzu? It takes over and chokes out or shades out everything else. Millions of acres of the South today are shrouded in
kudzu.

Jesus used an image of thorn bushes (think America's black-
berry and raspberry bushes) that can choke out a seedling that is
fighting for sunlight and moisture. All too often the thorn bushes
win. It happens spiritually, too—thorns and riches can choke out
a seed of faith that has sprouted in an unbeliever's heart. They can
even choke out a new spiritual insight in a mature believer's heart.
Seeds of faith are delicate; they must be protected and nurtured.

If God is stretching your faith with new kingdom insights,
don't let the cares of this world choke them out.

RAISED TO LIFE

And if Christ is not risen, then our preaching is
empty and your faith is also empty.
1 CORINTHIANS 15:14

When we look at the two sides of a coin, the two halves of a pair of scissors, or the two wings on a bird, it seems they are of equal value—that neither side nor half is more important than the other. We might look at the death and resurrection of Christ in a similar way—but we would be slightly wrong.

In 1 Corinthians 15 the apostle Paul does not say that without the *death* of Christ our preaching and faith are empty (verse 14). Nor does he say that without the *death* of Christ our faith is futile and we are still in our sins (verse 17). Instead, he says that without the *resurrection* of Christ all those things are true. It is a fine shade of difference, to be sure—but important. The death of Christ satisfied God's wrath against sin and paid the penalty for which only death would suffice. But in order to prove that the penalty of sin had been paid once and for all, death—the consequence of sin—had to be defeated. If Christ had not defeated death by rising from the dead, we would still be in our sins.

Give thanks to God today for the death of Christ—and especially for the resurrection of Christ and eternal life ensured by the empty tomb.

April 3

STAND UP AND SPEAK UP

*Nor do they light a lamp and put it under a basket, but on a
lampstand, and it gives light to all who are in the house.*
MATTHEW 5:15

hen the apostle Peter was confronted by a servant
of the high priest, he lost his tongue. Rather than
speaking up for Christ, he denied knowing the Savior. But after
the Resurrection and Pentecost, Peter couldn't keep quiet. "We
cannot but speak the things which we have seen and heard," he
told his critics (Acts 4:20). As *The Living Bible* puts it, "We cannot
stop telling about the wonderful things we saw Jesus do and heard
him say."

When we share the Gospel, we must stand up and speak up
for everyone to hear. Don't be deterred by criticism, and don't let
timidity keep you from telling others what God has done for you.
Listen to the advice of Jesus: "Return to your own house, and tell
what great things God has done for you" (Luke 8:39).

When we think of the wonderful things we've seen Jesus do
and heard Him say, and when we consider the great things He has
done for us, how can we be silent or hide our light under a basket?
Let's look up, stand up, and speak up for Him!

NEW EVERY MORNING

For His anger is but for a moment, His favor is for life; weeping
may endure for a night, but joy comes in the morning.

PSALM 30:5

salm 30:5 is an example of Scripture explaining Scripture. The second half of the verse is often quoted during times of trouble: "weeping may endure for a night, but joy comes in the morning." Weeping can sometimes last for *many* nights—or weeks or months, even years. But the first part of the verse explains the second: The psalmist is talking about relative periods of time—a "moment" compared with a "lifetime."

In other words, God's favor—His love, grace, mercy, comfort, and provision—is the dominant and permanent theme in our life with Him. His love and grace are never absent—contrary to what appears to us during moments of sadness or pain. Even in times of darkness we have every confidence that light will dawn again: "The LORD's mercies . . . are new every morning" (Lamentations 3:22–23). Even though the present may last more than one night, both the present and the future are in God's hands. Knowing that light always follows darkness, there is nothing in the future to fear.

If you are living in a dark time today, know that the Light of the World is lighting your path. Walking with Christ dispels all fear of the future.

April 5

PRACTICING PATIENCE

The testing of your faith produces patience.

JAMES 1:3

When we pray, "Lord, give me patience," what is the cause? A traffic jam? A spouse's irritating habit? A child's messy room? We know God will answer that prayer because we know He wants us to be patient; patience is a fruit of the Spirit (Galatians 5:22—"longsuffering"). But the reasons we pray for patience are several degrees removed from how the New Testament portrays the need for patience.

Over and over in the Epistles, patience is linked to persecution and troubles (2 Corinthians 6:4; Colossians 1:11). That is not to say that our need for patience in the everyday "trials" of life is inconsequential. But compared to persecution and trouble relating to one's faith—that calls for a deeper level of patience. In short, the deeper the trial, the deeper the lesson of patience learned. That doesn't mean we have to invent trials in order to learn patience; the trials will come on their own. But it does mean we must welcome them as teachers and tutors in the spiritual life.

Regardless of why you need patience today, embrace the cause and ask the Spirit to manifest patience in your response so "you may be perfect and complete, lacking nothing" (James 1:4).

In His Time

Our soul waits for the LORD; He is our help and shield.

PSALM 33:20

Our cell phone vibrates or rings while we are driving our car, and in our impatience to know what the call or text contains, we take our eyes off the road so that we can know immediately who is contacting us. This scenario ends in tragedy for hundreds of people each year who die trying to know *now*, rather than waiting until later to check their phone.

That reflects our age. Our attention spans are short, and we want things in a hurry. Our watchwords are *now, instant, quick, fast, rush.*

The Lord doesn't work that way. To Him, a thousand years are like a day, and a day is like a thousand years. He's in no hurry; He dwells in eternity. He knows our needs, and He works in His timing to do what's best. He waited four hundred years after the Old Testament to send the Messiah. Jesus waited till the fourth watch to rescue His disciples on the Sea of Galilee (Matthew 14:25).

The Bible tells us to wait on the Lord. Once we've done our best, we have to leave things in His hands and give Him time to work. Don't think God is inactive. In our waiting, He is working. He will work all for good—in His time.

PROVIDENCE

Indeed it was for my own peace that I had great bitterness.
ISAIAH 38:17

saiah faced great bitterness, but in the course of time it turned into peace. His burdens became blessings. What others meant for evil, God turned to good.

Tracing this truth through the Scripture, we find it's the universal experience for God's children. Joseph was betrayed by his brothers and imprisoned in Egypt; but in God's providence, he came into leadership. Moses was rejected by Pharaoh and driven from the land, but it led to the deliverance of Israel. Job faced the wiles of the devil; but in the end, he was twice as rich as before. Jesus was seized by His enemies and crucified, but He rose from the dead and established His Church. Paul was beaten and imprisoned in Philippi; but he planted a church there and wrote an enduring letter, in which he said, "I want you to know, brethren, that the things which happened to me have actually turned out for the furtherance of the gospel" (Philippians 1:12).

Are you having a tough day? Trust God with it and wait for Him. In His providence, He will turn your trial into a testimony.

KNOW LOVE, NO FEAR

*There is no fear in love; but perfect love casts out fear, because fear
involves torment. But he who fears has not been made perfect in love.*

1 JOHN 4:18

very verse of Scripture was written for a specific purpose and application. Yet so many verses have a broad
application. Take the apostle John's oft-quoted words in 1 John
4:18: "Perfect love casts out fear." John's immediate subject was
God's judgment. His point was that those who are secure in
God's perfect love have no reason to fear His judgment. So God's
love casts out the fear we may have about our sins. God's love in
Christ's sacrifice has paid for those sins. The heart that is full of
God's love has no room for fear of God's judgment.

How else might this truth apply? Think of all the times we
are tempted to fear: We fear the future—but God's love surrounds us and our future. We fear loving someone who has hurt
us—but God's love gives us assurance of His blessing for our
obedience. We fear finding our "place" in life—but God's love
assures us we are created and called according to His purposes.
The more we rest in the knowledge of God's love, the less fear we
will experience in any area of life.

If you are experiencing fear of any kind, ask God to show you
how His love can take that fear away.

April 9

STREAMS IN THE DESERT

He found him in a desert land and in the wasteland, a howling wilderness;
He encircled him, He instructed him, He kept him as the apple of His eye.
DEUTERONOMY 32:10

A television crew from Animal Planet was filming a scene on a deserted island in the South Pacific. Suddenly the crew spotted a man yelling and waving his arms. He was a genuine castaway, a stranded fisherman, suffering dehydration and sunstroke. The man had given up hope, said his prayers, and was prepared to die. The crew rescued him—and made a television program about the adventure.

None of us like to be cast into a desert place in life, but the Lord knows how to rescue us. He finds us where we are. He encircles us. He instructs us, and He keeps us as the apple of His eye.

If you're in a desert place, don't give up your hope. Desert places can become places of deliverance, and God can even turn spiritual deserts into times of refreshment. Isaiah 35 says, "The desert shall rejoice and blossom . . . for waters shall burst forth in the wilderness, and streams in the desert" (verses 1, 6).

Jesus often meets us in the desert places of life.

Trustworthy Authority

Then He appointed twelve, that they might be with Him
and that He might send them out to preach.

MARK 3:14

When considering matters of life, death, and eternity, nothing could be more important than authority. That is, who do we believe, and why? The world is full of people claiming to speak for God, but credentials are of the utmost importance. There are false apostles today just as there were in the first century (2 Corinthians 11:13–15).

The common denominator of apostolic authority in the first century was having seen and heard Jesus Christ in person: "How shall we escape if we neglect so great a salvation, which at the first began to be spoken by the Lord, and was confirmed to us by those who heard Him" (Hebrews 2:3). Spiritual and divine authority began with Christ and continued through those He appointed and sent out. Their authority was confirmed by "signs and wonders and mighty deeds" (2 Corinthians 12:12)—confirmation that was lacking among false apostles who sought to establish themselves through deceit and counterfeit means.

The reason the New Testament epistles are trustworthy is because they were written by those who were called to speak for Christ.

WHO OWNS YOUR BODY?

Or do you not know that your body is the temple of the Holy Spirit
who is in you, whom you have from God, and you are not your own?
1 CORINTHIANS 6:19

*I*f we borrow our neighbor's lawn mower, we might make sure it's clean and full of gas when we return it. If a teenager is given the family car to use for a social outing, he makes sure it is clean and undamaged (even topped off with gas) before handing back the keys. We might call it the "golden rule of borrowing": Treat the property of others in a manner consistent with the owner's expectations.

The Bible says that our human body is not our own; it is the temple of the Holy Spirit. The human body is part of the image of God in humans on earth—the physical manifestation of God's presence by the Spirit. Since our body belongs to God, we have an obligation to use it in ways that honor Him (1 Corinthians 6:20).

Beginning today, think of yourself as a steward of your physical body—another means for glorifying Him on this earth. All that we are belongs to God.

Our Replacement

Have mercy upon me, O God, according to Your lovingkindness; according to the multitude of Your tender mercies, blot out my transgressions.

Psalm 51:1

The concept of being replaced usually has a negative connotation. We work hard to become important and irreplaceable. While this mind-set has its benefits at work, it will not work when it comes to our relationship with God, where we are always on the receiving end. God does not need us.

We can ignore the truth and try to earn God's favor, or we can accept this truth and come to God in humility. In Luke 18, Jesus describes a Pharisee who is consumed with his own merit. His prayers reveal his blindness to his own shortcomings and to God's perfection and holiness. Meanwhile, a tax collector clearly sees his need for God's grace and forgiveness (verses 9–14).

God's mercy is revealed in the life, death, and resurrection of Christ. He stands in our place, and His perfection and purity make us acceptable to God. One way to remind ourselves of this is to pause, asking God to shine His light into any areas of our lives that we may need to confess or recommit to Him. This will keep our hearts tender and honest, and we will find deep joy in His compassion toward us.

April 13

THIRSTY HEARTS

And walk in love, as Christ also has loved us and given Himself for us, an offering and a sacrifice to God for a sweet-smelling aroma.
EPHESIANS 5:2

 e seek solace in physical comforts and people, forgetting that every sip of water and experience is a dim reflection of the eternal life and everlasting love Christ offers us. Our need for love is like our need for water: continuous. A single cup of water will not sustain us for a month, and a single experience of friendship will not sustain us for a lifetime. We long for more, wanting to know we are loved and valued.

When Jesus met the woman at the well, He spoke to her of life-giving water: drink once and be satisfied forever. This water would quench her thirst and become "a fountain of water springing up into everlasting life" (John 4:14). Jesus was offering Himself—all she had to do was ask. How often do we go through the day, forgetting to invite Jesus in? Jesus desires to satisfy our deepest needs and to transform us into His image, bringing life and hope to those around us. Do you know anyone who is thirsty?

Share the life-giving water of Christ to someone who is thirsty today.

The King Eternal

Now to the King eternal, immortal, invisible, to God who
alone is wise, be honor and glory forever and ever. Amen.

1 Timothy 1:17

here are two eternities in 1 Timothy 1:17. There is a King who reigns eternally, and there is praise that greets Him forever and ever. Because God is eternal, His praise is everlasting.

One of the reasons God promises us eternal life is so we can render everlasting praise. The Bible says, "Even from everlasting to everlasting, You are God" (Psalm 90:2). The cry of the holy ones in heaven is: "Blessing and honor and glory and power be to Him who sits on the throne, and to the Lamb, forever and ever!" (Revelation 5:13).

If Christians only think in terms of time, our lives are miserable. The Bible says that without the reality of the Resurrection and its ensuring eternal life, we are the most pitiful of people (1 Corinthians 15:19). But Christ *has* risen from the dead! The Day of the Lord is coming. Eternity is our inheritance. As we better contemplate the nature of our eternal King, we'll better cope with the tensions of time. Since we're going to praise Him forever, why not begin now? Why not start living with eternity in view?

April 15

YOUR BEST FRIEND

*"I have called you friends, for all things that I heard
from My Father I have made known to you."*
JOHN 15:15

t's possible to expect too much from a friend. No individual should be expected to sustain our spirits, to prop us up, to be responsible for always keeping us going. Only the Lord can do that. If we're expecting a friend to do what only Jesus can do, we'll be disappointed.

Our friends can pray for us, but only Jesus can answer our prayers and meet our deepest needs. Our friends can love us, but only Jesus is a friend who sticks closer than a brother. Our friends can give us a portion of their time, but only Jesus can be with us to the end of the world. Our friends can gather around us, but only Jesus can live within us.

Other friends can empathize and sympathize, but only the Lord Jesus Christ can read our thoughts and plumb the depths of our hearts. Our friends can give advice, but the Lord can direct our steps.

We thank God for friends—but our first resort should always be the Lord Jesus.

Learn the joy of having a divine Best Friend.

Obtaining Promises

. . . who through faith . . . obtained promises.

Hebrews 11:33

he Bible is full of promises, but how are they obtained? Can we purchase them like items in a store? Can we earn them like wages in a factory? Can we win them like dollars in a lottery? If you have a perplexity in your life presently, there's surely a promise in the Bible meeting your need. If you're worried about the future, there's a word from God to give you confidence. But how do you occupy that promise?

Through faith! It's like salvation. Christ has already purchased what we need, and it's available by grace. Our job is to receive it by faith, which means trusting Him to do just as He has said. God has given us the gift of faith that we can take what's unseen and make it part of who we are.

Hebrews 11 gives lots of examples of that, including Abraham (see Hebrews 11:8–18). He didn't know where he was going or how to find the land promised him, but he took every forward footstep with the assurance that God could and would unerringly guide him. We can do the same and through faith obtain the promises.

April 17

WHO DO YOU THINK YOU ARE?

For the LORD takes pleasure in His people . . . We are His workmanship.
PSALM 149:4 AND EPHESIANS 2:10

ow do you see yourself? Take confidence in this truth: You are the masterwork of God's creation and the masterpiece of His genius, the object of His love and the recipient of His grace. Psalm 139 says, "You made all the delicate, inner parts of my body and knit them together in my mother's womb. . . . It is amazing to think about. Your workmanship is marvelous—and how well I know it. . . . How precious it is, Lord, to realize that you are thinking about me constantly! I can't even count how many times a day your thoughts turn toward me. And when I waken in the morning, you are still thinking of me" (verses 13–18 TLB).

Zechariah 2:8 says that whoever touches us touches the apple of His eye. According to Isaiah 43:4, we are precious and honored in His sight. Isaiah 62:5 says, "As a bridegroom rejoices over the bride, so shall your God rejoice over you."

Remember this truth: You're not a loser or a piece of junk. You aren't beyond hope or help. The Lord made you in His image, redeemed you by His blood, and He takes great delight in you. He rejoices over you with singing (Zephaniah 3:17). You are a friend of God!

The Fatigue Factor

I know that You can do everything, and that no
purpose of Yours can be withheld from You.

JOB 42:2

The word *fatigue* frequently shows up in the headlines, preceded by a host of adjectives. Congress suffers budget fatigue. Sports teams lose because of travel fatigue. Trains derail because of driver fatigue. Soldiers face battle fatigue. Ministries go unfunded because of donor fatigue. There was even a report recently about young people suffering Facebook fatigue. All these reports—and more—are accurate. We are a society of tired people in a tired world.

But God isn't tired. "Have you not known? Have you not heard? The everlasting God, the LORD, the Creator of the ends of the earth, neither faints nor is weary" (Isaiah 40:28). Since God possesses all the power in the universe, He can do anything He chooses. He can do everything as easily as He does anything. Nothing is more difficult for God than anything else; He does all things with the same amount of ease. Nothing is too hard for Him. Nothing is remotely hard for Him. He never grows tired.

The Bible repeatedly reassures us of God's strengthening grace. So, take care of yourself, avoid unnecessary weariness, rest in Him, and draw from His strength.

April 19

NEVER GIVE UP

*Let us not become weary in doing good, for at the proper
time we will reap a harvest if we do not give up.*
GALATIANS 6:9 NIV

n Luke 18:1, Jesus told His disciples that "they should
always pray and not give up" (NIV). Paul told the
Galatians to remain faithful in good works, for they would reap a
harvest if they didn't give up.

Our culture today tends to give up too easily. Some give up
halfway through their marriage. Others give up on treatment
halfway through rehab. We're all tempted to give up on a diet, on
an exercise program, or on our educational goals. Some people
give up on their jobs before they've really persevered and done
their best. Pastors and Christian workers sometimes give up on
the ministry God has given them.

God calls us to do things that can be started in our strength,
but must be completed in His. If we've undertaken the task by
mistake and He clearly indicates we shouldn't be doing it—
well, then, abandon the project. Otherwise, never give up. Pray.
Persevere. Keep going. The harvest will come in due time, and
your work will be rewarded.

"We never give up," said Paul. "Though our bodies are dying,
our spirits are being renewed every day" (2 Corinthians 4:16 NLT).

THANKS FOR EVERYTHING

Now therefore, our God, we thank You and praise Your glorious name.

1 CHRONICLES 29:13

One of the most beautiful doxologies (hymn of praise) in the Bible comes at an interesting moment in Israel's history. David had led a "capital campaign" in the nation for funds to build the first temple in Jerusalem. The people responded generously, which led David to praise and thank God. Why did David thank *God* for what the *people* had done (1 Chronicles 29:10–12)? Because he knew that everything the Israelites had contributed for the temple had been given to them by God. They gave to the temple project because God had first given to them.

David summarized the whole experience in this part of his prayer: "But who am I, and who are my people, that we should be able to offer so willingly as this? *For all things come from You, and of Your own we have given You*" (verse 14, italics added). There is a danger in forgetting about those precious gifts from God. Remember what David said: Everything—every breath, every bite of food, every blessing of any sort—comes from God. The chair you are sitting in and the coffee or tea you are sipping, it all has come from God.

Let David's words inspire you right now, and always, to thank God for what He has given you. Especialiy when you give to Him.

April 21

KNOW YOUR ANGER

"Be angry, and do not sin": do not let the sun go down on your wrath.
EPHESIANS 4:26

We read that Jesus Christ was without sin (Hebrews 4:15). But we also read where He, on occasion, seemed pretty angry. For instance, He cleared the merchants and money changers out of the temple with a whip, turning over their tables and spoiling their goods (John 2:12–16). He also sorely rebuked the Pharisees for their hypocrisy, calling them lots of derogatory names (Matthew 23). And isn't anger sin? Apparently not always, since Jesus got angry but didn't sin in the process.

There are two things to remember about biblical anger. First, we need to consider its *design*. Jesus' anger was righteous indignation at how God was being dishonored by the Pharisees and how the temple was being used. Anger at unrighteousness and injustice is not sinful. Second, we should reflect on the *duration* of anger. Anger is an emotion that leads to action. But when anger is nurtured into bitterness and resentment, it becomes self-serving and sinful. That is why Paul used the psalmist's words to remind the Ephesians not to take their anger to bed.

If you are feeling angry, examine the *design* of your anger and keep its *duration* short. Otherwise, anger can become a foothold for the devil (Ephesians 4:26–27).

IF THEY WERE WISE

"He makes His sun rise on the evil and on the good,
and sends rain on the just and on the unjust."

MATTHEW 5:45

*J*esus told us to treat people as kindly as we can, for that emulates our heavenly Father. He shares His sun with everyone whether they are good or evil, and He waters the fields of both the righteous farmer and the ungodly landowner.

Were they wise, people everywhere would look to the sky, see the beauty of the sunrise, feel the refreshing drops of replenishing rains, watch the migration of the birds, and praise God for the genius of His Creation.

Were they wise, secularists and atheists and skeptics would notice the brilliance of the stellar heavens and their self-evident intelligent design, and they would praise the God of the stars. Were they wise, all the hedonistic, self-absorbed people on earth would pause to thank God for their pulsing hearts and breathing lungs and incredible brains.

The evidence of God's goodness is everywhere to be seen. Some people are blind to it, but they're the ones most needing our kindness. Let's praise God for His power, and let's share His compassion today even with those who don't believe in it.

April 23

EXAMPLES

*My brethren, take the prophets, who spoke in the name of
the Lord, as an example of suffering and patience.*

JAMES 5:10

The New Testament admonishes us to follow the right examples. Jesus said, "I have given you an example, that you should do as I have done" (John 13:15). Paul told us that the Old Testament biographies "became our examples" (1 Corinthians 10:6, 11). He told us to follow his example (Philippians 3:17) and called the Thessalonians "examples to all in Macedonia" (1 Thessalonians 1:7).

We become like those we admire. Our superficial society idolizes celebrities, sports figures, and media personalities, but these superstars seldom provide a wholesome model. Don't follow them. Instead, we should look around for the most measured and mature Christian we can find and emulate that person. We can open our Bibles to the stories of the heroes of the faith and see how they learned to walk with God in a corrupt world. Read Christian biographies. Read missionary stories. Learn about the heroes of Christian history, and take some pages from their books.

Most of all, stay focused on Jesus Christ, the hero of the ages, the most influential person who ever lived. He will not only show you how to live a successful life—He will live it *through* you by His Holy Spirit.

ANANIAS

But Peter said, "Ananias, why has Satan filled your heart to lie to the
Holy Spirit and keep back part of the price of the land for yourself?"

ACTS 5:3

here were three men in the book of Acts named Ananias.
The first was the man to whom Peter spoke in Acts 5.
Ananias and his wife sold a piece of land and claimed they were
giving all the proceeds to the church. They were lying, and their
lie was exposed to protect the church from deceit.

The second Ananias was a fervent disciple of Christ in
Damascus who had the joy of leading Saul of Tarsus to faith
in Christ and facilitating his baptism (Acts 9:1–19). Paul later
described him as a man of "good testimony" (Acts 22:12).

The third Ananias was the high priest who commanded that
Paul be struck on the mouth in Acts 23:2. The apostle responded
angrily, "God will strike you, you whitewashed wall!" (verse 3).

We encounter these same three men today. Some in the
church have a corrupting influence. Some in the world oppose
the spread of the Gospel. But here and there we encounter true
saints who maintain a good testimony and seek to win others to
the Lord Jesus.

What kind of Ananias are you?

LIFE TAKES TIME

And [Paul] continued there a year and six months,
teaching the word of God among them.
ACTS 18:11

he Internet has changed everything, not the least of which is time. To use an extreme example, it once took weeks for a sailing ship to bring letters from Europe to America. Now those messages, via text or e-mail, arrive at the speed of light—in a second or two, usually. This new way of thinking about time hasn't changed everything, though. Plants grow at the same speed they always have—and so do people.

When the apostle Paul first went to Corinth, he stayed there a year and a half, "teaching the word of God among them." Could he have stayed a shorter time if the Internet had been available? He certainly could have used it to access information, buy books, and send messages. But those benefits will never take the place of person-to-person discipleship. Some things just take time. The Internet doesn't help us pray faster, read faster, talk faster, weep or rejoice faster, heal faster, fall and rise faster, or forgive faster. And therein lies the danger. Everything in life is moving so fast now that we forget that our spiritual lives and transformations still take time.

Be patient with yourself and with others. Commit to a local community of believers, and help the church grow. Put down roots; stay in one place. And remember that nothing takes the place of how God works over time.

WHY AFFLICTION IS GOOD

It is good for me that I have been afflicted, that I may learn Your statutes.

PSALM 119:71

*J*oseph's rise to power in Egypt was amazing in a land that looked down on nomadic Semite shepherds like himself (Genesis 43:32; 46:34). We know the theological reasons—God promoted Joseph to power in Egypt to prepare a place for Jacob's family. But humanly speaking, why were the Egyptians so taken with Joseph?

A clue may be in Psalm 119:98–100, where the psalmist says God's Word made him "wiser than [his] enemies"; he had "more understanding than all [his] teachers." And how did the psalmist gain such a commitment to God's statutes? Through affliction (Psalm 119:71). Before Joseph was promoted to power in Egypt, he suffered in an Egyptian prison after being falsely accused (Genesis 39:20). Suffering and affliction accomplish one of two things. They either drive us *to* God and His Word or *away from* God. In Joseph's case, his affliction drove him back to the truths he knew about God, resulting in his knowing God better and better—something the Egyptians ultimately recognized as wisdom.

If you are suffering today, don't let it drive you away from God. Reach out to Him and embrace His promises.

O PRAISE HIM!

Let them praise the name of the LORD, *for He*
commanded and they were created.
PSALM 148:5

salm 148 is addressed to a varied crowd: angels, sun
and moon, stars of light, sea creatures, fire, hail, snow
and clouds, mountains and hills, fruit trees and cedars, cattle and
insects, kings and princes, you and me. We're all commanded
to praise Him who created us. "Let them praise the name of the
LORD, for His name alone is exalted" (verse 13).

In 1934, Admiral Richard E. Byrd spent five months alone
in Antarctica, where he nearly perished. It was so cold he could
hear his breath crystallize in the air; but he was there to study the
environment and to search for meaning in his own life. At first
he felt terribly alone in the frozen wastelands, but he soon became
overwhelmed with the genius of a Creator. "I am not alone," he
wrote. "The human race is not alone in the universe. . . . For those
who seek it, there is inexhaustible evidence of an all-pervading
intelligence."[1]

As Psalm 148 says: "Snow and clouds . . . let them praise the
name of the LORD, for His name alone is exalted" (verses 8 and
13). In a moment of solitude, stop and consider His greatness, and
"praise the name of the LORD."

WHEN WE PRAY

Devote yourselves to prayer, being watchful and thankful.
COLOSSIANS 4:2 NIV

When God made the universe, He made two dimensions of reality. There is heaven and earth. There is the spiritual and the physical. Colossians 1:16 says, "For by Him all things were created that are in heaven and that are on earth, visible and invisible . . ." Similarly, 2 Corinthians 4:18 says, "So we fix our eyes not on what is seen, but on what is unseen, since what is seen is temporary, but what is unseen is eternal" (NIV).

There is one time when we can step into the spiritual realm and venture into the invisible—and that's when we pray. When we pray, we are pulling aside the curtain and making contact with the spiritual realm. Prayer is accessing the unseen kingdom and drawing near to our heavenly Father.

John Newton wrote, "Thou art coming to a King, / Large petitions with thee bring; / For His grace and power are such, / None can ever ask too much." We're closer than we know to the invisible realm of the spiritual, and we have access whenever we say, "Our Father who art in heaven . . ." What a privilege to do that right now!

THE GOD WHO COUNTS

And it came to pass in the six hundred and first year, in the first month, the first day of the month, that the waters were dried up from the earth.
GENESIS 8:13

*I*magine 46,000 cups of tea. That's the count for Queen Elizabeth II. That statistic came to light when she became Britain's longest-reigning monarch, surpassing Queen Victoria's reign of 63 years, 7 months, and 2 days. Journalists calculated the number based on her two customary daily cups of tea.

History is full of assorted odd statistics. One of the reasons we trust the Scriptures is that the accounts are specific, precise, and unequivocal. Read about Noah, for example, and notice all the numerical references: He had three sons. The ark was 300 cubits long, 50 cubits wide, and 30 cubits high, with three decks and one door. The animals came two by two. It rained 40 days, starting when Noah was 600 years old (plus 2 months and 17 days). The waters prevailed 150 days. And so forth.

In other words, we serve a God who counts. He even counts the hairs of our heads and the days of our lives. He's a God who multiplies grace and calculates blessings. Why not give Him the sum total of your praise?

BLESSED TO BE A BLESSING

*"I will make you a great nation; I will bless you and make
your name great; and you shall be a blessing. . . . And in
you all the families of the earth shall be blessed."*

GENESIS 12:2–3

The next time you cut open a piece of fruit, pause to marvel at the abundance of seeds it contains. The seeds represent the process of renewal in nature, but they also represent an important necessity—plants require seeds to reproduce so that they do not become extinct! God blessed His creation so it could "be fruitful and multiply" (Genesis 1:28; 9:1). Even our own blessing of regeneration and salvation is to become a source of blessing to others.

The idea of "blessed to be a blessing" is seen earliest and most clearly in God's calling of Abraham. God didn't call Abraham out of Mesopotamia just to give him a richer life in Canaan. Yes, Abraham was blessed personally, but there was a greater purpose: "In you all the families of the earth shall be blessed" (Genesis 12:3). Through Abraham's faith and God's covenantal promise, generations of people have come to faith. "So then those who are of faith are blessed with believing Abraham" (Galatians 3:9).

Ask God to make you aware of someone who needs the blessing of God today. Plant a seed; share your faith; be a blessing.

MAY

*But God demonstrates His own love toward us, in
that while we were still sinners, Christ died for us.*

ROMANS 5:8

KNOWING ONE THING

For I determined not to know anything among you
except Jesus Christ and Him crucified.

1 CORINTHIANS 2:2

t times the complexity of the issues facing our world today seems overwhelming. In this global environment, the average person may feel inadequate to offer opinions on world-level issues, but that frequently doesn't keep us from offering an opinion.

The apostle Paul was highly educated, but he did not play the "I'm smarter than you" game. In his day, there were some teachers going about—Paul referred to them as "super-apostles" (2 Corinthians 11:5 NIV; 12:11 NIV)—who tried to impress others with their intellect. But Paul reminded the Corinthians that when he visited them he "did not come with excellence of speech or of wisdom" (1 Corinthians 2:1). Instead, he came knowing only one thing: "Jesus Christ and Him crucified." Paul was basically saying, "Let's focus on the most important thing first. If you know that one thing, it doesn't matter what you don't know." The biggest problem the world faces today is being reconciled to God. Knowing the answer to that problem is where all problem-solving begins.

Have you been reconciled to God through Christ? If you have, it means you can live confidently in a world of "grand ideas" with a heavenly destination in view. You may not know the answer to every question, but you know the One who does.

TAKE THE GIFT

For by grace you have been saved through faith, and that not of
yourselves; it is the gift of God, not of works, lest anyone should boast.

EPHESIANS 2:8–9

ou work hard in your vegetable garden and harvest an abundance of fresh produce. So, you collect a bag full of tomatoes, beans, cucumbers, and squash, and knock on your neighbor's door to share the bounty. As you hand her the gift from your garden, she asks if she can pay you something. You decline but understand. If it's not Christmas, a birthday, or an anniversary, people are uncomfortable with the idea of receiving a gift.

The human tendency to want to work for what we get, the feeling that what is not earned is undeserved, keeps many from understanding the Gospel of the grace of God. Salvation is no more free than the cost of growing vegetables. But just as you paid the price so your neighbor could have a gift, so Jesus Christ paid the price for salvation and offers it as a gift to us. We are "saved through faith, . . . not [by] works, lest anyone should boast" (Ephesians 2:8–9). Salvation "is the gift of God." When we pay for a gift, it ceases to be a gift at all.

There's only one thing to do with God's offer of the gift of salvation: Say thank you and embrace it.

EUREKA!

So then faith comes by hearing, and hearing by the word of God.
ROMANS 10:17

ou've no doubt had this experience: You've been pondering a problem for days without a solution, and then it hits you. Or you suddenly see an old situation in a brand-new light: "Wow! Now I get it!" It's the kind of "Eureka!" moment that brushes away the cobwebs and pulls back the curtain and lets the light in.

Those moments happen in the spiritual life as well—there is even a Greek word in the New Testament that, in a way, describes it happening. That word is *rhema*—it refers to a word, thing, or message. Normally, the "Word" of God is a translation of *logos*—a word, concept, speech. Because the two are similar, think of the Bible as the *logos* of God and a particular verse as a *rhema* of God. In Romans 10:17, Paul says that faith comes from hearing the *rhema* of God—a word or message that suddenly moves you to faith. The Holy Spirit quickens a truth about God to your heart, and you see something new, something that leads you to faith—either faith for the first time or faith in a new way.

As you are reading the Bible, both are important: *logos* and *rhema*. But be prepared for those moments when faith is quickened by a promise of God you are moved to believe. Be ready for a "Eureka!" moment every time you open the Bible to read. And then act on the faith that rises up within your heart and mind.

Pleasing God

For before [Enoch] was taken he had this testimony, that he pleased God.
HEBREWS 11:5

It is the classic theme of world literature—the need of a lesser being to please a greater being. Whether the greater being is a king, a tyrant, an ogre, or a fantastical being, the subject's need is to discover what the ruler demands and do it. Tension in the story builds as it looks less and less likely that the subject will be able to please the ruler.

The Bible is part of world literature, and it shares that theme with other great stories. The Bible's story—the necessity for man to please God—is at the same time more and less dramatic. First, God requires only one thing to be pleased: "But without faith it is impossible to please Him" (Hebrews 11:6). Everything else we might do to please the Creator God does not qualify unless it is preceded by faith. Second, there is a dramatic crisis and solution: God becomes a human being so dedicated to God that He lives a *perfectly* faithful life and dies to pay for the faithlessness of all other men. The life of pleasing God is illustrated simply by Enoch: "He pleased God."

If it is your desire to please God, always begin with faith. Our belief in Him seems to bring Him more pleasure than anything else.

May 5

WHY DO DOUBTS ARISE IN YOUR MIND?

And He said to them, "Why are you troubled? And why do doubts arise in your hearts?"

LUKE 24:38

As Christians, we place our faith in the Lord Jesus and believe what the Bible says about Him. We believe He died for our sins and rose on the third day. We believe He returned to heaven and is coming again. We believe those things because they are true. Our faith is rooted in clear thinking, and we know we can hold it with intellectual integrity.

Yet traces of doubt can still streak through our minds as it happened to the disciples in Luke 24. When Jesus appeared on Easter evening, they were terrified and thought He was a spirit. He allayed their fears with the reality of His presence, saying, "Why do doubts arise in your hearts? Behold My hands and My feet . . ." (verses 38–39).

If you suffer twinges of doubt, don't panic. Keep your eyes on Jesus. Look at His wounds. Study His resurrection. Look at how He changes lives. And the same Savior who convinced the disciples will strengthen your faith.

WHAT GOD CANNOT DO

God is not a man, that He should lie, nor a son of man,
that He should repent. Has He said, and will He not do?
Or has He spoken, and will He not make it good?

NUMBERS 23:19

nxious? Fearful? Worried? Depressed? Perhaps we need to remember what Joshua said: "Not a word failed of any good thing which the LORD had spoken to the house of Israel. All came to pass. . . . Behold, this day I am going the way of all the earth. And you know in all your hearts and in all your souls that not one thing has failed of all the good things which the LORD your God spoke concerning you" (Joshua 21:45; 23:14).

King Solomon made the same point at the dedication of the temple in 1 Kings 8:56, saying, "There has not failed one word of all His good promise."

Titus 1:2 says, "God, who cannot lie, promised."

Hebrews 6:18 adds, "It is impossible for God to lie"; and so, said the writer, that's why we "lay hold of the hope set before us." God has never broken, and will never break, a single promise—past, present, or future. Trust Him today with your anxiety, fear, worry, and depression. Lean on His power, love, grace, and mercy.

SATAN'S ULTIMATE GOAL

But now, stretch out Your hand and touch all that [Job]
has, and he will surely curse You to Your face!
JOB 1:11

Nothing hurts quite like betrayal. It can come in many forms: lies, a withdrawal of loyalty, a lack of defense, or disfavor. The effect is devastating. It's a universal feeling; everyone who has been betrayed suffers immensely. And the loss of confidence can take a great amount of time and effort to restore.

Satan's ultimate goal in spiritual warfare is to make us lose confidence in God, to feel betrayed by God, to make God seem disloyal and dishonest. If Satan tries to hurt us or disrupt our life, it is so we will call upon God and conclude He isn't listening. Satan wants to destroy our faith in the goodness and power of God. That was Satan's strategy with Job. Satan told God that Job was only faithful to God because God protected him. If God would allow Satan to make Job suffer, He would see that Job would give up on God. But Satan was surprised. When God allowed Satan to hurt Job twice, Job never faltered in his faith: "'Shall we indeed accept good from God, and shall we not accept adversity?' In all this Job did not sin with his lips" (Job 2:10).

If you ever find yourself feeling betrayed by God, even losing confidence in Him, you know Satan is at work. Stop the downward spiral and restore your faith. Trust in His goodness.

May 8

SIGNS OF LIFE

We know that we have passed from death to life, because we love the brethren.

1 JOHN 3:14

In earlier ages it was often hard to determine when someone was actually dead. Books of historical oddities are filled with accounts of people accidentally buried alive. Hans Christian Andersen was so petrified by the prospect that he kept a sign by his bed, bearing the words: "I am not really dead." Painter Auguste Renoir insisted doctors do whatever was necessary to prove he was dead before burial. George Washington told attendants to keep his body above ground for three days before burial.

According to Scripture, those without Christ are spiritually dead, but those who know Him are alive. If we're alive, there should be signs of life. People should instantly see that we're living in Christ. There should be no mistake about it. We should bear evidence of Christ's life—a love that consumes us, a joy that sustains us, a hope that brightens our outlook, a purity that maintains our holiness, and a commitment that makes others want to follow our Savior.

It's a tragedy when people don't know if we're dead or alive in Christ. Let the world know you're alive.

A GRANDFATHER'S INFLUENCE

For in the eighth year of his reign, while he was still young,
he began to seek the God of his father David.

2 CHRONICLES 34:3

King Manasseh was one of the worst men in history. He sat on Judah's throne fifty-five years and led his nation into a quagmire of idolatry, occultism, human sacrifice, lawlessness, violence, and moral confusion. Late in life, he turned to the Lord. His spiritual conversion was too late to influence his nation—but not his grandson.

Josiah was six years old when his grandfather died, and eight years old when he ascended Judah's throne. Remarkably, he was a God-lover who led Judah to unprecedented revival.

How can that be? Perhaps he'd been influenced by his grandfather's repentance. We can almost see old Manasseh, hands trembling with regret, pulling his grandson close and saying, "Son, one day you'll be king of Judah. Don't make the same mistakes I did. Try to reverse the damage I caused. Give your heart to the Lord and lead this nation righteously."

Grandparents cast a powerful shadow. Whatever your past mistakes, take every opportunity to shine the light of your testimony into the lives of your grandchildren and future generations. If you're the grandchild of a godly man or woman, continue that grandparent's legacy. God longs to give us unprecedented revival.

PAIN AND GAIN

And Pharaoh said to Joseph, "See, I have set you over all the land of Egypt."
GENESIS 41:41

*D*id you hear about the Christian who said his dream was to be a retired missionary? How about the person who wanted to be an author but not a writer? Or the little boy who said he'd like to be the Most Valuable Player on his team? These folks are looking at what only comes after years of work, practice, and suffering. Missionaries have to toil thanklessly, authors have to learn to write, and young athletes must practice repeatedly. It's a cliché because it is often true: there is no gain without a measure of pain.

Joseph didn't go to Egypt with his eyes set on becoming Pharaoh's prime minister. He spent more than a decade as a servant, a steward, and a prisoner, and risked his life as an interpreter of Pharaoh's dreams before God rewarded his faithfulness with a place of honor. Even for Jesus Christ, the cross preceded the crown. Life is all about gaining maturity, and maturity must be tested and perfected through trials.

The path to blessing and honor always goes through the land of testing and obedience. Stay on that path, and trust God for where it leads. Be faithful in the little and difficult things on the way.

GOOD FORGIVERS

"Forgive us our debts, as we forgive our debtors."
MATTHEW 6:12

The Bible is full of people who learned to forgive. Esau is one of the great forgivers in the Bible. His brother, Jacob, had exploited and deceived him, a story of sibling rivalry gone bad. But years later, when the brothers were reunited and Jacob feared his brother would try to kill him, Esau came instead with open arms and a forgiving spirit.

In the same way, Joseph forgave the brothers who had betrayed him. In fact, perhaps he had learned from his uncle Esau how to forgive others. Just as Job forgave the friends who had tormented him, Hosea forgave the wife who had betrayed him.

The prodigal's father is a picture of parental forgiveness. Stephen forgave his executioners in the last moments of his life. The early Christians forgave Saul of Tarsus for persecuting them and allowed him into their community of believers as the apostle Paul. Philemon forgave Onesimus for robbing him and accepted him as a Christian brother.

And, of course, the greatest master of forgiveness in the Bible is the Lord Jesus Himself who shed His blood to provide redemption and forgiveness of sins.

Is there someone you need to forgive? The Bible says, "And be kind to one another, tenderhearted, forgiving one another, even as God in Christ forgave you" (Ephesians 4:32).

Practice being a good forgiver.

Noah Walked with God

But Noah found favor in the eyes of the Lord. . . . *Noah was a*
righteous man, blameless in his time; Noah walked with God.

Genesis 6:8–9 NASB

e wonder if we live in the most evil age in history given the atrocities that happen around us. But it appears there has been an age when wickedness was even more widespread than in our own: the age described in Genesis 6. That age was so wicked that God "was sorry that He had made man on the earth" (verse 6). It was the age that prompted the Flood, after which God started over with Noah and his family.

Noah was an Adam-type man whom God trusted to be the new head of the human race. Noah wasn't sinless, like Adam before the fall, but he was righteous; he was a man who "walked with God." Genesis 6:9 suggests that he may have been the only human being of his kind on earth in that age, the only man who sought to follow God's will and who could be trusted with God's mission to preserve human and animal life on earth. Noah was faithful. In the face of probable derision and scorn from his community, he built an ark and preserved life on earth.

Noah raises this question: If God looked for one person who would be faithful to Him in a specific task, would His eyes rest upon you?

TROUBLE IS NORMAL

. . . strengthening the souls of the disciples, exhorting them
to continue in the faith, and saying, "We must through
many tribulations enter the kingdom of God."

ACTS 14:22

efore they mature in their faith and develop a biblical worldview, young Christians can be surprised when they endure hardships. Some early Christians believed Jesus would protect them from pain and suffering until it was time to enter heaven. Even though Jesus Himself suffered terribly, as did His apostles, it comes as a surprise to many Christians when they encounter pain and suffering.

But Paul made a priority of explaining to new followers of Christ that troubles in life are to be expected: "We must through many tribulations enter the kingdom of God." What exactly does "enter the kingdom" mean? It doesn't mean being saved; we don't have to suffer to enter God's eternal kingdom. But it does mean that a decision to enter the kingdom of God through faith in Christ should be made with the realization that suffering will follow. There are two kinds of trouble—the trouble from living in a fallen world and the trouble that comes from opponents of the Gospel who may attack us. Persevering through trials is part of our kingdom life.

Like the apostle Paul, we should recognize that tribulation is normal and allow trials to draw us into deeper communion with Christ (2 Corinthians 12:7–10).

THE SHIELD OF FAITH

Therefore take heart, men, for I believe God
that it will be just as it was told me.

ACTS 27:25

When the tragic shooting of nine people of faith occurred in a South Carolina church in 2015, the hearts of not only their families grieved, but the nation mourned as well. How could this happen? How could someone spend time with these lovely people in a Bible study and then turn on them? We will never have all the answers, but we do know that evil entered into the heart of that young man, and he acted with hatred and malice. It was an attack not only on these precious individuals but on people of faith. It is a reminder to us all to keep our shield of faith in place at all times.

What a poignant reminder that we need the shield of faith to protect us. No, physical violence isn't the greatest threat to most of us, but Satan is still on the attack. Without the shield of faith, it's easy to fall victim to the doubt Satan throws at us. We're tempted to doubt the outcome of our situations, the answers to our prayers, and the promises God has made. If we lay down our shield, we're fully vulnerable to the lies launched in our direction. But Satan has no answer to those who say, "Take heart . . . I believe God that it will be just as it was told me." Faith is the victory that overcomes the world.

UNENDING LOVE

Therefore, there is now no condemnation for those who are in Christ Jesus.
ROMANS 8:1 NIV

fter serving two terms as president, James Madison and his wife, Dolley, retired to Montpelier, their Virginia home. In Madison's final days, he was weak and bed-ridden. Madison's personal servant, Paul Jennings, wrote later in his memoir that Dolley Madison sat by her husband's bedside up to eighteen hours a day. She never left his side for more than fifteen or twenty minutes at a time.

We could easily say that very little could separate James Madison from the love of his wife, Dolley. Her love for him was constant. But we can say with greater confidence that nothing can separate the Christian from the love of God in Christ. Is it right to picture God by our side twenty-four hours a day, even while we are sleeping? Through the power of the indwelling Holy Spirit, that is a most appropriate image. The apostle Paul suggests a number of things we might think could separate us from God's love—the condemnation of sin, death, spiritual powers, things unimagined—and says none of them are that strong. Nothing can separate us from God in Christ.

If you are a Christian, remind yourself today that you are safe in God's presence. His love attends your every need in life or in death.

INSPIRATION OR IMPULSE?

Let nothing be done through selfish ambition or conceit, but in lowliness of mind let each esteem others better than himself.

PHILIPPIANS 2:3

wo men were riding their horses down a country road, discussing the question of motivation. One believed we're capable of pure motives, even without Christ. The other disagreed. They came to a ditch where a pig had gotten tangled up in fencing and was struggling to extricate himself. The latter gentlemen got down in the mud and managed to free the animal, though he ruined his clothing. Resuming their trip, the first man said, "There! That was a selfless act of kindness." But his friend replied, "No, it was pure selfishness. The only reason I helped that pig was to save myself from the guilt and torment of worrying about him all day."

Without Christ, it's impossible to operate from true love and godly motivations. But as we grow in Him, our motives gradually improve and we're increasingly compelled by His love, which is "poured out into our hearts through the Holy Spirit, who has been given to us" (Romans 5:5 NIV).

Only in Christ can we exhibit humility (lowliness of mind) and be motivated by biblical love rather than our own desires.

Playing Favorites

. . . remembering without ceasing your work of faith, labor of love, and patience of hope in our Lord Jesus Christ in the sight of our God and Father.

1 Thessalonians 1:3

irst Corinthians 13 might be Paul's most well-known passage, with the last verse being the most famous: "And now abide faith, hope, love, these three; but the greatest of these is love" (verse 13). It's no surprise to see these three virtues together; the New Testament groups them together frequently (Galatians 5:5–6; Colossians 1:4–5; Hebrews 6:10–12; 10:22–24; 1 Peter 1:21–22).

Paul elaborated on these three in the very first words he wrote to the Thessalonians. He commended them for their work of *faith*, labor of *love*, and patient *hope*. *Work* is most likely ministry-related activity. *Labor* is work, but it stresses the exertion and difficulty. And *hope* keeps us patient and helps us persevere. It is faith that fuels ministry, love that inspires us to serve others sacrificially and unconditionally, and hope in the Second Coming and eternal life that allows us to persevere in difficult times. Faith, hope, and love are a good checklist, a good gauge, for how we are doing in the Christian life. Kingdom work, love for others, and hope for the future.

Considering the frequency of their use and consistency in their union, perhaps faith, hope, and love should be our favorite virtues.

HAND GESTURES

You open Your hand and satisfy the desire of every living thing.

PSALM 145:16

*H*and gestures can communicate our innermost thoughts and emotions. Clenched fists reveal anger. White knuckles and trembling are usually the result of fear and nervousness. We close our hands around things we want to hold on to and open them to receive and give gifts.

God's generosity is described in the verse above. He created and sustains life. He opens His hand and satisfies the desire of every living thing. Our very existence is dependent on God. If we overlook God's generosity or find ourselves in the midst of a painful season, it's easy for a mind-set of scarcity to take over. We become afraid of losing what we have, and our hearts' stance becomes one of grasping as we seek to control our circumstances.

This is an exhausting place to be. Not only do circumstances remain outside our control, but we miss opportunities to participate in the joy of giving because we are focused on protecting what we have. We also miss God's gifts to us because we are focused on our lack. The first step to living with open hands is to embrace the truth of God's generosity. When we believe in God's goodness and His love for us, we find the freedom to receive and release His gifts.

DOES HE CARE?

When the Lord saw her, He had compassion on
her and said to her, "Do not weep."

LUKE 7:13

er tears blurred her vision. While we do not know if she saw Jesus, we know she did not reach out to him: Yet her son was dead and needed life. She knew Jesus was a healer, but what could He do for her? In the midst of her grief, Jesus saw her, and He had compassion. Instead of skipping to the happy end of this story, let's stop here: Jesus had compassion.

This simple phrase is found throughout each of the Gospels. An integral part of Jesus' character is His compassion. Sometimes we find it easier to pray for others than for ourselves. We subconsciously wonder, *Why would God help me?* We forget Jesus' compassion when we get stuck in this mind-set. The life-changing truth is that Jesus is good and He encourages us to ask Him for help. He never ran from disease, death, or wretchedness. We may not understand why certain prayers are answered quickly while others hang painfully in the air, but we can be assured that He sees us and He cares.

Fleeing and Joining

Let love be without hypocrisy. Abhor what is evil. Cling to what is good.

ROMANS 12:9

hristianity is known for its emphasis on love: God so *loved* the world, *love* your neighbor, *love* your enemies, and more. But there are times when we are told to hate—specifically, we are told to hate what is evil while we cling to what is good.

The two words Paul used in Romans 12:9 for "hate" (or "abhor") and "cling" are instructive. Indeed, they are almost opposites. The word for "abhor" is used only once in the New Testament—here in this verse. *Abhor* is a better translation than *hate* because it carries the idea of revulsion—of shrinking back with disgust and detestation. It is an active word, not passive; we are to actively pull away from that which is evil. *Cling*, on the other hand, is a word that means to glue something, to join to something else. Once joined, we are to "cling" to—to stay joined to—that which is good. So when it comes to evil, we are to back away in disgust, but we are to glue ourselves to that which is good—and stay joined to it.

Think about your own life—your practices, your thoughts, your entertainment choices, your words. Is there somewhere you need to back away, and somewhere else you need to cling more tightly?

May 21

WORD AND SPIRIT

The Spirit of the LORD *spoke by me, and His word was on my tongue.*
2 SAMUEL 23:2

here are some things that always go together: a person and her shadow, two sides of a coin, the blades of scissors—and the Spirit of God and the Word of God. It is the Word of God that establishes God's will in the earth, and it is the Spirit of God that enables, illumines, and empowers that Word.

For instance, when God spoke the world into existence, the Spirit was there (Genesis 1:2). When early Christians were "filled with the Holy Spirit . . . they spoke the word of God with boldness" (Acts 4:31). And the "sword of the Spirit" is "the word of God" (Ephesians 6:17). When the Bible exhorts Christians to "be transformed by the renewing of [their] mind[s]" (Romans 12:2), it means learning to think God's way instead of the world's way. It means to replace lies with truth. We do that by reading God's Word, which means the Spirit is the means of the transformation. It is the Spirit that gives understanding that leads to changed lives.

Don't neglect the daily reading and study of God's Word. A day missed is transformation delayed.

David's Epitaph

For David, after he had served his own generation by the will of God, fell asleep, was buried with his fathers, and saw corruption.

ACTS 13:36

Epitaphs on gravestones are not as popular as they once were. In previous generations, a person could write his or her own epitaph—a summary of one's life or legacy—before death, or leave the task to a friend or family member. The subject of epitaphs raises a good question: How would you want your life to be permanently remembered in one short sentence or phrase?

When the apostle Paul was preaching in a synagogue in Pisidian Antioch, Israel's King David had been dead and buried for a thousand years. But in leading up to talking about Christ's Resurrection, Paul cited King David as a man who was buried and whose body decayed in the ground. Unwittingly, Paul spoke what would have been a beautiful and simple epitaph for David: "He served his own generation by the will of God" (Acts 13:36). Bible students know that David was far from perfect. But in spite of his sins and errors in judgment, David had a heart for God (verse 22).

God doesn't hold us responsible for past or future generations. But He does ask us to serve Him in our own generation, as David did. There could be no greater legacy or remembrance.

A SACRED TASK

Whenever you come together . . . [l]et all things be done for edification.
1 CORINTHIANS 14:26

o understand edification, go back to the Old Testament building of the tabernacle in the wilderness: "Then have them make a sanctuary for me, and I will dwell among them" (Exodus 25:8 NIV). The Hebrews were instructed to *build* a dwelling place for God. Fast-forward to 1 Corinthians 3:16–17: "Don't you know that you yourselves are God's temple and that God's Spirit dwells in your midst? . . . God's temple is sacred, and you . . . are that temple" (NIV).

Edification means a building or the act of building. Just as the Israelites built a tabernacle as God's dwelling place, so the Church is the "building" we are constructing until Christ returns. And how do we build the Church? With God's wisdom by His Word and Spirit. In short, the truth of God is the "mortar" that binds the "living stones" (1 Peter 2:5) of the Church together. As we learn, apply, and share God's truth with each other, God's "building," the Church, gets stronger.

Are you mixing the mortar? Are you walking in the truth, applying the truth to your life and the lives of others? Ours is a sacred task, a sacred temple.

THE GIFT OF FORGIVENESS

*By faith the harlot Rahab did not perish with those who did
not believe, when she had received the spies with peace.*

HEBREWS 11:31

ometimes Christians wonder if they have committed
a sin that God cannot forgive. Or they wonder if they
have committed *the* unforgivable sin (Matthew 12:31–32). As for
the latter possibility, Jesus was speaking to Pharisees, who will-
fully rejected Christ's divine credentials as the Son of God. No
Christian is in danger of committing that sin.

As for committing a terrible sin that God cannot forgive,
the Bible is clear: all have sinned (Romans 3:23), and all may
receive eternal life (John 3:16). Because we live in societies that
are required to exact punishment for crimes, it is difficult to comprehend the idea that "if we confess our sins, He is faithful and
just to forgive us our sins and to cleanse us from all unrighteousness" (1 John 1:9). But He is! A pagan prostitute named Rahab
found that out personally. She threw herself on the mercy of the
Israelites' God when His people entered Canaan. And she was
forgiven her past and rewarded for her faithfulness (Joshua 2).

God withholds forgiveness from no one who needs and seeks
it. If that applies to you today, confess your sins and be forgiven.

COLD FEET

Asa became diseased in his feet, and his malady was
severe; yet in his disease he did not seek the LORD.
2 CHRONICLES 16:12

The story of King Asa occupies three chapters in 2 Chronicles. In chapter 14, we see him trusting the Lord, instituting revival, and rejoicing in victory. In chapter 15, he hears and heeds the prophetic message. But several years pass, and by chapter 16 Asa wants nothing to do with the Lord. His diseased feet couldn't find the right path. Somehow, he had lost the fire and faith of his earlier walk with God.

Why? Perhaps he stopped reading his Scriptures. Maybe his life became too busy for prayer. He might have allowed resentments to fester in his heart. Perhaps he fell into sin and his conscience was gradually dulled.

Whatever happened, Asa serves as a warning to us. We must keep close to the Lord every day, being quick to confess and turn from all known sin. Our hearts should break when we do wrong, knowing it was our sins that nailed Jesus to the cross. We each should keep a tender heart, one that is growing warmer, not colder. Ask God today for a tender conscience and a closer walk with Him.

CHRIST ALONE

"Behold I lay in Zion a chief cornerstone, elect, precious, and he who believes on Him will by no means be put to shame."

I PETER 2:6

uman beings are committed to making lists—and not just to-do lists. We create lists to rank all manner of things. Athletic teams are ranked, students in graduating classes are ranked, and music is ranked on the charts. *Fortune* magazine ranks the top companies, and *Forbes* magazine ranks the richest people.

The book of Hebrews does some ranking of its own, but in a different way. The world ranks groups of equals to see who is number one. And while Hebrews ranks Jesus Christ as number one, it is not because He is first among equals. He is number one in all of creation because He has no equal. The first three verses of Hebrews 1 summarize why Christ is superior to angels, Moses, priests, and everyone else—because only Christ has taken away our sins and has sat down at the right hand of God as a sign of the Father's approval of what Christ accomplished. No one else has done for us what Christ has done for us.

Christ sets Christianity apart from all other religions. He is the only person who had the remedy for human sin and was qualified to carry it out on our behalf. For that and more, today He deserves our praise.

TRUST GOD'S PROVISION

And Elijah said to her, "Do not fear; go and do as you have said, but make me a small cake from it first, and bring it to me; and afterward make some for yourself and your son.

1 KINGS 17:13

The widow glanced at all she had left: a handful of flour and a little oil. As she went outside to gather sticks for her and her son's last meal, she was preparing herself for the end. When she met the prophet Elijah and he requested water and bread, she explained her situation.

Elijah encouraged her to look beyond her circumstances to God's provision, saying "Do not fear" (1 Kings 17:13). As she prepared Elijah's meal that day and each day that followed, she had a choice to either trust God's provision or to protect the little she had.

When God prompts us to serve, it's easy to focus on our resources instead of on God's glory. It's easy to list our lack of resources as an excuse or to mistakenly take the glory for ourselves when we have the resources. We forget that everything we have comes from God. His glory is tangible and real. Elijah asked the widow to set aside fear and to serve based on the God she was serving.

God is powerful, and all glory belongs to Him. He changes circumstances and redeems even the darkest of circumstances. In the midst of situations the world sees as hopeless, we can cling to Elijah's words, "Do not fear."

LEARNING TO SAY, "THANK YOU"

Therefore by Him let us continually offer the sacrifice of praise to God, that is, the fruit of our lips, giving thanks to His name.

HEBREWS 13:15

One of the first things parents do with their children is teach them to say, "Thank you." Later, children learn to write thank-you notes for Christmas and birthday gifts. The expression of gratitude is a learned trait, and "Thank you" hopefully becomes a spontaneous response.

"Thank You" to God is a form of worship, springing from a sense of gratitude. Saying "Thank You" to God is a learned expression of worship in response to His gifts. Worship is also a sacrifice. At the very least, we sacrifice time, talent, and treasure in worshiping God, all of which could have been spent differently. The first act of worship recorded in human history was an act of sacrifice by Cain and Abel (Genesis 4:1–4). While Cain's sacrifice was based on selfish interests, Abel's sacrifice was pleasing to God and cited as exemplary (Hebrews 11:4). Upon learning what God has done for him, the Christian should respond first with the "sacrifice of praise" (Hebrews 13:15)—the sacrifice of saying, "Thank You."

Use your desire to worship God as a measure of your gratitude to Him.

DOUBLE BLESSINGS

But this I say: He who sows sparingly will also reap sparingly,
and he who sows bountifully will also reap bountifully.
2 CORINTHIANS 9:6

hen it comes to stewardship, our giving to God is like a farmer sowing seed in a field. If we sow abundantly, we reap abundantly; if we sow sparingly, we reap sparingly. But can that principle be applied to other areas of life besides financial stewardship?

Paul suggests it can. Before he wrote the words of 2 Corinthians 9:6 to the Corinthians, he wrote to the Galatians: "Do not be deceived, God is not mocked; for whatever a man sows, that he will also reap" (Galatians 6:7). The context of that verse was not finances but the moral life: Sow to the flesh and reap destruction; sow to the Spirit and reap life. In other words, sowing and reaping is a general principle of God's economy that applies to all areas of life. Take love and compassion, for example. If we sow compassion toward others, we will reap compassion from others. Being a compassionate person (or a kind, loving, generous, patient person) is a path to a double blessing for the receiver as well as the giver.

If you need compassion today, sow compassion toward others—double your blessings.

NOT OF THIS WORLD

"I have given them Your word; and the world has hated them
because they are not of the world, just as I am not of the world."

JOHN 17:14

After His last sermon in the Gospels, which is recorded in John 13–16, Jesus paused to pray for His disciples, and His words are preserved in the next chapter, John 17. In verse 14 He prayed, "I am not of the world." Being eternally God, Jesus entered the world via a virgin birth and left the world by ascending to heaven from the Mount of Olives. He was truly "not of the world."

But the preceding phrase in verse 14 is mind-bending, for it says of us, His followers, "They are not of the world, just as I am not of the world." We don't belong to this world any more than Jesus did. Our citizenship is in heaven, our eternal home is there, and our values are determined from there—just like Him. These aren't easy days to be a Christian, but no such days have ever existed. The challenges of living a Christian life in today's culture can't be used as an excuse for not walking with God. Stay true to Him no matter what the world says. If you sometimes feel out of place on planet Earth, remember that you are a citizen of heaven. What you feel is a longing for your native land.

HOW TO BE SECURE

But whoever listens to me will dwell safely, and
will be secure, without fear of evil.

PROVERBS 1:33

*I*s there a better word than *insecure* to describe how many people feel today? The economy, world events, the breakdown of cultural norms and traditions—certainly none of those events contributes to feelings of security. Is it possible to feel secure in the modern world? According to Solomon, yes.

The first nine chapters of the book of Proverbs are words of advice from a father to his immature son. The teachings, principles, and exhortations are designed to turn a naive youth into a wise man (or woman). "Wisdom" is personified in Proverbs 1:20–33—she is given her own voice as she speaks to the simple and foolish young men of the day. She warns them against ignoring her wise words, saying she will ignore them in their day of trouble if they don't heed her advice. But if they do listen and obey, they will "dwell safely, and will be secure, without fear of evil." In other words, it is possible to live confidently regardless of what happens around us. Security comes from listening to, and obeying, what God says about walking in His ways.

There is no better way to live in peace and security than to live according to the precepts of God's wisdom and teachings.

JUNE

*Therefore let those who suffer according to
the will of God commit their souls to Him
in doing good, as to a faithful Creator.*

1 PETER 4:19

JESUS IN ME

Be of the same mind toward one another. Do not set your mind on high things, but associate with the humble. Do not be wise in your own opinion.
ROMANS 12:16

The apostle Paul never lived with Christ, learning from Him during His earthly life. Paul's personal knowledge of Jesus was based on visions (Acts 9:1–8; 23:11; 2 Corinthians 12:1–4) and what he was told by the other apostles. And yet Paul's knowledge of Christ was profound—it infiltrated what he wrote to the early churches.

Paul's simple words to the Roman church in Romans 12:16— be like-minded, not high-minded; associate with the poor and humble; don't be conceited or wise in your own eyes—parallel the words he used to describe Jesus in Philippians 2:5–11. After repeating some of the same admonitions to the Philippians as he wrote to the Romans, Paul said, in short, "Be like Jesus." Jesus was humble, leaving heaven to associate with poor sinners; He wasn't conceited or wise in His own eyes; He considered our needs more important than His own; He humbled Himself before the will of God.

Our calling as Christians is not so much to *imitate* Christ as to allow the *indwelling* Christ to live His life through us (Galatians 2:20; 5:22–23). Yield yourself today to the Holy Spirit, who is *in* you to manifest Christ *through* you (Romans 8:14).

FAMOUS LAST WORDS

The time of my departure is at hand. I have fought the good fight, I have finished the race, I have kept the faith.

2 TIMOTHY 4:6–7

he apostle Paul focused on Christ to the end. His final words are found in 2 Timothy 4, written shortly before Nero's soldiers beheaded him. Three things occupied Paul's mind.

First, Paul wanted to continue *God's work* till the last moment. He told Timothy, "Get Mark and bring him with you, for he is useful to me for ministry" (verse 11). Second, Paul wanted to study *God's Word* as long as possible, telling Timothy to bring "the books, especially the parchments" (verse 13). Third, he wanted *God's will* to perfectly unfold in his life with every passing minute and forever. He wrote, "The Lord stood with me and strengthened me, so that the message might be preached fully through me. . . . And the Lord will deliver me from every evil work and preserve me for His heavenly kingdom" (verses 17–18).

We stay centered in Christ when we focus on His work, His Word, and His will. When we keep the core of our souls strengthened, we can withstand Satan's threats. Whatever comes, we can praise the Lord, saying, "To Him be glory forever and ever. Amen!" (verse 18).

June 3

LISTENING EARS

*They found Him in the temple, sitting in the midst of the
teachers, both listening to them and asking them questions.*
LUKE 2:46

*L*istening is such a simple act," wrote management
consultant Margaret J. Wheatley. "It requires us to be
present, and that takes practice, but we don't have to do anything
else. We don't have to advise, or coach, or sound wise. We just
have to be willing to sit there and listen."[1]

Jesus certainly knew how to advise, coach, and communicate His wisdom. The teaching of the ages rolled off His tongue,
and His Words change our lives. Yet He also knew how to listen.
He freely gave the present of listening ears. He heard the cries
of widows, the perplexity of disciples, the voices of children, the
confusion of rulers, and the voice of His Father.

According to Proverbs 20:5, people's hearts are like deep
waters, "but a man of understanding will draw [them] out." Those
who listen have a way of uncovering the needs of others. We can't
solve everyone's problems, but sometimes listening is enough. Let
every one of us be swift to hear, slow to speak (James 1:19).

LIGHT SWITCH

For it is the God who commanded light to shine out of
darkness, who has shone in our hearts to give the light of the
knowledge of the glory of God in the face of Jesus Christ.

2 CORINTHIANS 4:6

*I*n the beginning, the world was dark and void until God's words flipped a switch and there was light. While it may be hard to imagine a world without light, we have experienced other types of darkness: discouragement, disappointment, and sorrow, to name a few.

Trusting God in the darkness is difficult. We pray for Him to instantly change our circumstances; and while He sometimes does, we often find ourselves waiting for Him in a hard place. Paul was familiar with waiting and challenges. In 2 Corinthians 4:7–15, Paul described being persecuted and struck down. Instead of requiring God to intervene with a bright light from heaven, which he had experienced before on the road to Damascus, Paul patiently relied on God to sustain him. Although unseen, God's goodness, presence, and strength were at work. Paul knew that having God in his life was enough. God was all the light he needed.

June 5

BORN TO RULE

But one testified in a certain place, saying: "What is man that You are mindful of him, or the son of man that You take care of him?"
HEBREWS 2:6

ton College (founded in 1440) is a boarding school in England for boys aged thirteen to eighteen, traditionally from England's privileged class. Nineteen British prime ministers have been educated at Eton (Churchill attended a similar school, Harrow) along with countless political elites. Eton is known as the chief nurse of England's statesmen. Unofficially, it is said that Eton students learn they are "born to rule."

Not all Eton graduates rule England, of course. But there is a class of people in this world who were born to rule: human beings. In Genesis 1, mankind is given dominion over all of creation (verses 26–28). And in Hebrews 2, the writer quoted David, the psalmist, who said, "And You have crowned [man] with glory and honor. You have made him to have dominion over the works of Your hands; You have put all things under his feet" (Psalm 8:5–6; Hebrews 2:7–8). So, what happened? Sin. But the last Adam (1 Corinthians 15:45) has come to restore what the first Adam lost.

Remember who you are in Christ: born to rule, then born again and destined to regain your place of honor and glory.

HOLDING POSSESSIONS LIGHTLY

And Jesus said to him, "Foxes have holes and birds of the air have nests, but the Son of Man has nowhere to lay His head."

MATTHEW 8:20

It is easy to pass over some things Jesus said because their meaning is not obvious. Or perhaps the meaning is clear but demanding. Would Jesus really ask us to do *that*?

When a man declared his desire to follow Jesus, He warned the man that it was not a comfortable life—Jesus had nowhere to sleep at night. And when another young man asked what it would take to inherit eternal life besides keeping God's laws, Jesus told him to sell his many possessions and give the proceeds to the poor. In both cases, Jesus was illustrating the temporal nature of life on this earth. Homes, goods, wealth—all these are possessions that can confuse us about the nature of our true home. We must be cautious about putting down permanent roots on earth and losing sight of the new earth to come.

Following Christ means having the same detached relationship to the things of this earth that He did. As you follow Christ, hold lightly that which you will one day leave behind.

"WHATEVER HE SAYS TO YOU, DO."

Then Pharaoh said to all the Egyptians, "Go to Joseph; whatever he says to you, do."

GENESIS 41:55

In Genesis 41, God raised up Joseph to refocus and reprioritize the nation of Egypt during a prolonged period of drought and famine. During a national crisis, Joseph knew what to do, and everyone looked to him for answers. When the people cried to Pharaoh, he simply replied, "Go to Joseph; whatever he says to you, do."

That reminds us of another Bible story. In John 2, the wedding party in Cana faced a similar crisis—though far less serious. They ran out of wine during their festivities. Mary, the mother of Jesus, took things in hand. Speaking of her Son, she echoed the words of Pharaoh: "Whatever He says to you, do it" (John 2:5).

We all face shortages at one time or another. It might be lack of funds, lack of energy, lack of answers, or lack of wisdom. Sometimes we cope with needs that seem to have no provision, or crises that seem to have no answer. When problems come, we must refocus on our Lord Jesus Christ. We must go to Him. Whatever He says, do it. He will meet the need.

STAND FIRM

But Peter and the other apostles answered and said:
"We ought to obey God rather than men."

ACTS 5:29

hink how often God's will is challenged in life. Examples range from national issues, like government-sanctioned abortion, to private matters, like the temptation to shade the truth on a tax form or other legal document. It's so easy to believe that we are not accountable to God to do the right thing *in every single situation* in life.

It is especially true when we are trying to do what pleases God and we are met with opposition or criticism—and we are standing alone in our desire to please God. That was young David's situation when Israel was confronted by the Philistine giant, Goliath (1 Samuel 17). Everyone from King Saul to David's own brothers was an obstacle in his path. Yet he refused to back down. David knew that God's name was at stake and needed to be defended. So, he put his faith in God and went into the battle, armed with the only things he knew how to use—faith and a sling—and was victorious.

God does not promise physical victory in every confrontation. But He does expect faithfulness and commitment to Him. If you are being opposed in your desire to please God, clothe yourself in God's armor and stand firm (Ephesians 6:10–18).

THE CLOCK IS TICKING

For this purpose the Son of God was manifested, that
He might destroy the works of the devil.

I JOHN 3:8

*I*n athletic games that are played for a set number of minutes, like basketball and football, the closer the clock gets to the final seconds, the more intense the play becomes. In fact, coaches practice plays to use when time has almost expired. Immediacy increases intensity in athletics—and in spiritual warfare.

Has the world ever been in more dire straits than it is now? Revelation 12:12 tells us that the devil "knows that he has [but] a short time" left to disrupt God's plans on earth. It should come as no surprise that the closer we get to the end of the age and the second coming of Jesus Christ, the more Satan will increase his activity. Wars, discord, disease, strife, immorality, and more are evidence of Satan's work. But what Jesus started when He came the first time—destroying the works of the devil—will be concluded when He comes again.

The great hope of the Christian is that one day we, and the world, will be free from the attacks of God's enemy. Satan knows the clock is ticking and that he will one day be removed forever (Revelation 20:10).

REALITY AND RELATION

As the bridegroom rejoices over the bride, so shall your God rejoice over you.

ISAIAH 62:5

*M*ost Christians understand the idea that God created man in His image (Genesis 1:26–27). Every member of the human race was to bear the image of God throughout the earth to represent God's dominion and authority over His creation. We might say that individuals bearing the image of God are to represent the *reality* of God in their character and behavior.

But there is another dimension to God that is represented by communities of individuals: the *relational* part of God. Starting in the garden of Eden (Genesis 2:24), God used marriage as a metaphor for how He relates to those whom He loves. Beginning with Israel, God has related to His people as a bridegroom relates to his bride (Isaiah 54:6–8; 62:5; Hosea 2:19–20). Then, in the New Testament, we find Paul using marriage to illustrate the relationship between Christ and His Church (and vice versa) (Ephesians 5:22–33). As individuals, we bear witness to the *reality* of God, and in associations with others we illustrate the *relational* dimension of God. Both are powerful witnesses to a watching world.

Each of us should consider: *What do people see of God and His love when they see us?* May our lives reflect God's love—as the portrait of God's image to others.

DON'T FORGET

Now I beg you, brethren, through the Lord Jesus Christ, and through the love of the Spirit, that you strive together with me in prayers to God for me.
ROMANS 15:30

The apostle Paul was traveling from Corinth to Jerusalem with money for the Jerusalem church. Knowing the Jews in Jerusalem would be eager to persecute him, he wrote to the church in Rome, asking for their prayers "that [he] may be delivered from those in Judea who do not believe" (Romans 15:31).

Prayer is often the forgotten ingredient in spiritual warfare. In Paul's classic passage on the believer's spiritual armor (Ephesians 6:10–18), prayer is often neglected. But it is Paul's final admonition: "With all prayer and petition pray at all times in the Spirit, and with this in view, be on the alert with all perseverance and petition for all the saints" (verse 18 NASB). It is as if Paul was saying, "Once you are clothed with God's armor against Satan, you must win the battle on the field of prayer!" He made the point by asking for prayer for himself against the temptation to fear the repercussions from preaching the Gospel (verses 19–20).

Be clothed with God's spiritual armor—but don't neglect to pray for strength and steadfastness against "the wiles of the devil" (Ephesians 6:11).

COVER UP

He who covers his sins will not prosper, but whoever
confesses and forsakes them will have mercy.

PROVERBS 28:13

here are two ways of covering sin. The first is by our own effort, which, in our society, is called a cover-up. Every political junkie knows that politicians get into more trouble covering up their crimes than by committing them to begin with, and the same is true for us. If you have a secret habit, a guilty conscience, or a moral failure, Proverbs 28:13 is a warning. Do not try to cover it up or explain it away.

There's another way of covering our sin, and that's by confessing it. Psalm 32:1 says, "Blessed is he whose transgression is forgiven, whose sin is covered." Isaiah said, "The iniquity of Jacob will be covered. . . . For He has clothed me with the garments of salvation, He has covered me with the robe of righteousness" (Isaiah 27:9; 61:10).

Hidden sin yields the crop of guilt, but confession brings release and peace. Is there something in your life that needs to be covered? Don't try to hide it. Confess it, and let the blood of Jesus Christ cover your guilt with its crimson flow.

LIFT HIM UP

You have made him a little lower than the angels; You have crowned him with glory and honor, and set him over the works of Your hands.

HEBREWS 2:7

*I*n terms of classification, there seems to be a gradu-ated order to creation. God Himself is over all, Lord of all, eternal and omnipotent. Below Him is the angelic order—fabulous beings of light and glory. Below them are humans, created "a little lower than the angels" (Psalm 8:5), and placed on earth to tend it. Below humans are animals—sheep, oxen, beasts of the field, birds, and fish (Psalm 8:6–9).

According to Psalm 8 and Hebrews 2, Jesus Christ moved down the chain to redeem the human race. Though He was God Himself, He became human—a little lower than the angels—in order to die for our sins. Following His resurrection, He ascended back to heaven to reassume the glory He had with the Father before the world began (John 17:5). "Therefore God also has highly exalted Him and given Him the name which is above every name . . . in heaven . . . and . . . on earth" (Philippians 2:9–10).

We'll never fathom all Jesus did for us; but the more we study it, the more we are able to comprehend and appreciate His great gift of salvation.

Don't Lose the Joy

*Restore to me the joy of Your salvation, and
uphold me by Your generous Spirit.*

Psalm 51:12

*J*oy is one of the greatest gifts accompanying our salvation. Professor Lewis Smedes wrote, "You and I were created for joy, and if we miss it, we miss the reason for our existence! Moreover, the reason Jesus Christ lived and died on earth was to restore to us the joy we have lost . . . His Spirit comes to us with the power to believe that joy is our birthright because the Lord has made this day for us."[2]

The Bible calls it "joy unspeakable and full of glory" (1 Peter 1:8 KJV).

When we allow disobedience to fester in our lives, it depresses our joy. When David sinned against God, he spent a year without joy before confessing his failure and asking for a restoration of joy.

Don't wait as long as David. The joy of our salvation is too precious to allow sin to steal it away. Confess your wrongdoing; turn from it now with God's help. He will restore your joy and uphold you with His generous Spirit.

You can be joyful again!

TRADITIONS

Therefore, brethren, stand fast and hold the traditions which
you were taught, whether by word or our epistle.
2 THESSALONIANS 2:15

Many adults today are assuming a greater share of responsibility for their aging parents. In Jesus' day, He criticized some who sidestepped that responsibility based on a Jewish tradition that had evolved. They made "the word of God of no effect through [their] tradition" (Mark 7:13). This tradition said money could be dedicated to God and thus not be used to help one's parents. That is an example of keeping the letter but violating the spirit of the law. It was a tradition that essentially negated God's Word.

Traditions are not wrong in and of themselves—they are simply practices or teachings passed from one generation to another. If the practices or teachings conform to God's Word, they are good and should be preserved—like the traditions Paul exhorted the Corinthians and Thessalonians to keep (1 Corinthians 11:2; 2 Thessalonians 2:15). The challenge is discerning which traditions are pleasing to God and which are not.

Think about the religious traditions in your own life today. How many are conscious choices, consistent with Scripture, and how many are not?

ROCK PILES

*I will remember the works of the Lord; surely I
will remember Your wonders of old.*

PSALM 77:11

lthough the tools for capturing memories have in-
creased, we are just as forgetful as the Israelites when
it comes to God's goodness. When the Israelites crossed over the
Jordan River with Joshua, they were commanded to pick up rocks
from the riverbed to create a monument of remembrance. The
rocks were a symbol and a tangible reminder of God's deliverance, power, and compassion.

While we may not hear a voice from heaven commanding us
to gather rocks, Scripture urges us to remember the work of God
in our lives. We have cameras, journals, and computers at our dis-
posal, and yes, even rocks. When we keep tangible reminders of
God's goodness, we are strengthened to trust God with today and
the future. Just as crossing the Jordan was not the final challenge
the Israelites faced, we will continue to be faced with difficulty
throughout our lives. Instead of being surprised by it, we can gaze
at our rocks of remembrance and have confidence that the God
who helped us then is the same God of today. He never changes,
and He delights in strengthening and delivering His people.

DINNER INTERRUPTED

Therefore submit to God. Resist the devil and he will flee from you. Draw near to God and He will draw near to you. Cleanse your hands, you sinners; and purify your hearts, you double-minded.

JAMES 4:7–8

*D*iners were minding their own business in a sushi restaurant in Studio City when a man came in and threw a thirteen-foot python on the floor. Patrons at the Los Angeles eatery scattered as the serpent slithered around, looking for dropped pieces of sushi. It turned out the man had argued with a restaurant employee, left, gone home to fetch his snake, and returned to create a scene.

It worked.

Something akin to that happens in homes and dining rooms all the time. The old serpent, the devil, drops in with a *thud* to create friction, rage, contention, jealousy, dissension, and division. Sometimes we bring him into a situation and drop him into the middle of our relationships. We do it with negative attitudes, harsh words, and ungodly habits.

The Bible tells us to resist the devil so he will flee from us. If we're harboring anger, bitterness, or frustration that's hurting our family, we should confess it. If we're indulging in an impure practice that's damaging our home, we must turn from it. As we draw near to God, He lovingly draws near to us.

A Trustworthy Source

For of Him and through Him and to Him are all
things, to whom be glory forever. Amen.

Romans 11:36

The best journalists are careful to find trustworthy sources. If a journalist cites incorrect information, his reputation is damaged and the piece is discredited. Wasted are the hours he spent researching, writing, and editing. Although most of our lives will remain off of the printed page and out of the limelight, the principle of selecting credible sources serves as a good reminder.

If journalists are this careful with their printed words, how much more careful should we be with the sources we choose to base our lives upon? As we live out our own stories, we can choose to listen to the world's wisdom or to seek God's wisdom. If we choose the wrong source, our life becomes a dim reflection of what it could be.

We can turn to Christ as our unfailing source because everything was created through Him for His purposes. He never lies and has promised to be with us through every season on earth and for all eternity spent with Him. As we build our lives upon His truth, we can have confidence in the security and power of His Word.

GOD IS ON TIME

*The Lord is not slack concerning His promise, as some
count slackness, but is longsuffering toward us.*

2 PETER 3:9

*D*id you know "I promise" is not found in the Bible? The
implication is that when God makes promises, He
doesn't have to add the words "I promise" to convince the hearer
that He means what He says. When a parent says something to a
child and the child replies, "Do you promise?" it may be an indication that somewhere in the past a word given was not a word
kept. Jesus said, "But let your 'Yes' be 'Yes'" (Matthew 5:37).

The greatest challenge we have in embracing the promises
of God is the variable of time. Even the apostles were anxious
for God to keep His promises about "[restoring] the kingdom to
Israel." Jesus reminded them that they should not worry about
"times or seasons which the Father has put in His own authority" (Acts 1:6–7). In other words, trust the *what* without worrying
about the *when*. We forget that God's promises flow from the
perfection of His character. For a promise to be made and not
kept would be to allow a chink in the unassailable nature of God
Himself.

If there is a promise in Scripture you are depending on, let
time be a test of your faith and God's faithfulness. God's promises are always kept.

NO PLACE FOR THE DEVIL

. . . nor give place to the devil.

EPHESIANS 4:27

*B*oy Scouts, infantry soldiers, and wilderness explorers are required to have a working knowledge of topography. The key root in *topography* is the Greek word *topos*, or "place." So topography is the science of place—as in the places laid out on a map. In the New Testament, *topos* is translated "place," "locale," or "opportunity." When it occurs in Ephesians 4:27, it means not to give the devil a place or opportunity. The New International Version translates that verse as, "Do not give the devil a foothold." That works—a "foothold" being a "place" where a climber can insert his foot when scaling a cliff. A foothold was needed by soldiers seeking to gain entrance to an enemy stronghold or fort.

So, what gives the devil this place, opportunity, or foothold? Sinful anger, Paul wrote in Ephesians 4:26. The longer anger remains in the human heart, the greater an opportunity, the more secure a foothold, it becomes. All the devil needs to get his foot in the door of the human heart is for us to nurture our hurt feelings, anger, or resentment.

Keep short accounts. Fill in the footholds. Erase the sinful places from the map of your heart. Give the devil no opportunity. If the emotion of anger appears, make sure it has a godly purpose.

GOD OF THE IMPOSSIBLE

Jesus said to him, "If you can believe, all things are possible to him who believes."

MARK 9:23

he word *impossible* occurs nine times in the New King James Version of the Bible, and most of the references tell us that this word doesn't appear in God's regular vocabulary.

- Matthew 17:20: "Nothing will be impossible."
- Matthew 19:26: "With men this is impossible, but with God all things are possible."
- Mark 10:27: "With men it is impossible, but not with God."
- Luke 1:37: "With God nothing will be impossible."
- Luke 18:27: "The things which are impossible with men are possible with God."

Hebrews 6:18 tells us it is impossible for God to lie, and Hebrews 11:6 adds that without faith it is impossible for us to please Him. It demonstrates how important it is to cast our impossibilities in God's hands. Just as He parted the sea for Israel, reversed the events in Esther, raised Jesus from the dead, and converted Saul of Tarsus, God is capable of reversing our irreversible problems.

MIRROR FOR LIFE

For the word of God is living and powerful, and sharper than any two-edged sword, piercing even to the division of soul and spirit, and of joints and marrow, and is a discerner of the thoughts and intents of the heart.

HEBREWS 4:12

*I*t has been said that to truly know oneself it is necessary to live in relationship with others. As we see our life reflected in the life and response of others, we discover more about ourselves. Others are like a mirror in which we see reflected our true selves.

But people are cloudy mirrors at best. It is only by seeing ourselves face-to-face in a perfect relationship that we discern who we truly are. As we see our imperfections reflected in perfection, we get an idea of what we want to become. Such a face-to-face encounter with perfection in the person of Jesus Christ awaits us when we "see Him as He is" (1 John 3:2). Until the day we see the Living Word face-to-face, looking into the written Word is where we will find a true picture of who we are and who God created us to be. The apostle James even wrote about "[looking] into the perfect law of liberty" to find God's blessing (James 1:22–25).

Renew your mind through meditating on God's Word, and you will find God's "good and acceptable and perfect will" for your life (Romans 12:2).

June 23

ETERNAL FOCUS

*For [Abraham] waited for the city which has
foundations, whose builder and maker is God.*

HEBREWS 11:10

*P*arents are sometimes heard telling their young adult children, "You need to stop dreaming about the future and get a job today!" Some adults can't stop thinking that their true destination in life is just around the corner. Instead of sowing seeds today, they dream only of a harvest (Proverbs 12:11).

Just the opposite is true of some Christians. Instead of keeping our eyes focused on our eternal calling, we become enamored with "today"—the things of this world that are only temporal (1 John 2:17). The writer to the Hebrews singled out Abraham and Moses as examples of those who lived their lives by faith in the future. Abraham might have been traveling to Canaan, but he knew he was destined for an eternal city. And Moses didn't mind giving up the riches of Egypt because "he looked to the reward" God had planned for him in eternity (Hebrews 11:26).

Both the present and the future are important, but only one will last forever. In fact, our present life is to be lived with our eternal life in mind (1 Corinthians 3:11–15). Whatever your plans are for today, fulfill them for eternal reasons.

186

SUFFICIENCY IN CHRIST

And He said to me, "My grace is sufficient for you, for My strength is made perfect in weakness." Therefore most gladly I will rather boast in my infirmities, that the power of Christ may rest upon me.

2 CORINTHIANS 12:9

The apostle Paul had a problem that he never specifically identified (2 Corinthians 12:7). It could have been a physical ailment (see Galatians 4:15; 6:11), or it could have been attacks from false apostles (2 Corinthians 11:13–15). Or it might have been something else entirely. Whatever the problem, we know it was uncomfortable. Otherwise, Paul would not have asked God three different times to remove it.

God's answer to Paul was no when it came to removing the problem. But the answer was yes when it came to giving Paul new and deeper insight into what it meant to be in Christ. Before God's revelation to Paul of the sufficiency of grace, Paul viewed his problem as an interference in his life and ministry. After God's revelation, Paul viewed his problem as an opportunity to give thanks—not for the problem, but for how the problem allowed him to experience deeper dimensions of Christ's sufficiency (2 Corinthians 12:10).

You likely have some kind of problem today—perhaps large, perhaps small. In any case, your problem is a reason for placing your trust and hope in Christ. In Him there is sufficient help and comfort for any problem.

June 25

Do What Is Right

Trust in the LORD, and do good.

PSALM 37:3

*I*t took some courage, but a Texas Girl Scout Troop helped nab a shoplifter while they were selling cookies at a Houston supermarket. From their table near the entrance, they watched a suspicious man wheel his shopping cart out the door and toward the curb. The girls were suspicious because none of the items were in bags and the man looked as if he was trying to sneak out. They alerted authorities, who found $2,000 in stolen merchandise in the man's possession—not just groceries but small appliances and alcohol as well. "He was stealing a lot of stuff," said one girl. "We caught [a] bad guy."[3]

Sometimes while minding our own business throughout the course of a day, we're confronted with a challenge—a wrong to right, a correction to make, a task to finish, or a soul to influence. Most people look the other way, apathetic or frightened. But remember that the word *bold* is a New Testament adjective for God's people (Acts 13:46); and the Lord expects us to be of "good courage" (Psalm 27:14; 31:24).

Having faith will give us courage even when the challenge seems intimidating or the task seems impossible. We must always trust God and do what is right.

DEMONSTRATE YOUR LOVE

"A new commandment I give to you, that you love one another;
as I have loved you, that you also love one another."

JOHN 13:34

hink about what the following words have in common with *love*: *address, report, dream, risk, force, joke, license, tour, plan, whisper, stand, peel, hammer, fly, delay, comb, loan, permit, yawn, shape,* and *judge*. All those words are both nouns and verbs, things and actions. And the digital revolution has given us even more: *tweet, google, e-mail, text,* and others.

Love as a verb is nothing new. Jesus Himself commanded His disciples to "love one another." And John said that God "so loved the world" that He sent Christ to save it (John 3:16). The apostle Paul wrote his famous treatise on love in 1 Corinthians 13, where he primarily talked about *love* as a noun. And even though he didn't use the verb *to love* in 1 Corinthians 13, he described love in action terms: "Love suffers long and is kind; love does not envy; love does not parade itself, is not puffed up" (verse 4), and so on. In other words, true love is best identified by what it does.

The next time you tell someone, "I love you," make sure that person can reply, "I know," because he or she has seen your love in action.

June 27

THE GIFT OF PRAYER

Epaphras, who is one of you, a bondservant of Christ, greets you, always laboring fervently for you in prayers, that you may stand perfect and complete in all the will of God.

COLOSSIANS 4:12

arianne Adlard, a bedridden girl in 1860s London, read about the success of evangelist D. L. Moody and longed for his ministry to touch her own local congregation. She prayed, "O Lord, send this man to our church." In 1870, Moody was indeed invited to speak at Marianne's church; but that morning there was no response to his message. Marianne prayed earnestly that afternoon. In the evening Moody asked if anyone wanted to give their lives to Christ. A flood of people rose to their feet. Moody was so surprised, he had them sit down while he clarified his invitation. Still they stood. In a ten-day period, four hundred people professed faith in Christ.

Like Marianne, Epaphras wrestled in prayer for the church he loved, asking God to work among the people. He believed his greatest ministry to others was in prayer.

When we present the needs of others in prayer to God, we're exercising throne power—the power of coming to the throne of grace so another soul can receive mercy and grace to help in time of need. Only heaven knows the power of such a ministry.

SHUN JEALOUSY

Jealousy [is] as cruel as the grave; its flames are
flames of fire, a most vehement flame.

SONG OF SOLOMON 8:6

*I*t seems nothing could be crueler than the grave, but according to Song of Solomon, there's one thing as bad— jealousy. That's what caused Lucifer to rebel against God. It's what caused Cain to kill Abel, and Jacob's sons to sell their brother Joseph into slavery. It's why King Saul devoted his life to killing David. According to Mark 15:10, the Jewish leaders handed Jesus over to Pilate because of envy and jealousy.

That means it's no small thing to feel pangs of jealousy toward another.

If someone receives a higher grade, makes a larger salary, wins a race, achieves a victory, or experiences more prosperity in some way, are you jealous? Yes, we're all tempted to feel jealous, because the tree of envy grows from the soil of pride. But *love* is God's supernatural attitude that allows us to rejoice in the success of others. The Bible says, "Love suffers long and is kind; love does not envy" (1 Corinthians 13:4).

If you feel jealous toward another, ask God for His supernatural attitude of love. It can make all the difference.

June 29

THE JUDGE OF ALL THE EARTH

True and righteous are His judgments.

REVELATION 19:2

*I*n Genesis 18:25, Abraham asked a question that puts things in perspective: "Shall not the Judge of all the earth do right?" As humans, we recoil from the concept of judgment. We question why God would condemn the world. We wonder about those who have never heard the message of the Gospel. We can't fully understand the presence of evil in the universe or the suffering that fills our world. Sometimes we're uncomfortable with the biblical concepts of God's wrath, vengeance, and judgment.

In the end, we will come to Abraham's conclusion in Genesis: the Judge of all the earth will do right. We'll agree with the angels in Revelation: "True and righteous are His judgments." God's wisdom knows how to handle sin, and His purity demands its condemnation. His grace is extended to us fully and freely, and His Cross frees us from condemnation.

Without the judgment of God, sin and suffering would be unhindered, unfettered, and unending. God's judgment is certain, but it's wise in its application and crucial for our happiness. We can praise Him for His judgments, for the Judge of all the world will do right. He is—and always will be—true and righteous.

WORDS OF LOVE

Therefore comfort one another with these words.

1 THESSALONIANS 4:18

he phrase "one another" occurs fifty-three times in the New Testament epistles. That frequency of use indicates just how relational the Christian life is meant to be. We are given the responsibility to look out for the needs of others as well as for our own. And that applies to the "one anothers" in marriage—husbands and wives who encourage each other.

There are lots of ways to encourage one's spouse. We tend to focus on things that require investments of time, talent, and treasure—gifts, trips, flowers, and date nights. And those are well worth the effort. But the tool of encouragement that is probably more helpful than any other is also the least expensive: encouraging words. When Paul wrote to the Thessalonians to "encourage one another with these words," he was referring to truth about the Rapture and the future of deceased loved ones. It was just a word, but that's all it took to provide hope and certainty. And the same can be true in marriage. A true word from a spouse can convey the certainty of love and hope in a moment.

If you are married, decide to share an encouraging word with your spouse at least once a day. The right words can become building blocks to a stronger union. If you are unmarried, look for someone to share a kind word with today. An often overlooked and undervalued gift is a word of encouragement.

July

Also with the lute I will praise You—
And Your faithfulness, O my God!
To You I will sing with the harp,
O Holy One of Israel.

Psalm 71:22

THE END OF EVIL

"An evil man out of the evil treasure brings forth evil things."
MATTHEW 12:35

he concept of evil has returned to the world's vocabulary. Because of atrocities by jihadists in the Middle East, we've seen beheadings, crucifixions, genocide, and murder by immolation. Many secularists try to avoid the term *evil*, for they don't want to admit the existence of God-ordained absolute moral values. Yet the Bible uses the word *evil* nearly five hundred times, and the presence of evil in today's world is hard to deny.

According to Jesus, evil actions proceed from evil hearts of evil people. Notice the triple evil in Matthew 12:35: evil people, evil treasures, evil things. At its core, evil is anti-Christian and anti-Christ. One day the ultimate Antichrist will appear as evil personified. Until then there will be forerunners of the Antichrist in the world (1 John 2:18), but God knows how to protect His children from the evil one (2 Thessalonians 3:3).

Jesus dealt a mortal blow to evil by rising from the dead, and He will banish evil forever when He returns. Evil is not an eternal part of our lives. We can be assured the Antichrist—and all antichrists—will be terminated in the end.

LAW OF IMITATION

*And be kind to one another, tenderhearted, forgiving
one another, even as God in Christ forgave you.*

EPHESIANS 4:32

The Latin phrase *lex talionis* refers to the "law of retaliation," illustrated by the biblical instruction of "eye for eye, tooth for tooth" (Exodus 21:24). The biblical guideline was meant to limit punishment, not mandate it; and the New Testament suggests a better response to wrongdoing: love and grace instead of retaliation.

Nothing is more impulsively human than retaliation, and nothing is more supernaturally surprising than the extension of grace in all things—especially when one has been wronged. And in Ephesians 4:32, there is a reason for such an unnatural response: We should extend grace to others because of the grace that has been extended to us by God. It takes a measure of disregard and contempt to say, "Even though God has extended grace to me, I choose not to extend that same grace to others." God had every reason not to extend grace to humanity, but He did anyway. And He calls us to do the same. We can know it's the right thing to do when we feel a natural resistance to doing it.

Instead of the law of retaliation, practice the law of imitation. Do for others what you have seen God do for you.

July 3

UNSEARCHABLE

Great is the LORD, and greatly to be praised;
and His greatness is unsearchable.

PSALM 145:3

he artist Chester Harding visited the aged Daniel Boone in 1819 to paint the explorer's portrait. During their time together, Harding asked Boone if he had ever been lost in the wilderness. "No, I was never lost," Boone replied, "but I was bewildered once for three days."[1]

When it comes to our relationship with Christ, we're not lost, but we are often bewildered. Our God is limitless and incomprehensible. Though He has revealed much of Himself to us, our minds are too finite to grasp His full glory. He does things that are "unsearchable, marvelous things without number" (Job 5:9). Isaiah said, "The everlasting God . . . neither faints nor is weary. His understanding is unsearchable" (Isaiah 40:28). The apostle Paul exclaimed, "Oh, the depth of the riches both of the wisdom and knowledge of God! How unsearchable . . . !" (Romans 11:33). According to Ephesians 3:8, His riches are unsearchable.

Though we cannot search Him out, He searches for us. He died for us and three days later rose again. We're still bewildered by it all—and incredibly blessed!

WARNING SIGNS

*And the L*ORD *God of their fathers sent warnings to them by His messengers, rising up early and sending them, because He had compassion on His people.*

2 CHRONICLES 36:15

*I*f a society doesn't have "warnings," it doesn't care for its citizens. Depending on where we live, we need warning sirens to alert us to the dangers of tornadoes or tsunamis. We need notifications that warn us of severe weather. We need warning labels on products that may be harmful. News outlets have an obligation to warn viewers of local scams or regional epidemics.

A warning is an attempt to prevent another person from running into danger or encountering harm. The Bible is full of warnings. Sin produces sorrow, immorality brings heartache, moral depravity causes despair, and disregard for grace results in judgment. When we ignore God's greatest warnings and continue to live in sin, we miss His grace, His Gospel, and the glory He wants to give us. That's why the apostle Paul told the Ephesians, "Therefore watch, and remember that for three years I did not cease to warn everyone night and day with tears" (Acts 20:31).

If our Gospel contains no warnings, we're not preaching the "whole counsel of God" (verse 27). If we fail to heed the warnings God sends us, we're endangering our souls.

July 5

BE READY

Here am I! Send me.
ISAIAH 6:8

One day, a Florida supermarket employee noticed an elderly customer struggling to bend over and tie his shoelaces. The employee walked over, bent down, and tied the man's laces for him. A fellow employee snapped a picture of the two, whose backs were turned, and posted it on Facebook. It quickly generated two hundred thousand "likes." When local news programs picked up the story, it went viral.

Why should such a simple deed generate so much attention? Perhaps it's because the world is starved for love. In the darkness, even the flicker draws attention. The Gospel gives us the opportunity and mission to reach out with acts of kindness and to show compassion to those around us. When the Lord sends us into the world, it's both to *preach* and to *practice* the Gospel.

It's wonderful to take mission trips to needy areas of the world; but every day when we leave our driveway, we're taking a mission trip into a needy world. Learn to pause as you leave home each day and say, "Here am I! Send me." Be ready and willing to preach and practice the Gospel. Embrace small tasks that you can do for Him each day.

EXTRAVAGANT LOVE

"The Spirit of the Lord GOD is upon Me, because the LORD has anointed Me to preach good tidings to the poor; He has sent Me to heal the brokenhearted, to proclaim liberty to the captives, and the opening of the prison to those who are bound."

ISAIAH 61:1

God's love for us is like an intricately cut diamond. The longer we examine each facet, the deeper our understanding of it. Jesus used the father in the story of the prodigal son to describe His heart and affection for the lost (Luke 15:11–32). When the prodigal returned home, the father could have cut him off from the family. This was the acceptable course of action against a person who had brought such shame upon his family. It was naive of the son to think he could return home, even as a servant.

But this father does the unexpected. When he sees his son in the distance, he runs to him, embracing and kissing him. The father is more concerned with having his son return than with hearing why he returned. He is given a robe, a ring, and shoes—these are visible signs to the community that the son is a part of his family.

We serve a loving God: He searches for us and runs to us. He embraces us and adopts us into His family. When God's love touches our lives, we are inspired to seek and love the lost as Jesus did.

July 7

CRACKED POTS

But we have this treasure in earthen vessels, that the
excellence of the power may be of God and not of us.
2 CORINTHIANS 4:7

veryone knows what it's like to be disappointed by someone we love or admire. Our husbands, wives, children, or parents sometimes let us down. Our heroes stumble. Our leaders falter. It can devastate us and damage our relationships, because we place high expectations on those we love. Sometimes we forget they are broken people just like we are.

According to 2 Corinthians 4:7, we are all earthen vessels, jugs of clay, easily chipped. *The Voice* translates 2 Corinthians 4:7 like this: "But this beautiful treasure [the Gospel] is contained in us—*cracked* pots made of earth and clay—so that the transcendent character of this power will be clearly seen as coming from God and not from us."

God blesses us cracked pots in spite of our sinful, undeserving nature; and high on His list of blessings is forgiveness. As we look to Him alone, He gives us grace (He imparts a million blessings we don't deserve) and mercy (He withholds a million judgments we do deserve).

If He gives grace and mercy to cracked pots like us, perhaps we need to extend the same to those we love.

BLINDED BY PRIDE

When Jesus heard it, He said to them, "Those who are well
have no need of a physician, but those who are sick. I did not
come to call the righteous, but sinners, to repentance."

MARK 2:17

hildren will sometimes fake an illness to get out of school and may even convince themselves they are sick. The Pharisees had the opposite problem. They convinced themselves they were better than others and avoided those they saw as lower than themselves.

Jesus confused them. His authority and healing power could have allowed Him to choose His associates and to gain status in the synagogue. Instead, He was moved with compassion toward those who called upon Him: the sick, destitute, and unclean.

Pride makes us blind to the work of God. We forget His sovereignty. Pride also blinds us to our own need for a Savior, and we withhold grace from those we feel do not deserve it. It is important to confess our pride or we will end up like the Pharisees, taking God's grace for granted and missing opportunities to lead others to Christ. If we are not careful, pride will distance us from others and from God.

VICTORY OVER FEAR

Yet in all these things we are more than conquerors through Him who loved us.
ROMANS 8:37

In the history of warfare, victors have rarely, if ever, done away with their enemies completely. Rather, the defeated group lays down its arms and surrenders to the victor. To one degree or another, the victorious group stays alert to its enemy's presence. Being victorious doesn't mean the threat of war is eliminated. But it does mean the immediate crisis has passed.

One of the Christian's enemies in spiritual warfare is fear. But we have been given power, love, and a sound mind to overcome fear and defeat it (2 Timothy 1:7). Once defeated, will fear cease to approach us? No. Fear is always there, lurking in the shadows, waiting for the right moment to attack. But if we live in a state of victory, never letting down our defenses, fear cannot attack and defeat us. Regardless of how fearful the circumstance, "we are more than conquerors through Him who loved us."

The secret to living victoriously over fear is living moment by moment in Christ: "It is no longer I who live, but Christ lives in me" (Galatians 2:20). Christ was never stymied or overcome by fear, and we should not be either. If we are afraid, it is us, not Christ in us.

BLESSED

"Blessed are the pure in heart, for they shall see God."

MATTHEW 5:8

ack to the basics." We hear that phrase a lot—so many things in life can be "fixed" when we return to basic principles. That lesson was at the heart of Jesus' Beatitudes (Matthew 5:3–11). Nine times He said, "Blessed are [those] . . ." referring to people who put the kingdom of God first.

Blessedness is more than happiness. It is akin to the Hebrew concept of *shalom*, or peace, the contented, stable, peaceful relationship one has with man and God. Blessedness is an Old Testament concept that was picked up by Jesus in the Sermon on the Mount. In Psalm 1—the psalm chosen to introduce Israel's hymnbook— the psalmist begins just as Jesus did: "Blessed is the man who . . ." The psalmist says we are blessed when our "delight is in the law of the LORD" (verse 2). That is, we are blessed when our thoughts and actions are consistent with God's values and priorities as found in Scripture. It's the same message Jesus gave to His audience: Center your heart on God, and you will know Him now and forever.

It's good to be happy in this world, but even better to be blessed by God. Blessing comes from getting back to spiritual basics.

THE VICTOR

Now I saw heaven opened, and behold, a white horse.
And He who sat on him was called Faithful and True,
and in righteousness He judges and makes war.

REVELATION 19:11

rchaeologists in Montana have analyzed five thousand artifacts of a battle that occurred in 1876. That's when Lieutenant Colonel George Armstrong Custer led his army to disaster at the Little Bighorn. Custer's troops were slaughtered to the last man; and even now whenever we hear the name Custer, we think of one of history's worst defeats.

One day that's how we'll think of the Antichrist. Despite his threats, charisma, power, technology, militarism, wealth, and satanic energy, he and his army will be defeated suddenly and decisively at the moment Christ returns. In one swoop, Jesus will put down all rebellion against Him when He returns in victory at the end of history. The Bible says, "And then the lawless one will be revealed, whom the Lord will consume with the breath of His mouth and destroy with the brightness of His coming" (2 Thessalonians 2:8). The devil and all his forces are defeated. They were defeated at the Cross. They are defeated now in our lives. They will be defeated forever at Christ's return.

There is only one Victor, and His name is Jesus.

THE POWER OF "NO"

My son, if sinners entice you, do not consent.

PROVERBS 1:10

emptation has been around since the days of Adam and Eve, but it's never been as virulent as today. Sexual temptation, especially, has been intensified by technology, and it tends to reach people earlier in life. Still, we read in 1 Corinthians 10:13 that no temptation has overtaken us except what is common to humanity, and God is faithful to provide pathways of escape. He did this for Joseph in Genesis 39. When tempted by Potiphar's wife, Joseph was able to say no because he had established his convictions before the crisis. His moral principles were set in advance, so Joseph instinctively resisted the lure of lust.

Temptation has many guises, but God gives power over all forms of temptation. Our greatest weapons are: (1) a preset determination to obey God; (2) memorized Scripture on needed topics; and (3) prayer. Jesus told us to watch and pray so we don't fall into temptation (Matthew 26:41).

Don't wait until the moment of crisis. Plan ahead, hide God's Word in your heart, and pray in advance for victory, holiness, and a life pleasing to God.

July 13

AT PEACE

The wicked flee when no man pursueth, but
the righteous are as bold as a lion.

PROVERBS 28:1 KJV

eople alongside the Monongahela River in western Pennsylvania are nervous about an alligator lurking about. Police, consulting with zookeepers and the Coast Guard, suspect the gator hitched a ride on a barge from a warmer spot down South. The creature may never be found or captured, say authorities, but several sightings have left local residents nervous about swimming, fishing, or letting their dogs play in the water.

In biblical times, people were equally nervous about lions prowling around. Two famous biblical characters faced an attacking lion. Judges 14:5 describes how a lion came roaring against Samson; and David told King Saul of the time he had slain a lion who attacked his flock (1 Samuel 17:34–35).

We have a powerful lion that is tracking us—hoping to inflict harm and instill doubt and fear in our lives (1 Peter 5:8). But he's no match for the Lion of Judah (Revelation 5:5). Keep your focus on your risen Lord and trust fully in Him and His gift of salvation. His strength will be yours in the time of trouble. God is greater than any foe that Satan may place in your path. He will guard and keep you in peace.

STAND FOR RIGHTEOUSNESS

Therefore you are inexcusable, O man, whoever you are
who judge, for in whatever you judge another you condemn
yourself; for you who judge practice the same things.

ROMANS 2:1

e are all disappointed when someone we know, or *thought* we knew, shocks us by being involved in an immoral or illegal activity. Our disappointment is the deepest when the guilty party has previously stood for the very opposite behavior he has been found guilty of. It seems harder to forgive when the H-word—*hypocrisy*—is involved.

Judging another person for some act while practicing the same thing ourselves is plainly hypocritical. Jesus said it bluntly: "Hypocrite! First remove the plank from your own eye . . ." (Matthew 7:5). So what should we do? Should we never stand and speak for righteousness for fear that we might one day commit the very sin we stand and speak against? Should we never call out sin when necessary? No, we should always stand and speak for righteousness—but with a serious measure of grace, knowing that "there, but for the grace of God, go I" (see 1 Corinthians 10:12; 15:10). And if we do fail or fall, we must repent with equal grace and humility.

When others fail, let us forgive them and pray that God will keep us from the same end.

July 15

THE GREAT COMMISSION

*How shall they hear without a preacher? And how
shall they preach unless they are sent?*

ROMANS 10:14–15

he story of the Church is interwoven with the history of missions. It's the record of an endless parade of characters who have been sent—and who have willingly gone. Take, for example, Robert Morrison, who was born in Scotland in 1782. He became a Christian as a teenager and joined a prayer meeting that met every Monday in his father's workshop. The London Missionary Society sent him out in 1807 as the first Protestant missionary to China, and his story is more exciting than a movie.

Morrison served twenty-seven years and saw fewer than a dozen people come to Christ during the entirety of his ministry. Yet he opened the door and paved the way for the millions of conversions that have reshaped the story of modern China.

The priority of the Church is the Great Commission, to go into the world and preach the Gospel. We must share Christ wherever we are, and we must keep sending others to go where we cannot. The results may sometimes seem meager, but don't be discouraged. Your labor in the Lord is not in vain.

July 16

DIVINE DEPENDENCE

Draw near to God and He will draw near to you.

JAMES 4:8

mergency medical care for wounded soldiers is amazing. Soldiers who, in a previous era, would have died on the battlefield are now surviving. But they often recover with life-changing and often debilitating results. Soldiers who have survived the loss of one or more limbs awake from their surgeries with a new realization: *I'll never be able to do this on my own.*

Strong, self-sufficient soldiers have to accept the humbling reality that they need others around them to help them adapt to a new life. If there is a silver lining in such an experience, it is learning the lesson afresh that we were not created by God to live life alone—even the healthiest among us are dependent. Jesus said as much when He told His disciples, "Without Me you can do nothing" (John 15:5). That was not a statement of ego on Jesus' part; it was a way of stating the truth that man was created to live in dependence upon God. And God gives the grace needed to live such a life of leaning on Him (James 4:6).

If you feel the need for God in your life, that's exactly how you are supposed to feel. You were never intended to do life on your own.

211

July 17

Finding Purpose

For we are His workmanship, created in Christ Jesus for good works,
which God prepared beforehand that we should walk in them.
Ephesians 2:10

To understand the intricacy of a new invention, one must interview the inventor. To pinpoint the meaning of a painting, one must consult with the artist. Although some people prefer to leave their work open for interpretation, others are eager to share the purpose and meaning they intended to instill into their work.

If we are struggling to understand the purpose and meaning of our life, we should seek out the One who created us. Scripture states that God not only created us; He also designed and designated good works for us to do. As we seek Him and follow His guidance, He will direct our steps. We don't need to worry that we will miss God's plan for us.

This truth frees us from the cage of our limited perspective. Realizing God's power and redemptive plan frees us from striving, regret, and shame. Our lives have purpose. What areas of your life are difficult to entrust to God? As you begin opening these areas up to Him through prayer, they become opportunities for your faith and trust to increase.

MULTIPLIED GRACE

*This is a faithful saying and worthy of all acceptance, that Christ
Jesus came into the world to save sinners, of whom I am chief.*

1 TIMOTHY 1:15

he apostle Paul is often called "the apostle of grace" because his writings are filled with references to the grace of God. *Grace* appears eighty-three times in Paul's epistles, especially when he wrote about his past and present.

First there's the grace of forgiveness. Paul referred to himself as the "chief" of sinners. For him, his pre-Christian life of persecuting the Church of Jesus Christ was beyond the pale (1 Corinthians 15:9). He never seemed to get over the fact that the grace of God was greater than all his previous sins (Romans 5:20). Regardless of our past sins, we each feel the same way: How could God forgive all I have done and said? But He does.

Then there's the grace of endurance. Even as a mature Christian, Paul suffered in various ways, and he was not shy about asking God to relieve his suffering. On at least one occasion, God granted him grace to endure rather than removing the cause of his suffering (2 Corinthians 12:7–10). Regardless of our present situation, that same grace is sufficient for our every need.

God knows every detail of your past sins and present situation. And His grace is sufficient for both.

July 19

NOTHING HIDDEN

And there is no creature hidden from His sight, but all things are naked and open to the eyes of Him to whom we must give account.
HEBREWS 4:13

he front (obverse) of the Great Seal of the United States appears in many settings associated with the president. The back (reverse) side was never made into a seal, but its design can be seen on the back of the United States one-dollar bill. A distinctive feature is the unfinished pyramid with an eye appearing in glory above the pyramid. Such an image of an eye has been used in history to represent God's omnipotence and providence—the fact that He sees and watches over all things.

It is certainly a biblical image. The writer of 2 Chronicles 16:9 says "the eyes of the LORD" survey all the earth, while the psalmist says "the LORD looks from heaven [and] He sees all the sons of men" (Psalm 33:13–14). The writer to the Hebrews put it more dramatically: "And there is no creature hidden from His sight"—suggesting that mankind would prefer to hide some things from God. The writer also suggests that hiding is a bad idea since we "must give account" to Him who sees everything.

Today, consider the "everythings" of your life. Is there anything you hope God doesn't see? Ask God for grace to live a life you will be glad for Him to see.

LOST AND FOUND

"For the Son of Man has come to seek and to save that which was lost."

LUKE 19:10

*J*esus said His mission was "to seek and to save that which was lost." The Jews to whom He said those words were confused. How could they be lost? After all, they were the chosen people of God.

People today who hear the biblical term *lost* have an equally hard time comprehending the meaning. Lost from who or what? In the Jews' case, God had rebuked the spiritual leaders of Israel, her shepherds, for allowing their "sheep" to wander off into carnality and captivity. He said through the prophet Ezekiel, "I will seek what was lost and bring back what was driven away" (Ezekiel 34:16). The Jews were lost because they had wandered away from God, and they needed to be found. That's what Jesus meant in the three parables He told about the lost sheep, the lost coin, and the lost son (Luke 15:3–32). Jesus was fulfilling God's promise to seek "the lost sheep of the house of Israel" (Matthew 10:6; 15:24).

But His mission was extended to all of God's creation—to reconcile the world back to God (2 Corinthians 5:18–20). If you are apart from Christ, you are lost. But Christ has come to seek and save you today.

July 21

TOO CLOSE?

"And the second, like it, is this: 'You shall love your neighbor as yourself.' There is no other commandment greater than these."
MARK 12:31

It's easier to love people from afar so that we experience them in small doses. Then, when they begin to wear on our nerves, we can retreat and take a break. This is one of the challenges and opportunities of marriage: there is less distance. Spouses sleep in the same bed, wake in the same house, and return to the same home each day.

Great marriages do not happen by accident. It's easy to drift into negative patterns, which can create distance and defensiveness toward one another. It takes intention and energy to grow and build a meaningful relationship. Marriage can be a catalyst for growth when we intentionally spend time reflecting on our marriage, forgiving and giving grace to one another, praying through areas of tension, and, perhaps most important, taking responsibility for our weaknesses, mistakes, and negative tendencies.

When we surrender our marriages and relationships to God and seize the growth opportunities, God will transform our view of ourselves, our spouses, and our relationships. Whether you are married or single, invite God and His perspective into your relationships with others today.

COMMUNITY

Finally, all of you be of one mind, having compassion for one another; love as brothers, be tenderhearted, be courteous.

1 PETER 3:8

One of the most distinctive changes between the Old Testament and the New Testament was terminology. In the Old Testament, God and Israel's relationship was theocratic: God was King and Israelites were His subjects as defined by divine covenants. But in the New Testament the relationship became familial: God is Father and Christians are His children (Romans 8:12–17). The phrase "children of God" occurs ten times in the New Testament, not at all in the Old Testament.

Families live "communally"—that is, they hold things in common. The body of Christ, therefore, is a family community that shares in the grace and gifts of God equally. And the New Testament is filled with images of what that community of believers should look like. It should share in love, unity (comm*unity*), forgiveness, tenderheartedness, compassion, courtesy, generosity, and more. Family members are to love one another as God the Father loves the family (Ephesians 4:32).

Consider how you might strengthen the ties that bind you closer to your brothers and sisters in Christian community—in your own family and the family of God.

Seated with Christ

Do you not know that the saints will judge the world? And if the world will be judged by you, are you unworthy to judge the smallest matters?
I Corinthians 6:2–3

*I*n 1 Corinthians 6, Paul chided the Corinthians for failing to resolve difficulties without suing one another. We should be able to settle matters with each other, he said, because one day we'll judge the world. It's hard to foresee how that will happen, but similar verses reinforce the point. The Bible teaches we will reign with Christ and have part in His kingship. When He judges the world, we'll be there to agree with His judgment.

Jesus told His disciples in Matthew 19:28, "You who have followed Me will also sit on twelve thrones, judging the twelve tribes of Israel." Revelation 3:21 adds, "To him who overcomes I will grant to sit with Me on My throne." The Bible says, "If we endure, we shall also reign with Him" (2 Timothy 2:12). In Revelation 20, John envisioned God's faithful children reigning with Christ a thousand years.

If we'll one day judge the world, shouldn't we be able to work out our disagreements now? Think of a troubled relationship in your life and ask God for wisdom to improve it.

GET SOME REST

He said to them, "Come with me by yourselves
to a quiet place and get some rest."

MARK 6:31 NIV

The disciples endured a stressful period in Mark 6. At the start of the chapter, they were caught in a riot in Nazareth. In mid-chapter, they went out two by two to practice their ministry skills. Then John the Baptist was executed. By the time we get to verse 31, we're told "there were many coming and going, and they did not even have time to eat." That's when Jesus gave them a command: "Come with me by yourselves to a quiet place and get some rest" (NIV).

Our Lord often said, "Come *to* Me," but here He said, "Come *with* me." Never leave Jesus behind when you take a break or a vacation. Your soul needs rest as well as your body. And notice the words "by yourselves." Don't drag the world around with you. Turn off your phone and ignore your e-mail. Find "a quiet place," not a loud and pulsating spot. And note those final words: "Get some rest."

God doesn't want you to live in perpetual weariness. He wants you to take care of yourself so you can better serve Him.

OUR GUIDE THROUGH LIFE

LORD, *You have been our dwelling place in all generations. Before
the mountains were brought forth, or ever You had formed the earth
and the world, even from everlasting to everlasting, You are God.*
PSALM 90:1–2

he next time you are near a lake or a seashore, spend
some time observing the movements of sailboats on the
water. Though some larger sailboats have small motors to use in
case of an emergency, for normal use they are totally dependent
on the wind. Their pilots can change the direction of the boat to
a degree, but it is the wind that is in charge.

Sailboats existed for thousands of years before the apostle
Peter's day; as a fisherman, he knew the value and power of
the wind. So when he wrote about how God inspired the Old
Testament prophets to write their books, he used an image akin
to sailing: men "spoke from God as they were carried along by
the Holy Spirit" (2 Peter 1:21 NIV). Just as the wind carries along
a sailboat, so the Holy Spirit was the power and source behind
the writers of Scripture (2 Timothy 3:16). But the same image
applies to our daily life as Christians. When we are filled with
and yielded to the Spirit, He is the power who silently guides us
through life. Yes, our hand is on the rudder, but it is the wind of
the Spirit that fills our sail. Trust Him to guide and empower you.

July 26

ABBA FATHER

*"In this manner, therefore, pray: Our Father
in heaven, hallowed be Your name."*

MATTHEW 6:9

nglish *father* was *vader* in Dutch, *fadēr* in early
German, *vater* in later German, and *fader* in Middle
English. And all those words were built on Latin *pater,* which
was very close to Greek *patēr.* But all those Western spellings
were a radical departure from Aramaic, the language Jesus
spoke. He would have pronounced *father* as *abba,* derived from
Hebrew *ab.*

In fact, Jesus' use of "father" represented a major shift in how
the Hebrews used the term—almost exclusively to refer to human
fathers. God was rarely called "Father" by the Jews (Isaiah 63:16;
64:8; Jeremiah 31:9; Malachi 2:10), but Jesus called God "Father"
(*Abba*—Matthew 11:26) and taught His disciples to do the same
(Matthew 6:9). But this was not the formal, Victorian *father* of the
English language. This was the *abba* of the Hebrew family unit—
the "papa" or "daddy" used by children the world over today
(Mark 14:36). Jesus introduced a new way to relate to God—a
familial way of fondness and closeness.

However you view and address your earthly father, feel free to
address your heavenly Father the way Jesus did—as *Abba* Father.

July 27

YOUR PRAYER IS HEARD

Do not be afraid, Zacharias, for your prayer is heard; and your wife Elizabeth will bear you a son, and you shall call his name John.

LUKE 1:13

*P*erhaps you know those who have become cynical toward Christ because of unanswered prayer. They've been disappointed, and their disappointment has settled into indifference or bitterness. We understand their feelings, but such reactions don't take into account the examples of the Bible. Many biblical heroes grappled with unanswered prayer—Abraham wanting a son; Moses longing to lead Israel out of Egypt; Paul desiring freedom from his thorn; even Jesus asking for the cup of suffering to pass.

God did answer their prayers, just not as they expected. Prayer isn't a matter of getting our wishes fulfilled on earth, but of God's drawing us into His will and working all things for His good.

The angel Gabriel told aged Zacharias, "Do not be afraid, Zacharias, for your prayer is heard." What prayer? Years before, Zacharias and Elizabeth had pleaded earnestly for a child. They had grown into old age thinking God hadn't answered their prayers. But not a syllable of their petitions had been neglected by the Almighty.

Don't worry. God always answers the sincere prayers of His faithful people, though it be at His time, in His way, and for His glory.

DAILY GRACE

*Catch us the foxes, the little foxes that spoil the
vines, for our vines have tender grapes.*

SONG OF SOLOMON 2:15

The small problems of life aren't always small. Consider what happened at the McMillen Community Center in Fort Wayne, Indiana, when a little squirrel managed to get into the place. The building was under construction and due to open within weeks. The furry guy chewed into some wiring and caused a power surge that fried three HVAC systems and destroyed the building's heating, ventilation, and air-conditioning units. The damages exceeded $300,000.

Perhaps you're not facing traumatic, life-altering events right now; but the little foxes are trying to ruin the vines, and the little squirrels are short-circuiting your happiness. God's grace is endless and amazing, but it also comes in small doses and daily allotments. The same grace that keeps us from losing our souls in hell also keeps us from losing our tempers in the office. The same grace that transports us to heaven also gives us composure when our flights are delayed or the traffic is jammed up.

God's grace is infinite, but accessible. It's an ocean of grace, but it also falls in gentle drops at our feet. It's more than enough for the little problems you'll face today.

July 29

A SHOCKING REVELATION

I wait for the LORD, my soul waits, and in His word I do hope.
PSALM 130:5

*I*n the chaos of everyday decisions and demands, it's easy to forget God is guiding us. The story of Esther reminds us that although we may not see the fruition and impact of His plans immediately, He is working on our behalf. Esther was an orphan, raised by her uncle, and became queen to a foreign king. When an evil plan to annihilate the Jews was announced, she had a choice: to believe that God had orchestrated her ascension to the throne to save the Jews or to hide her identity for the sake of self-preservation.

Although we may never experience such a shocking revelation, we are faced with the same choice. Will we trust God or trust ourselves? Jesus frequently referred to Himself as a shepherd, and a good shepherd does not leave his sheep to fend for themselves. A good shepherd protects and leads his sheep. Will you trust Him today? God in His wisdom knows what is best.

SEEKING THE LOST

*"But we had to celebrate and be glad, because this brother of
yours was dead and is alive again; he was lost and is found."*

LUKE 15:32 NIV

ome things only work in pairs: shoes, socks, gloves, the
two parts of scissors, the two wings of a bird, the two
sides of a coin. And that applies to Jesus' mission in the world:
seeking and finding. It makes no sense that Jesus Christ would
come into the world to seek those who are lost and not find them.

Jesus was criticized by "Pharisees and scribes" for socializ-
ing and sharing meals with "sinners" (Luke 15:1–2). Earlier, Jesus
had answered their objections in a word: "I have not come to call
the righteous, but sinners, to repentance" (Luke 5:32). "Sinners"
were those who needed to be found—those He came seeking. To
amplify the point, He told three stories about "finding." A single
sheep was lost and found, a coin was lost and found, and a son
was lost and found (Luke 15:3–32). He meant that He associated
with sinners—and found them—because they knew they were
lost; they knew they needed finding, unlike the Pharisees.

If you have been found by Jesus, it is because He came seeking
you. If you want Him to find you, tell Him you are lost and want
to be found.

His Will

When the Most High divided their inheritance to the nations,
when He separated the sons of Adam, He set the boundaries of
the peoples according to the number of the children of Israel.
Deuteronomy 32:8

hess may be the most popular board game in the world. Many public parks have permanent chessboards and benches installed that are almost always filled with friendly competitors. Secondary schools are incorporating chess into their curricula because of the game's ability to strengthen mental agility. Chess is challenging; a sense of control comes from moving the pieces around.

It is no surprise that some have compared the world to a chessboard on which God moves the pieces according to His will. While there are verses that speak to God's sovereign control over the nations (Job 12:23; Daniel 2:21), there are also verses that speak to man's choices (Deuteronomy 30:19). And therein lies the mystery: God has a will for the world (not just for Christians), but He incorporates our choices into the perfection of His will. We should never view the world as "out of control," regardless of how it may appear.

God's will is that "all should come to repentance" through faith in Christ (2 Peter 3:9).

AUGUST

Let us hold fast the confession of our hope without
wavering, for He who promised is faithful.

HEBREWS 10:23

August 1

FIVE PEOPLE TO LOVE

Let brotherly love continue.

HEBREWS 13:1

ccording to Hebrews 13:1, we must live in brotherly love. We're to love everyone with the love of Christ, but Hebrews 13:1–8 gives us five people we must love in particular.

1. The stranger. Verse 2 says, "Do not forget to entertain strangers, for by so doing some have unwittingly entertained angels."
2. The prisoner. Verse 3 says, "Remember the prisoners as if chained with them."
3. The person to whom you are married. Verse 4 says, "Marriage is honorable among all."
4. The Lord Himself. Verse 5 says, "Let your conduct be without covetousness . . . for He Himself has said, 'I will never leave you nor forsake you.'"
5. The church worker, your pastor, or teacher. Verses 7 and 8 tell us, "Remember those who rule over you, who have spoken the word of God to you, whose faith follow, considering the outcome of their conduct."

In which of those five areas are you strongest? Weakest? Let's take Hebrews 13:1 seriously and let brotherly love continue.

LIVE FEARLESSLY

If that is the case, our God whom we serve is able to deliver us from the burning fiery furnace, and He will deliver us from your hand, O king.

DANIEL 3:17

*P*ower and *ability* are synonyms, and the book of Daniel has examples of both—and the lack of both. For example, the royal counselors of kings Nebuchadnezzar and Belshazzar did not have the power/ability to interpret dreams and cryptic writing. Daniel did because of his relationship with God. It wasn't Daniel's power; it was God's power working through him.

Because Daniel and his three friends had an intimate relationship with God and had full confidence in His sovereignty, they lived free of fear. When faced with the prospect of being burned alive in a furnace, Daniel's friends expressed confidence in God's ability to protect them. They didn't need to *see* God exercise His power; it was enough for them to know He had it. So they told the king, "We know God is *able* to save us, but even if He doesn't display His *power*, we are fine with that. We trust Him regardless of the outcome" (Daniel 3:17–18, paraphrased). God's ability dispelled fear.

Are you confident in God's power and ability? If so, you do not have to fear. You can live fearlessly, trusting in God's decisions.

August 3

GOD'S GUIDEBOOK

However, when He, the Spirit of truth, has
come, He will guide you into all truth.
JOHN 16:13

*D*riving the 469 miles of the Blue Ridge Parkway is an explorer's delight. From northern Virginia to the Tennessee–North Carolina border, there are wonders around every bend in the mountainous road. You may see wildlife, a pioneer cabin, gorgeous vistas, a country church, a stream or waterfall—the beauty never ends. The Parkway is not for the hurried; it is for the expectant—those eager for new experiences and discovery.

And the same is true for the Christian life—if, that is, we take seriously the foundational biblical truth that our God is a guide through life. Even though we do not know what is around every bend in the road, God does. There are encounters, discoveries, people, events, opportunities, blessings, and challenges to be found. Instead of being shocked at a circumstance or event, we should look at our path through the lens of heaven. There is a time, season, and purpose for everything (Ecclesiastes 3:1–8). There is something to rejoice in, give thanks for, and pray about around every curve (1 Thessalonians 5:16–18).

Today, trust that the Holy Spirit is guiding you into all truth. Live with eyes and arms open to embrace what you discover.

A Time to Recharge

*And He said to them, "Come aside by yourselves
to a deserted place and rest a while."*

MARK 6:31

Rechargeable batteries are nothing new. An early version of them was invented in 1859 by French physicist Gaston Planté. But imagine how surprised Planté would be if he could see how dependent we've become on his invention. The modern world wouldn't exist without batteries. They run our vehicles, devices, computers, and toys. Batteries are little boxes of energy that keep things powered up, but they must frequently be connected to an external power source, or they run down and die—usually at the worst time.

Just like batteries, we are created by God with internal reserves of physical, emotional, and spiritual energy. But we need frequent recharging, or we'll wear ourselves out. We're not perpetual motion machines. After we've expended energy, we must rest and become replenished.

We do this physically by resting, mentally by meditating, and spiritually by leaning on the Lord in faith and fellowship. Jesus told His disciples to come with Him to a quiet place and get some rest. That's a divine command from Him who made us. Don't be afraid to take some time for yourself. This is a great time to recharge. Remember: *if your output exceeds your intake, your upkeep will be your downfall.*

THE PLACE OF GRACE

Let us therefore come boldly to the throne of grace, that we may obtain mercy and find grace to help in time of need.

HEBREWS 4:16

*M*ost people are familiar with the story of the Wizard of Oz. Dorothy and her three companions follow a yellow brick road to the Emerald City to ask the Wizard of Oz for what they need: Dorothy needed to get home to Kansas, the Scarecrow needed a brain, the Tin Man needed a heart, and the Cowardly Lion needed courage. They discover, of course, that the Wizard is a fraud.

But the idea of approaching a throne for help is much older than *The Wizard of Oz*. The writer to the Hebrews encouraged his readers to "come boldly to the throne of grace" to find "mercy" and "grace to help in time of need." What else would one expect to receive at a throne of *grace* but grace? And therein lies an important theological and practical truth: regardless of what we think we need in terms of help, we really only need one thing: the grace of God. When God pours out His grace, we receive what He knows we need: provision, endurance, wisdom, patience, strength, resistance, courage, and more.

If you are facing a need right now, regardless of the specifics, go to the throne of grace and ask God for that which you are certain to receive: the grace of God.

REMEMBER THE PURPOSE

*For whom He foreknew, He also predestined to be conformed to the image
of His Son, that He might be the firstborn among many brethren.*

ROMANS 8:29

The nineteenth-century historian Thomas Carlyle wrote
that "the man without a purpose is like a ship without
a rudder—a waif, a nothing, a no man. Have a purpose in life
and having it, throw such strength of mind and muscle into your
work as God has given you." Simply stated, God created man for
a purpose.

That purpose was revealed immediately at the dawn of creation. Man was to be an earthly steward of God, being a caretaker
of creation and filling the earth with people who reflect His glory.
But when sin disrupted God's narrative, an additional purpose
was added: populating heaven with people who reflect the image
of Jesus Christ. Christians are part of the Church, the bride of
Christ, and are called to fulfill Christ's own purpose of bringing
"many sons to glory" (Hebrews 2:10). As marriages are called to
exemplify the relationship between Christ and His Church, one
of the purposes of marriage is to serve Christ's calling and commission. Before you were ever born, God had a purpose for you.

OUR NIGHT LIGHT

The day is Yours, the night also is Yours; You have prepared the light and the sun.

<small>PSALM 74:16</small>

he book of Psalms is full of nocturnal verses. Psalm 1 tells us to meditate on God's Word day and night. Psalm 16:7 says, "My heart also instructs me in the night seasons." According to Psalm 30:5, "weeping may endure for a night, but joy comes in the morning." Psalm 77 reminds us to sing at night (verse 6), and Psalm 92 speaks of God's faithfulness to us every night (verse 2).

Psalm 134, one of the shortest chapters in the Bible, was written to priests on the graveyard shift: "Behold, bless the LORD, all you servants of the LORD, who by night stand in the house of the LORD! Lift up your hands in the sanctuary, and bless the LORD. The LORD who made heaven and earth bless you from Zion!"

Sometimes our "nights" are metaphorical as we go through dark seasons in life. But sometimes they're literal, for we often have trouble sleeping, sometimes due to anxious cares. Remember, you can lift up your hands in the night seasons as well as in the light, for both the day and night belong to the Lord.

August 8

YOUR GROWTH CHART

Being confident of this very thing, that He who has begun a good work in you will complete it until the day of Jesus Christ.

PHILIPPIANS 1:6

A friend who hasn't seen your new baby for a while says, "I can't believe how much she's grown!" After being out of town for a week, we return and marvel at how our tomato plants are so much taller. Grandparents come for a visit and are amazed at how their teenage grandson is now taller than they are. Over time, growth is obvious; in the moment, it's impossible to see growth taking place.

The same is true of our spiritual growth. Remember these truths: (1) God's purpose is to to grow His children into the image of His firstborn Son, Jesus Christ (Romans 8:29). (2) Growth happens consistently and continually, even when we think the opposite of growth is happening (Romans 8:28). (3) We *will* grow up to full maturity in Christ—God has promised it (Philippians 1:6). (4) All growth requires nurturing. If we provide the nutrients of obedience and faithfulness, God promises He will grow us up in Christ.

When you look for spiritual growth in your life, don't stand patiently in front of a mirror. Take the long view—trust in the promises of God's Word—and you should see the evidence of God at work in your life over time.

My Strong Refuge

Be my strong refuge, to which I may resort continually; You have given the commandment to save me, for You are my rock and my fortress.

PSALM 71:3

When our lives progress according to our plans, we feel confident and secure. We value our independence and sense of control. This sense of security dissipates when we face trials, difficulty, or loss. Instead of feeling secure, we become acutely aware of our vulnerability. As our plans unravel, we realize the limitations of our control and power. As Christians, we may wish for an exemption from suffering, but this was never promised to us. In the midst of our insecurity, we have a choice.

We can be like trees whose roots grow deep into the ground to withstand the winds shaking them, or we can allow the circumstances to separate us from God, our strength and foundation. He is the only one who can provide the power and peace we need to survive trials. The security offered by other sources is temporary. God alone is steadfast and constant.

Start a list of God's attributes and the ways He has worked in your life. This can serve as a reminder when you face trials. When we remember who God is and His faithfulness to us in the past, we are encouraged to continue depending on Him as our strong refuge in the midst of new challenges.

A FRAGRANT SCENT

Rejoice always.
I THESSALONIANS 5:16

ave you heard about the man who smelled good no matter where he was or what he was doing? His skin and clothing and very being seemed to exude a pleasant fragrance. He worked in a perfume factory and breathed its aromas every day. They filtered into his clothing, penetrated his skin, and even filled his lungs. He became a walking perfumery.

That's the way we should be as Christians. The Bible says, "For we are to God the fragrance of Christ among those who are being saved and among those who are perishing" (2 Corinthians 2:15). We exude the aroma of joy, for in His presence is fullness of joy (Psalm 16:11).

You might have heard that "Jesus wept" (John 11:35) is the shortest verse in the Bible, but that's only true in the English translation. In the original New Testament Greek, 1 Thessalonians 5:16 is shorter—"Rejoice always." The two verses are related. Because Jesus wept, we can rejoice. He doesn't want us to live in perpetual discouragement, sadness, or doubt. The joy of the Lord is the strength of our days (Nehemiah 8:10). We have a reason to rejoice.

EXPERT COUNSEL

*Happy is he who has the God of Jacob for his help, whose
hope is in the LORD his God, who made heaven and earth,
the sea, and all that is in them; who keeps truth forever.*

PSALM 146:5–6

Who will help me? Our natural response to challenges is to react in our own strength. We strategize and try to think our way to a solution. When that fails, we turn to those around us. Have you experienced this? What did you do?

While these methods sometimes work, we have forgotten our most powerful ally. This simple refrain from a children's song reminds us, "He's got the whole world in His hands." True wisdom and help come from the One who not only holds the world, but created it. If we are struggling to trust God's insight and sovereignty, all we need to do is spend time in His creation. The details, structure, and creative coloring of each plant and creature point to God's power.

Instead of running to God as an afterthought, we can start with Him. We are His creation and He knows what we need. God knows more about you and your situation than any other being, including you. He is also the only one who can control the outcome. When we realize this, we will seek His expertise and help first. As we surrender ourselves and our situation to His expertise, we gain the hope and confidence of knowing that He is in control and that He loves to help us.

REWARDS OR REGRETS?

God has numbered your kingdom, and finished it; . . . you have
been weighed in the balances, and found wanting; . . . your kingdom
has been divided, and given to the Medes and Persians.

DANIEL 5:25–28

*J*esus frequently used images from the agrarian world to illustrate His teaching. On one occasion, Paul did the same in Galatians 6:7. Like seeds that eventually come to fruition and harvest, so all people will reap the fruit of their lives. To point out the seriousness of this truth, Paul warned his readers, "Do not be deceived, God is not mocked," when it comes to holding man accountable.

God is long-suffering and always leaves room for repentance. To illustrate, He allowed the ruler of Babylon, Belshazzar, seventeen years to repent of his ways before finally stepping in and judging king and kingdom alike. It happened on the night of Belshazzar's drunken feast, when a hand appeared and wrote a message of judgment on the wall. The words of the message suggested that God's evaluation had been a process, and that night was the harvest. Belshazzar reaped what he had sown.

Life is a process of sowing seed by word and by deed, and the harvest is inevitable. Make sure that your judgment results in rewards instead of regrets (1 Corinthians 3:11–15).

DEVOTED

*Ezra had devoted himself to the study and observance of the Law
of the Lord, and to teaching its decrees and laws in Israel.*
EZRA 7:10 NIV

re you familiar with phrases about having our *daily devotions*? Where did that term originate? We don't know when the word *devotions* was first used for our periods of Bible study and prayer, but it's appropriate. The word *devotion* means "earnest affection for a person or a cause." It's a better term than the word *commitment*. We can be committed to a cause out of sheer duty; but to be devoted implies commitment plus affection.

When we're devoted to learning God's Word, it helps to have the right study tools. The primary point is having a Bible; and a good study Bible is indispensable. Many Christians also use a personal notebook to record their thoughts. A concordance (either online or in book format) can help locate all the occurrences of particular words in Scripture. And a simple, one-volume commentary can yield helpful insights on difficult passages.

As our children head back to school, it's time to don our backpacks and enroll in the Ezra School of Bible Study—devoting ourselves to the study and observance of God's Word and to teaching it to others.

A TIME TO REFLECT

Reflect on what I am saying, for the Lord will give you insight into all this.

2 TIMOTHY 2:7 NIV

*I*f you visit Mount Rainier, take time to drive three miles past Paradise until you come to the Reflection Lakes. There your enjoyment of Rainier's grandeur will be doubled, because its majestic slopes are duplicated on the canvas of the waters. If you can't visit the Pacific Northwest this fall, don't worry. Reflecting lakes are everywhere. They are God's mirrors, allowing us to take in His creation from two perspectives at once.

The word *reflect* means to "reproduce," to cast back an image. It also means to "meditate, ponder," and "think." When we reflect, we're looking at something a second time, taking it in, studying it again, pondering.

This is a good season to review your life and reflect on God's mercies. Take time to contemplate the mountaintops of His unchangeable nature, the treetops of His lofty reign, the colors of His grace, the clouds of His anticipated return. Take time to meditate on a verse He's given you or a Scripture you're memorizing.

Reflect on all this, and the Lord will give you fresh insights for living.

August 15

A CONFIDENT PROMISE

*Nevertheless we, according to His promise, look for new
heavens and a new earth in which righteousness dwells.*

2 PETER 3:13

Consider how you feel when you're in a relationship with a person—spouse, friend, coworker, boss—who has *never* been untrue in word or deed. The longer that person goes without betraying your trust, the higher your confidence soars. But should something untrue be said or done, your confidence crashes. It can take a long time to restore trust.

We serve a God who has never been untrue in word or deed. In fact, Jesus called Himself "the truth," personifying the quality that is an attribute of God (John 14:6). While man is constantly redefining truth—Pontius Pilate famously asked, "What is truth?" (John 18:38)—Jesus and the psalmist declared that God's Word is truth (Psalm 119:160; John 17:17). And God's promises are part of His Word (2 Peter 1:2–4). Jesus said that the Christian's place in eternity, in God's family, is eternal—that is a promise that will be eternally true (John 10:28). Nothing can separate the Christian from the love of God in Christ (Romans 8:38–39).

Whatever your need may be today—provision, protection, perseverance—cling to the promises from the One who has never been untrue.

DEALING WITH DISASTER

"When you pass through the waters, I will be with you; and through the rivers, they shall not overflow you. When you walk through the fire, you shall not be burned, nor shall the flame scorch you."

eading about the Israelites standing on the shore of the Red Sea, we can imagine their distress over the advance of the Egyptian army. *Has God forgotten us?* This question visits each of us from time to time when everything around us seems to be crumbling: the loss of a job, broken relationships, or even the loss of loved ones.

It's hard to trust an invisible God. Like the Israelites in their moment of distress, we do not know God's plan; the Israelites were not expecting God to part the water before them. It would have been easy to abandon faith and become cynical. Instead, we can apply Moses' exhortation to ourselves, "Do not be afraid. Stand still, and see the salvation of the LORD. . . . The LORD will fight for you, and you shall hold your peace" (Exodus 14:13–14). God delights in carrying us through even the darkest of times. He is at work in our situation. Trust in Him, and allow this promise to strengthen your spirit today.

A Costly Sacrifice

On the next day, when [the Samaritan] departed, he took out two denarii, gave them to the innkeeper, and said to him, "Take care of him; and whatever more you spend, when I come again, I will repay you."
LUKE 10:35

What is the most you have ever given, spontaneously, to a person in need? A dollar? Five, ten dollars, or more? How about the equivalent of what you earn in two days? There are 260 working days in the year (52 weeks x 5 days per week). Divide 260 into your annual salary and see what you come up with. Would you give that much money to a person in need—*someone you didn't know?*

That's what the "good Samaritan" did who stopped to help a man who had been beaten and robbed on the road from Jerusalem to Jericho. The Samaritan tended to the injured man's wounds, then took him to an inn and gave the innkeeper two denarii—the equivalent of two days' wages—to look after the injured man (Matthew 20:2). He even promised the innkeeper he would cover any additional expenses incurred when he passed that way again. Writing a check for two or three hundred dollars today sounds like a lot. And it is! But love and compassion are costly and require sacrifice.

Giving until it hurts means we have crossed the line between convenience and sacrifice.

WORRY FREE

"But when they arrest you and deliver you up, do not worry . . ."

MARK 13:11

On December 28, 1900, the *(Toronto) Daily Mail and Empire* ran this headline: "Illness Slight, Worry Killed Him." The story said, "James McIntosh, of 535 Talbot Avenue, Braddock, worried himself to death. That is the opinion of his attending physician. McIntosh came to Braddock a year ago with his young wife, coming from London, Ontario. On Christmas Eve, McIntosh was attacked with acute laryngitis, and he feared he would not get well, although Dr. G. E. Blair, who attended him, told him there was no danger. He worried continually, and in 48 hours was a corpse. His excessive worry is said to have affected his heart."[1]

Twice the Lord told us not to worry. The first time had reference to our food, clothes, and daily needs, and Jesus told us not to worry about those things for the heavenly Father knows our needs (Matthew 6:27–34). The other time is when we're persecuted or imprisoned. Even then, we're not to worry, for God will show us what to say and do (Matthew 10:19). He's in control, even though it may appear otherwise at times.

So make this a worry-free day. Trust instead.

Why We Worship

Give unto the Lord *the glory due to His name;*
worship the Lord *in the beauty of holiness.*
Psalm 29:2

*S*ome things in life are negotiable, others are not. Civil laws are nonnegotiable. The physical laws of the universe, like gravity, are nonnegotiable. Going to the gym, raking the leaves, purchasing a desired item—these, and other things in life, are negotiable. That means we can allow our feelings to help determine our course of action.

Nonnegotiables in the kingdom of God are expressed as commands. Sometimes we are told they are laws, as in the Ten Commandments (Exodus 20:1–17), and other times their status as commands is implied by how they are written. As suggested by Hebrew grammar, worshiping God is not negotiable: "worship the Lord" is an imperative form (1 Chronicles 16:29; Psalm 29:2; 96:9). We think of worship as an emotional act born out of love and gratitude—and those are good reasons to worship God. But what if we don't feel love and gratitude? At that point we worship God because of "the splendor of his holiness" (niv). That is, we worship Him because He deserves to be worshiped as our Creator God.

Don't let feelings be an obstacle to worship. Worship God because of who He is and what He deserves—and feelings will follow.

GOD'S REMEDY

And if Christ is not risen, your faith is futile; you are still in your sins!

1 CORINTHIANS 15:17

The "ostrich effect" is a term used by financial professionals to describe the avoidance of risky financial situations by denying the risk actually exists. The label comes from the long-held (false) belief that ostriches bury their heads in the sand to avoid seeing an approaching predator or other danger. (They supposedly do this to ingest sand and pebbles that help to grind up food in their gizzard.)

Denying reality is a human weakness, the most dangerous form of which is to deny the reality of sin. To deny we are dead in our trespasses and sins doesn't change the fact that we are (Ephesians 2:1). To believe that we can be saved by good works in spite of our sin doesn't change the fact that we can't (Ephesians 2:8–9). When the apostle Paul wrote to the Corinthians about the resurrection of Jesus, he said that if the Resurrection didn't happen, we are still in our sins. Without Christ's death and resurrection, the reality of our being in our sins hasn't changed.

When it comes to sin, denial is a life-or-death matter. Thankfully, God has provided a remedy for those who want to be saved from their sin.

August 21

SLEEP WELL

When I remember You on my bed, I meditate on You in the night watches.
PSALM 63:6

cientists and researchers aren't sure why we sleep. When we don't sleep, we are tired, less alert, irritable, and have poorer memory. So, we sleep to prevent those things from happening. We do know this: the mind is active while we sleep. Many believe it is helpful to give the mind positive and peaceful thoughts while drifting off to sleep.

And what could be more positive and peace-inducing than thoughts of God's love and care? Meditating on Scripture before going to sleep is encouraged by verses such as Hebrews 4:12: "Scripture is alive and active, able to separate soul from spirit, able to reveal the thoughts and intents of the heart" (paraphrase). Why not give our minds "food for thought" that is alive and active, truth the Holy Spirit can use even as we sleep to create ideas, desires, insights, and motivations for our life? And if we awake from sleep in the night with a troubled heart, a whispered prayer to God for rest and peace is better than tossing and turning (Philippians 4:6–7).

Give your mind and body the rest it needs by sleeping peacefully in the knowledge that God is at work in you for His own good pleasure (Philippians 2:13).

LOVE YOUR ENEMY

"But I say to you, love your enemies, bless those who curse you, do good to those who hate you, and pray for those who spitefully use you and persecute you."

MATTHEW 5:44

he word *tradition* in Greek comes from two words: *para* ("beside") and *didomi* ("to give"). Therefore, a tradition was something given alongside something else. In first-century Jewish culture, traditions were teachings of the Jewish elders that they gave alongside the law of Moses. Those traditions were often given equal, if not more, weight than the Law itself.

In the Sermon on the Mount, Jesus calls into question one of those traditions: "You have heard that it was said, '. . . Hate your enemy'" (Matthew 5:43). Nowhere in the Old Testament were the Jews taught to hate their enemies. Did some Israelites express hatred for the enemies of God? Yes (Psalm 139:21–22)—but not because they were commanded to. Instead, the Law taught the Jews to treat their enemies with kindness (Exodus 23:4–5).

The definition of *enemy* is a sliding scale. We all have those for whom feelings of dislike, resentment, and even hatred are evoked. But those feelings are to be replaced by Jesus' teaching: Love your enemy. Or in the words of both Testaments, love your neighbor (Leviticus 19:18; Luke 10:27, 36–37).

YOUR RESURRECTION BODY

The Lord Jesus Christ . . . will transform our lowly body
that it may be conformed to His glorious body.

PHILIPPIANS 3:20–21

lthough it's true that we're inwardly renewed by the Lord day by day, we're nonetheless outwardly perishing (2 Corinthians 4:16). Our aging bodies experience pain, illness, and death. But one day, God's children will be changed in the twinkling of an eye. Our resurrected bodies will be raised, glorified, and transformed into the pattern of the body of the risen Christ. That means: (1) Our bodies will be physical, real, and recognizable (Luke 24:36–43). (2) Our racial and gender identities will likely continue into heaven (Revelation 7:9). (3) We will be incapable of dying (1 Corinthians 15:50–54). (4) We'll be free from pain and tears (Revelation 21:4). (5) We may have extra dimensional qualities like those of Jesus, who could move in and out of locked rooms (Luke 24:30–31). (6) We'll forever be in the prime of life, like the Lord at His resurrection.

We'll have indestructible bodies in an ideal environment, and so shall we ever be with the Lord. These truths may not relieve your physical pain or disability right now, but perhaps they'll encourage you to look forward to what God has planned.

CLEAN GARMENTS

Now Joshua was clothed with filthy garments,
and was standing before the Angel.

ZECHARIAH 3:3

he prophet Zechariah once had a vision in which the high priest of Israel in postexilic times, a man named Joshua, stood before the Lord in filthy garments. Joshua was embarrassed, especially because Satan was there, pointing out every flaw and failure. But the Angel of the Lord—likely a reference to Christ— issued a command: "Take away the filthy garments from him. . . . See, I have removed your iniquity from you, and I will clothe you with rich robes" (Zechariah 3:4). Joshua was clad in clean clothes and equipped to minister without sin or shame, and Satan was defeated.

We are God's people even when others treat us like underdogs, even when Satan makes us feel like second-class citizens, even when we're down on ourselves. We're valuable to God. He loves us, and Jesus died to cleanse our sins, to clothe us with the garments of His righteousness, and to use us for His glory.

If you've had some kind of failure or relapse, don't dwell on it. Confess it. If others look down on you, don't obsess over it. Keep your eyes on the Lord.

August 25

WISE INVESTING

The law of Your mouth is better to me than
thousands of coins of gold and silver.

PSALM 119:72

riting two hundred years after Christ, Bishop Cyprian of Carthage said of the Scriptures, "[They] are nothing else than divine commands, foundations on which hope is to be built up, buttresses by which faith is to be strengthened, nourishment wherefrom the heart is to be comforted, helps whereby to steer our way, ramparts whereby salvation is to be preserved; and thus, while they instruct the teachable minds of believers on earth, they also lead them on to the heavenly kingdom."[2]

There has never been a book like the Bible—inspired by God and penned by men, deep enough to study for a lifetime but concise enough to hold in our hands. Every page is a treasure. Psalm 19:10 says the Word of God is more desirable than fine gold. Proverbs 3:15 says it's more precious than rubies. And Psalm 119:72 says it's better than thousands of coins of gold and silver.

When you invest yourself in the Bible, you're the richest person on earth.

"NOT RESENTFUL"

Resentment kills a fool, and envy slays the simple.

JOB 5:2 NIV

he word *resentment* comes from the Latin term *sentire*, which means "to feel." When you put the *re-* in front of it, it means "to feel again." When someone offends us, we feel anger or shame. As we recall the event, we keep dredging up those emotions, and they harden into resentment. Sometimes the memories get stuck in our heads and we replay them over and over. When this happens, it destroys love, tears down marriages, ruins friendships, and devastates our internal peace of mind.

If that's happening to you, study how Paul advised Timothy to handle his conflicts with false teachers: "Don't have anything to do with foolish and stupid arguments, because you know they produce quarrels. And the Lord's servant must not be quarrelsome but must be kind to everyone, able to teach, not resentful" (2 Timothy 2:23–24 NIV).

We can't avoid feelings of anger when we're offended or hurt, and it takes time to process difficult emotions. But don't replay the offense over and over in your mind. Give the hurt to the Lord, learn to release the bitterness, and uproot resentment before it uproots you.

August 27

GONE, GONE, GONE, GONE

*Purge me with hyssop, and I shall be clean; wash
me, and I shall be whiter than snow.*

PSALM 51:7

ave you ever bundled up for a walk through the snow on a sunny day? If so, you know you need to grab your sunglasses along with your scarf because the reflection of the sun on the snow is blinding. Underneath the snow there may be dirt and mud, potholes, and decaying leaves. But all is covered, hidden, and washed white by the dazzling blanket of snow. It's as pristine as sheer light.

That's a picture of God's forgiveness. Two verses in the Bible talk about how His love covers a multitude of sins (1 Peter 4:8 and James 5:20). The blood of Christ cleanses us from all sin, covers a multitude of failures, and washes us whiter than snow. Perhaps you remember the little Sunday school song that said, "Gone, Gone, Gone, Gone! Yes, my sins are gone. / Now my soul is free, and in my heart's a song. / Buried in the deepest sea, yes, that's good enough for me. / I shall live eternally, Praise God! My sins are gone!"

That's the way God's children should feel today—whiter than snow.

HE NEVER SLUMBERS

*I will both lie down in peace, and sleep; for You
alone, O LORD, make me dwell in safety.*

PSALM 4:8

ow are you sleeping? All kinds of things can disrupt
our rest, but believers shouldn't stay awake night after
night from fear and worry. In the book of Daniel, King Darius
didn't sleep a wink in chapter 6, but Daniel rested just fine in the
lions' den. The next morning he told the king, "My God sent His
angel and shut the lions' mouths" (verse 22).

The same angels guard us, and not just the angels! God
Himself watches over His children by day and night. According
to Psalm 121:4, our heavenly Father watches over us and He neither slumbers nor sleeps. With God on our side, we can have
peace amid opposition and rest in troubled times.

Try some adjustments to your evening routine. Instead of
rehearsing your problems at bedtime, review your favorite Bible
verses. Thank God for three or four specific blessings you've experienced during the day. Choose a promise as a pillow. In peace, lie
down and sleep, for the Lord makes you dwell in safety.

EVER-PRESENT HELP

Your servant has killed both lion and bear; and this
uncircumcised Philistine will be like one of them, seeing
he has defied the armies of the living God.

1 SAMUEL 17:36

When the shepherding lad David went to check on his brothers in the army, he was alarmed to find them paralyzed with fear because of the threats of a Philistine giant named Goliath. The whole army seemed stupefied, from King Saul down to the lowest ranks. David offered to take on the giant, but his brothers were scornful and Saul was doubtful. "You are a youth," Saul said (verse 33). But David told him how he had killed the lion and the bear that had threatened his flocks. In verse 37, he said, "The LORD, who delivered me from the paw of the lion and from the paw of the bear, He will deliver me from the hand of this Philistine."

And God did.

Our Lord's past performance of faithfulness is an ever-present comfort during times of distress. One of the reasons God allows trials is to strengthen our faith for the future. Don't waste yesterday's lessons by forgetting the deliverance of God. The same God who delivered you from the lion and the bear will give you victory and grace today and tomorrow.

PREPARED FOR BATTLE

. . . praying always with all prayer and supplication in the Spirit, being watchful to this end with all perseverance and supplication for all the saints.

EPHESIANS 6:18

*W*hen we pray, our thoughts are centered on "our side" of the prayer: time, place, and our need. Even after we pray, our attention is on the answer we hope to receive. Again, all that activity is on our side of the prayer. But what about "God's side" of our prayers? What happens in heavenly places, at the throne of God, when we pray? Simply put, we don't know—and it is fruitless to speculate. But we should not ignore the glimpses behind the curtain that Scripture offers.

First, prayer is linked to spiritual warfare—it was the last thing Paul mentioned in his description of the Christian's spiritual armor (Ephesians 6:18). Anticipating conflicts in Jerusalem, Paul requested prayer for his deliverance before arriving (Romans 15:30–33). Jesus labored so mightily in prayer that an angel had to minister to Him (Luke 22:43–44). And Daniel 10 gives us a glimpse of the actual three-week spiritual warfare in heaven that surrounded Daniel's prayers.

The next time you pray, thank God for the strength to persevere and that His will is always done.

GREATER WORKS

"Most assuredly, I say to you, he who believes in Me, the works that I do he will do also; and greater works than these he will do, because I go to My Father."

JOHN 14:12

he world's population was around 200 million in the first century. For Jesus to reach all those people individually would have been humanly impossible. Even with the assistance of twelve helpers (Luke 9:1), even with seventy helpers (Luke 10:1), human limitations would have caused the Great Commission to fail.

Jesus lived His life by the power and wisdom of the Holy Spirit, who was given to Him by the Father without limit (John 3:34). No number of men and women operating in their own strength could accomplish the Great Commission in their own fleshly power. So Jesus returned to heaven and sent the Holy Spirit to fill and empower His helpers so they could do even greater works (more works) than Jesus Himself did in His three years of ministry on earth. Indeed, He said it was to His disciples' advantage that He should leave them and send the Holy Spirit in His place (John 16:7).

If you are facing a task you feel is impossible, remember that Jesus sent His Spirit to enable you to do what He Himself would do if He were here—and more.

September

Your mercy, O Lord, is in the heavens;
Your faithfulness reaches to the clouds.

Psalm 36:5

September 1

SUPERNATURAL STRENGTH

I can do all things through Christ who strengthens me.
PHILIPPIANS 4:13

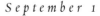oday's entertainment industry has its pantheon of mythology—gods born in the pages of comic books: Iron Man, Captain America, Spider-Man, Wonder Woman, the Fantastic Four, Batman, and, of course, the Man of Steel. Why are we so obsessed with superheroes? Perhaps we like to think there's a little superhero inside each of us.

Superheroes are figments of the imagination, but supernatural strength is available to all of God's children. We can say with the apostle Paul, "I can do all things through Christ who strengthens me." That doesn't mean we're faster than a speeding bullet, more powerful than a locomotive, or able to leap a tall building in a single bound. It means God will enable us to do all that He has called us to do and strengthen us in our inner being to accomplish His perfect will today. The Bible says, "The eyes of the LORD run to and fro throughout the whole earth, to show Himself strong on behalf of those whose heart is loyal to Him" (2 Chronicles 16:9).

Tackle today's work in the strength He provides, and trust Him to work powerfully within you.

MINDFUL OF YOU

When I consider Your heavens, the work of Your fingers, the moon and the stars, which You have ordained, what is man that You are mindful of him?

PSALM 8:3–4

When the ancients looked up at the heavens, they didn't know what they were seeing. We may know more about the universe than they did, but we still know relatively little. The *observable* universe is thought to be 92 billion light-years in diameter—and one light-year is 6 trillion miles. So do the math: 92 billion times 6 trillion equals . . . well, it equals a long way from one side of the observable universe to the other. And what about the *unobservable* part?

Based just on what they saw and understood of the heavens, the ancient biblical writers were overwhelmed with their smallness measured against its immensity. And they were amazed that God invested time and attention in them. When we have problems in life, they seem very large—and they are. But when we consider that God is powerful enough to have created the universe, we realize He is more than capable of meeting our needs.

God cares about you and your needs. Bring them to Him in a spirit of worship and thanksgiving, knowing that He is mindful of your place in His creation.

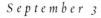

September 3

A WELCOMING DELEGATION

When Paul saw them, he thanked God and took courage.
ACTS 28:15

*I*n Acts 28, the apostle Paul grappled with disappointment, fatigue, and a sense of failure. He had hoped to be on his way to Spain as a free man, but he had encountered a series of unfortunate events—hostility, arrest, a near flogging, a prolonged legal battle, a terrifying storm, a shipwreck, a snakebite, and a forced march to Rome, where prison awaited him. Imagine even one of those things happening to you!

But as Paul approached the city of Rome, he looked up and saw a delegation of brothers and sisters coming to meet him. At the sight of his friends, his spirits revived. He thanked God and took courage. As we visualize the scene in our minds, we can almost see a smile coming to his face, a grateful whisper on his lips, and a bounce entering his steps.

You and I have people like that in our lives, too, but perhaps we don't thank God enough for them. Take a few moments today to appreciate those who strengthen you and give you courage. Thank God for the blessings that abound, including your brothers and sisters in Christ.

ALWAYS FAITHFUL

*For this reason I also suffer these things; nevertheless I am not
ashamed, for I know whom I have believed and am persuaded that
He is able to keep what I have committed to Him until that Day.*

2 TIMOTHY 1:12

The Latin phrase *Semper Fi*—short for *Semper Fidelis*—is
well-known to United States Marines and their families.
It means "always faithful" or "always loyal," and it has served as
the motto of the Marine Corps since 1883. On the Marine Corps
emblem, an eagle holds a ribbon in its mouth, inscribed with *Semper
Fidelis*. The words "always faithful" suggest there is never a time
when a Marine will not be faithful to his or her duty to country.

The Marine Corps motto could well serve as a motto for the
Christian life. The apostle Paul made the point that "it is required
in stewards that one be found faithful" (1 Corinthians 4:2). And
Christians are nothing if not stewards—of creation, of spiritual gifts, of the Gospel, of time, talent, and treasure, and of the
grace of God. There is never a day when we are not expected to
be faithful to God, never a day when we can allow fear of the
future to replace faith in the God who knows the future. Writing
from prison in his final letter, Paul knew that better days were
right around the corner in the presence of his Lord. In the deepest
sense, nothing could really touch or harm him.

If you are a follower of Christ, let *Semper Fidelis* be your
watchword today and every day: Always Faithful.

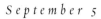

THE FRUIT OF OUR LIPS

Therefore by Him let us continually offer the sacrifice of praise to God, that is, the fruit of our lips, giving thanks to His name.
HEBREWS 13:15

*S*ometimes when two people are together, one will hear these words: "Hello? You seem to be a thousand miles away." The response comes: "Sorry—I was thinking about something that happened earlier today. What were you saying?" It's possible to be in the same place without really connecting or engaging; we might as well be somewhere else.

Even though we know God is always with us (Hebrews 13:5), if we are not engaging with Him, there is little benefit from His presence. So how do we engage with God? Always being mindful of Him, living in an attitude of prayer, and responding to His Word. But what about praise? Praising God is the same as praising a friend or family member; it suggests that the person we are praising is "in the room" and receiving our praise. When we offer the sacrifice of praise to God, we give our attention to Him; we sing to Him, we speak to Him, and we humble ourselves before Him—all reminders that He is present with us.

When you feel distant from God, restore the sense of His presence by offering Him the "fruit of [your] lips"—your praise.

PENNED PRAYERS

The LORD *God is my strength; He will make my feet like
deer's feet, and He will make me walk on my high hills.*

HABAKKUK 3:19

When was the last time you wrote a prayer with pen
and ink? We have many methods of prayer, and we
should try all of them. But we have two great encouragements to
add written prayers to the mix—our Bibles and our hymnals.

In the Bible, many of our heroes wrote out their prayers.
Study the Psalms, for example, and notice how many are written
prayers. The prophets, such as Jonah and Habakkuk, left us with
recorded prayers on the printed page. The apostle Paul composed
prayers for most of his congregations.

In the hymnbook, many of our great songs are prayers written to God and designed to be read and sung to Him. Think of
the hymn "How Great Thou Art." The words aren't written *about*
God but addressed *to* Him: "O Lord my God, when I in awesome
wonder . . ."

Sometimes we have trouble focusing our thoughts in prayer
or harnessing our emotions. In such times, it's often helpful to
write out a prayer and perhaps then share it verbally. God can
read as well as He can hear; He knows your scribbling as well as
He knows your soul.

AMAZING FORGIVENESS

For You, Lord, are good, and ready to forgive, and
abundant in mercy to all those who call upon You.
PSALM 86:5

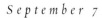hen a young man massacred nine Christians at the end of a Bible study at Emanuel AME Church in Charleston, South Carolina, journalists were amazed at how quickly the families of the victims expressed their willingness to forgive the shooter. The loved ones certainly didn't condone the man's actions or excuse him from the consequences of his crimes. But they didn't want to harbor lifelong animosity, and their statements left reporters speechless. One mourner, whose seventy-year-old mother had perished, told the shooter, "You took something very precious away from me. I will never get to talk to her ever again. I will never be able to hold her again. But I forgive you, and have mercy on your soul."[1]

When you express forgiveness toward others, you're simply passing on the forgiveness you have experienced personally from God. When we come to Him in confession and repentance, He grants abundant pardon; He forgives our debts. Knowing God has forgiven your sin provides a way for you to release any bitterness you feel toward others.

FEAR NO EVIL

*Why should I fear in the days of evil, when the
iniquity at my heels surrounds me?*

PSALM 49:5

evelation devotes several chapters to the coming days of evil and tribulation. Reading these passages, we sense the time drawing near. We're astounded at the evil of our days and are prone to worry about the evils to be unleashed on earth.

But remember: the times have always been evil. Genesis 6:5 says of man in Noah's day, "Every intent of the thoughts of his heart was only evil continually." Moses described his people as "this evil generation" (Deuteronomy 1:35). Isaiah called the people of his day "a brood of evildoers" (Isaiah 1:4). Jesus referred to His generation as evil (Matthew 12:39). Paul told people in his age to redeem the time "because the days are evil" (Ephesians 5:16).

Perhaps the evil is worse now; we're closer to the end than we've ever been before. But evil has been around since the garden of Eden, and God's plan for victory was designed before the world began. The Bible tells us to fear no evil. Because Christ triumphed, we will also overcome evil in the end. Trust Christ in this evil age and redeem the time, for the days are evil.

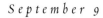

September 9

BLESSINGS FROM ABOVE

The backslider in heart will be filled with his own ways,
but a good man will be satisfied from above.

PROVERBS 14:14

*D*eep beneath the streets of New York City is a cavern more than a hundred years old known as the Williamsburg Trolley Terminal, which is an abandoned subway station. Engineers are turning it into a park. They are devising an ingenious system for piping in real, live sunshine using a series of mirrors and focusers that bounce the light through pipes from huge sunlight collectors above ground.

We're living in a dark world, but God pipes His sunshine into our lives every day. His goodness shines down from above. James said, "Every good gift and every perfect gift is from above, and comes down from the Father of lights, with whom there is no variation or shadow of turning" (James 1:17).

The thankful heart rejoices in God's gifts, including the blessings of eternal life, which come down through Him from above. Jesus said, "You are from beneath; I am from above" (John 8:23). Let's thank God for the sunlight of His blessings, reflected into our lives by Him who is the mirror image of heaven—Jesus Christ our Lord.

268

THE FINE LINE

"Listen to Me, you stubborn-hearted, who are far from righteousness:
I bring My righteousness near, it shall not be far off."

ISAIAH 46:12–13

*A*re you stubborn? If so, is your stubbornness a good quality or a bad one? When stubbornness means dogged determination to do the will of God, it's good. Perhaps a better term would be *perseverance*—a quality the Bible upholds as the core of character (Romans 5:4). But when stubbornness is another word for self-will, it's a destructive force. The Bible says, "For rebellion is as the sin of witchcraft, and stubbornness is as iniquity and idolatry" (1 Samuel 15:23).

There's a fine line between stubborn self-will and godly perseverance, and often the Lord uses crises in our lives to move us from one to the other. Take the patriarch Jacob, for example. His story in the book of Genesis is filled with selfish and stubborn choices, which caused pain to himself and others. But by the end of the story, God had used a series of crises in his life to turn his stubbornness into sanctified perseverance.

We can't avoid pressure in life, but we should always remember that whatever crisis we face is God's way of reshaping our stubborn hearts into models of perseverance and character.

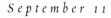

September 11

WE BELONG TOGETHER

Husbands, likewise, dwell with them with understanding, giving honor to the wife . . . as being heirs together of the grace of life.

1 PETER 3:7

wo old men sat in a coffee shop, talking about the recent death of one man's wife. The widower told the story of how he saw her, fell in love with her, and married her. He explained how she made him a better husband and daddy— and made him a better worker and a better Christian. Then one day she became ill. It took two years of decline, weakness, and medication before the Lord took her home. During that time, the man continued to work twelve hours a day, and then would come home and take care of her, ultimately feeding her and carrying her to bed at night. At her passing, he was lost. His friend said, "That must have been hard taking care of her." The widowed man responded, "It was my privilege to serve my queen."

That is God's view of marriage. Two people serving one another in love, making each other better. God is powerfully in favor of married love. It's true that marriage isn't for everyone. Neither Jesus nor Paul married; their God-ordained mission in life precluded it. But marriage is God's idea. He defined its terms in the garden of Eden, and He blesses those who value its purpose and purity.

CHARACTER COUNTS

And [God] said, "Your name shall no longer be called Jacob, but Israel;
for you have struggled with God and with men, and have prevailed."

GENESIS 32:28

iven names (first names) came first in history, with
surnames (last names) being added later. It's easy to
see how some name combinations were formed: John the miller
became John Miller; Thomas the blacksmith (or ironsmith)
became Thomas Smith; Joseph the farmer became Joseph Farmer.
Surnames were also derived from geography, nature, and character traits.

That last category—character traits and responsibilities—
describes how many biblical names were assigned or changed.
For example, Jacob ("tripper" or "supplanter") received his name
because he grasped his firstborn twin brother, Esau's, foot when
they were born. And later, Jacob "tripped" Esau up by stealing
his birthright and blessing from their father, Isaac. But then God
humbled Jacob in an encounter and changed his name to Israel—
"he who struggles with God." Characteristically, Israel the nation
took Israel the patriarch's name, and rightfully so: Israel as a
nation has struggled all its life with God, and remains in that
struggle today.

If God were to ascribe a name to you, based on character,
what would it be?

HEAVEN ON EARTH

But you have come to Mount Zion and to the city of the living God,
the heavenly Jerusalem, to an innumerable company of angels.
HEBREWS 12:22

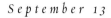n his 1933 novel *Lost Horizon*, British author James
Hilton introduced the world to "Shangri-La," a kind of
heaven on earth in the Kunlun Mountains of Tibet, a secluded
place where people hardly aged and lived very long lives in a society free of conflict and strife. It was another expression of man's
quest to create heaven on earth.

The Bible suggests that we can experience heaven while still
living on earth! The writer to the Hebrews says that we "have
come" (past tense) to Mount Zion, Jerusalem on earth, but also to
"the heavenly Jerusalem." We "have come" to the "church of the
firstborn who are registered in heaven . . . to Jesus the Mediator
of the new covenant" (Hebrews 12:22–24). Look around you—are
you in heaven? Not physically, but spiritually you are united with
heavenly reality if you are in Jesus Christ. Until our life on earth
is over, we are seated with Christ in heavenly places (Ephesians
1:3).

When your life on earth is a challenge, avail yourself of the
heavenly access that is yours in Christ.

PRIORITIES

"And this is eternal life, that they may know You, the only
true God, and Jesus Christ whom You have sent."

We hear a lot about priorities in life, and there are many. Every area of life—family, work, personal—has its own set of priorities. But is there one that stands above all others? It could be said that attaining eternal life is more important than any other goal in life. After all, eternal life was the gift of God in the beginning, and it is what was lost due to sin. So reestablishing that status could be seen as Priority One in life.

"But I have already achieved that priority," you say. "After all, Jesus said that knowing the Father and the Son is eternal life. I know the Father through faith in Christ and have eternal life." Yes, knowing Christ is where eternal life begins, but by its very definition it never ends. All of our earthly, temporal life should be lived in light of the eternity we possess and the presence of God we anticipate. We should be living *now* the same way we will live in heaven *forever*.

As the season changes, ask whether your life is changing as well. Is your life taking on more and more of a Christlike quality every day—becoming less temporal, more eternal?

Irrevocable Conviction

*I call heaven and earth as witnesses today against you, that I
have set before you life and death, blessing and cursing; therefore
choose life, that both you and your descendants may live.*

Deuteronomy 30:19

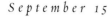hen someone is *convicted* of a crime and sent to prison,
he becomes a *convict*. Barring any judicial errors, a
decision (*conviction*) has been reached that is unchangeable; the
convict must serve the sentence. A *conviction* can also be made at
the personal level. We can *convict* ourselves to a permanent position regarding commitments, beliefs, and values. We can become
a *convict* for Christ when we choose to follow Him permanently
and irrevocably.

Jesus was a self-determined *convict*—a person with immovable
convictions. He refused to give in to Satan's temptations in the wilderness (Matthew 4:1–11). And He lived as a servant to God the
Father, refusing to give up His *convictions* even when it resulted
in His physical death (Philippians 2:6–8). Choosing one's *convictions* is what Moses (Deuteronomy 30:19) and later Joshua
(Joshua 24:15) offered the Israelites. And we are given that same
choice (Luke 14:26–27).

Sentence yourself today to a lifelong, irrevocable *conviction* of
faithful obedience to Christ.

EDUCATIONAL ENCOUNTER

*Also God said to [Jacob]: "I am God Almighty. Be fruitful
and multiply; a nation and a company of nations shall proceed
from you, and kings shall come from your body."*

GENESIS 35:11

The list of those whom God saved out of carnality and
rebellion into a life of spiritual maturity is long. But
that's the whole point, isn't it? God's goal is to transform us into
the image of Christ (Romans 8:29)—and He will use all means
necessary (Romans 8:28).

Who would have thought that, in his younger days, a schem-
ing man like Jacob would become the father of twelve sons from
whom would arise the multitudes in the nation of Israel? And
yet that is what God did through a painful encounter with Jacob
(Genesis 32:22–30). In fact, Jacob lived with a limp after that
encounter, and his descendants refused to eat the meat in an
animal's hip socket in memory of Jacob's encounter and transformation (Genesis 32:31–32). In short, God will do whatever it takes
to conform us to the image of His Son—even allow us to experience pain and live with reminders of our "educational encounter"
with Him.

Let God have His way in your life today. The sooner we say,
"Yes, Lord" to Him, the sooner we become like Him.

OVERCOMERS

Little children, it is the last hour; and as you have heard that the Antichrist is coming, even now many antichrists have come, by which we know that it is the last hour. . . . But you have an anointing from the Holy One.
1 JOHN 2:18–20

One day the world will welcome history's most charismatic leader, a man whose oratory will sway the masses, whose magnetism will amaze the media, and whose mouth will blaspheme God. But we needn't wait for the evil he will bring, for it is already here. The spirit of the Antichrist is in the world now.

In Jesus' name, we can stand against the spirit of the Antichrist today; and John told us how to do it in 1 John 2: "Do not love the world or the things in the world. . . . the lust of the flesh, the lust of the eyes, and the pride of life. . . . You have an anointing from the Holy One. . . . Therefore let that abide in you which you heard from the beginning. . . . Abide in Him" (verses 15–27).

Except for divine intervention, this world is a lost cause. Don't fall in love with it. You have an anointing from God. You can abide in God's truth every day as you abide in Christ. You can overcome. "For whatever is born of God overcomes the world. And this is the victory that has overcome the world—our faith" (1 John 5:4).

BEHIND THE SCENES

Then it came to pass, when Pharaoh had let the people go, that
God did not lead them by way of the land of the Philistines,
although that was near; for God said, "Lest perhaps the people
change their minds when they see war, and return to Egypt."

EXODUS 13:17

On the way *out of* Egypt, God protected Israel from *military* danger by sending them deep into the Sinai Peninsula (Exodus 13:17–18). And God sent them *into* Egypt to protect them from a *moral* danger in the land of Canaan (Genesis 38).

Without going into the unsavory details, some in Jacob's family—specifically, Jacob's son Judah—became involved in serious immorality because of his family's close proximity to Canaanites. It became apparent that if Jacob's sons and their families were to remain faithful to the Lord, they needed to leave Canaan until they were morally and spiritually stronger. So God sent a famine on Canaan, arranged for Jacob's son Joseph to provide a place of refuge for Jacob's family in Egypt, and kept them there for four hundred years, separated from the Egyptians in a corner of the land (Genesis 46:31–34).

Don't be too quick to judge inconvenient circumstances in your life. God may be at work behind the scenes to protect you from something more serious.

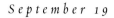

SUSTAINING JOY

Do not sorrow, for the joy of the LORD is your strength.
NEHEMIAH 8:10

he apostle Paul is the classic example of discovering and experiencing joy in difficult circumstances. "Joy" and "rejoicing" are mentioned twelve times in his short letter to the Philippians—written while he was under house arrest in Rome with an uncertain future ahead of him.

What does it mean to have joy in difficult circumstances? At least two truths make joy possible. First, Moses told the second generation of Israelites who had survived thirty-eight years of wilderness wanderings, "You shall rejoice in all the good things the LORD your God has given to you and your household" (Deuteronomy 26:11 NIV). That is, we can rejoice because of God's *care* for us in difficult times. Second, the fact that we are citizens of heaven means that we are in Christ in the heavenlies. That is, we can rejoice in difficult situations because of our *citizenship* in heaven, where we are fully protected.

If you are a Christian today, God has *cared* for you and made you a *citizen* of heaven. He will continue to care for you and sustain you with the resources of heaven itself. Both truths make good reasons for having joy in the Lord today.

THE LAST WORD

"You shall not bear false witness against your neighbor."

EXODUS 20:16

There are at least two ways to be untruthful about another person. One, it is possible to tell a lie—to say that someone did or said something that he didn't. The other way is *not* to tell the truth when you know someone is under a false impression. Staying quiet in the presence of a lie can be as wrong as telling the lie.

Ten of Jacob's sons, who were also brothers of Joseph, the eleventh son, were guilty on both counts. First, they misrepresented what happened to Joseph; they pretended they didn't know how Joseph's torn, bloody coat got that way. They even pretended not to know if the coat was Joseph's. Then, when Jacob reached a wrong conclusion about Joseph's fate—that he had been killed by a wild animal—the brothers remained silent, knowing that they had sold Joseph, alive and well, to Midianite traders. Not to worry—God always gets the last word when it comes to truth, as He did in Joseph's case (Genesis 39:19–23; Matthew 12:36).

First, purpose never to traffic in falsehoods yourself. Second, purpose never to remain silent in the presence of a lie (Ephesians 4:15). The false reports of man are always subject to the final reports of God.

FOLLOW HIS VOICE

"My sheep hear My voice, and I know them, and they follow Me."
JOHN 10:27

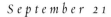

efore the days of video chat services, the telephone was the link between far-flung loved ones—and still mostly is. An anxious parent calls a child at college, "I just needed to hear your voice." A discouraged husband on a business trip calls his wife to hear the sound of her voice. A frightened child calls out from her bed at night, "Mom?" and is reassured by the returning voice: "I'm right here, sweetheart."

The human voice can bridge distances and bring comfort like nothing else. It is the same with the voice of God. We think of Him as being in heaven and sometimes forget that He is in us and with us as well. And even though we don't hear His audible voice, we can "hear" His voice at any time through His Word and the way the Spirit applies the Word to our life individually. Just as a child can recognize a parent's voice in the dark, so we can recognize God's voice in our darkest moments. Jesus said His sheep hear His voice and follow Him. His voice tells us that we are never separate from Him.

When you wonder where God is in your life, listen to His voice through His Word and prayer to remember that He is near to you. And when you hear His voice, be prepared to follow Him.

GOD'S AMAZING LOVE

For whom the LORD loves He corrects, just as a
father the son in whom he delights.

PROVERBS 3:12

ost Bible readers know that the story of Joseph and the family of Jacob moving to Egypt takes up the last major section of Genesis: chapters 37–50. We meet Joseph as a teenager in Genesis 37 and see him buried at the end of his life in Egypt in Genesis 50. The story flows smoothly except for one part: Genesis 38. If you connect the last verse of Genesis 37 with the first verse of Genesis 39, the story flows beautifully. But Genesis 38 has nothing to do with Joseph and appears to be just a snapshot of Jacob's family in Canaan.

Since God inspired the writing of Scripture (2 Timothy 3:16; 2 Peter 1:20–21), we know that Genesis 38 is there for a reason. And the reason is this: It explains *why* God sent Joseph to Egypt to prepare a place for Jacob's family to live in isolation from the world. It reveals the serious moral compromises Jacob's family was making in Canaan that could have ruined the future of Abraham's descendants. It proves that God loves His people enough to protect and preserve them through drastic measures if needed.

And God loves us that much as well. He loves us enough to do what we may be unwilling to do ourselves to protect our spiritual life.

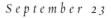

September 23

THE MASTER'S JOB

*Now may the God of peace . . . make you complete
in every good work to do His will.*

HEBREWS 13:20–21

The big idea of stewardship in Scripture is built on a fundamental premise: It was the responsibility of the master to furnish his steward with everything he needed for his assigned task. The master's job was to provide the resources; the steward's job was to use the master's resources according to his will.

It could be said that stewardship is the defining theme of the God-human relationship. In Genesis 1, God made man the steward of His creation (Genesis 1:28). The New Testament calls followers of Christ His servants—which is another way to define a steward (Romans 1:1). Paul says that bishops are stewards of God, meaning overseers of His Church (Titus 1:7). Paul called himself a steward "of the mysteries of God" (1 Corinthians 4:1). In every case, God as Master provides what the steward needs to fulfill his or her calling. Paul wrote that the Bible can make the Christian "complete, thoroughly equipped for every good work" (2 Timothy 3:16–17). And the writer to the Hebrews praised God for making Christians complete "to do His will" (Hebrews 13:21).

With all of the biblical examples we have before us, you can be certain that whatever God has called you to do, He will furnish you with the resources to complete it.

PLANS

A man's heart plans his way, but the LORD *directs his steps.*
PROVERBS 16:9

hink for a moment about all the plans you have in place right now: You plan to finish reading this devotional; you plan to take care of chores and tasks this weekend; you plan to do certain things next week; you plan to accomplish some family objectives this fall; you plan to take a vacation, get involved in a committee at church, retire, enjoy your senior years, and spend eternity with Christ. We live with plans—from the small to the sacred and everywhere in between.

Scripture commends plan-making—especially Proverbs (3:5–6; 16:1–4, 9; 19:21; 20:24). Proverbs even commends the ants for planning for the winter by storing up food in the summer (Proverb 6:6–8). Yet for human planners, there is one caveat when it comes to making plans: God's plans always take precedence over ours. Every plan we make should carry the conscious addendum, "As the Lord directs." In a parable the apostle James taught, planners are told to say, "If the Lord wills . . ." (James 4:15).

So, make your plans for this weekend, this fall, and the coming year. Just allow God to direct your steps. And trust that if He changes your plans, it is a chance to walk by faith (2 Corinthians 5:7).

ABUNDANT BLESSINGS

*"I have come that they may have life, and that
they may have it more abundantly."*
JOHN 10:10

hy is it easier to lament the things we *don't* have rather than praise God for the things we *do* have? The latter is the important list, and it's so long that there's not enough paper in the world to list all the items that make up the abundance of our blessings. The Bible says that God is abundant in mercy and abundant in kindness (Numbers 14:18; Nehemiah 9:17). He gives us an abundance of peace, and with Him is abundant redemption (Psalm 37:11; 130:7). And He *abundantly* pardons (Isaiah 55:7).

Jesus said, "The thief does not come except to steal, and to kill, and to destroy. I have come that they may have life, and that they may have it more abundantly" (John 10:10).

Part of stewardship is keeping track of our blessings and counting them daily. Yes, we could also keep a ledger of things we *don't* have, but why focus on that? "God is able to make all grace abound toward you, that you, always having all sufficiency in all things, may have an abundance for every good work" (2 Corinthians 9:8). With the abundant blessings we receive daily, our heartfelt response should be to praise God "from whom all blessings flow."

ELEPHANT TRACKS

And the God of peace will crush Satan under your feet shortly.
The grace of our Lord Jesus Christ be with you. Amen.

ROMANS 16:20

For Bowling, twenty-seven, an engineer, quit his job to see the world, but in Thailand he got more than he bargained for. While hiking in the Phu Luang Wildlife Sanctuary, he encountered an elephant charging at him like a freight train. Bowling instinctively stepped forward and held up his hand in a halting motion. The elephant stopped, turned, and fled in the opposite direction.

At times, Satan charges us like a stampeding elephant or a roaring lion. He can be intimidating. He may even appear to be winning. He reduced Job to the ash heap, sifted Peter like wheat, caused Christ to die for our sins, and hindered Paul from visiting the Thessalonians. According to the book of Revelation, he will dominate the entire world during the Tribulation.

But when we hold up the Cross, Satan's power is broken. His defeat is certain, and the God of peace will crush him under our feet shortly. Until then, we have all we need for victory—the grace of our Lord Jesus Christ.

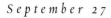

September 27

FREE FALL

But Jesus looked at them and said to them, "With men this is impossible, but with God all things are possible."
MATTHEW 19:26

ould you ever bungee jump? What would it take for you to trust the bungee cord and harness enough to fall from a ledge, believing it would hold you? For most of us, the tension between fear and the desire to experience the exhilaration of the fall will be resolved in fear's favor, and we can only imagine what it would feel like to safely free-fall.

When it comes to the invitation of Jesus in our lives, it takes courage to step out in faith. The disciples left their careers and families and planned futures to follow Jesus. Although they sometimes failed, Jesus patiently and lovingly led them.

Sadly, the rich young ruler could not see past the loss of his riches. The apprehension he felt in response to Jesus' invitation was resolved in fear's favor. He walked away from the Creator of the world, who offered him more than he would have ever lost. What is Jesus inviting you to do? If we look past what He is asking and remember His power and faithfulness, we will soon discover the courage to take that leap of faith—knowing He will hold us firmly in His grasp.

FRIENDS

The LORD *repay your work, and a full reward be given you by the* LORD *God of Israel, under whose wings you have come for refuge.*

RUTH 2:12

ristotle made the following observation about friendship: "My best friend is the man who in wishing me well wishes it for my sake."

The Bible often exhorts us to care for one another. In the book of Ruth, for example, Boaz extended kindness toward Ruth; and she thanked him in return, saying, "What have I done to deserve such kindness? . . . I am only a foreigner."

"'Yes, I know,' Boaz replied. 'But I also know about everything you have done for your mother-in-law. . . . May the LORD, the God of Israel, under whose wings you have come to take refuge, reward you fully for what you have done'" (Ruth 2:10–12 NLT). This story has gratitude all around—Ruth to Naomi, Boaz to Ruth, Ruth to Boaz—and is a great example to us.

Do you have a friendship that needs tending? Mend it with thanksgiving.

IN THE NAME OF JESUS

*Then Peter said, "Silver and gold I do not have, but what I do have I
give you: In the name of Jesus Christ of Nazareth, rise up and walk."*
ACTS 3:6

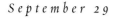

ome people are employed to speak for another person or
institution—the White House press secretary does that
every day. The press secretary regularly meets with represen-
tatives of the press and is the spokesperson for the United States
government—especially the president—on topics regarding poli-
cies, recent national or world events, and issues of the day.

Something similar happens when Christians represent Jesus
Christ in the world. It is Christ's power and authority being represented, not that of the believer. When Peter and John healed
a man outside the temple in Acts 3, Peter disclaimed his own
authority and said, "In the name of Jesus Christ of Nazareth, rise
up and walk."

We pray to the Father "in Jesus' name" not because it is a
magic formula, but because it is only in Christ that we have access
to the Father. When we pray in Jesus' name, we are asking God
to hear the prayer as if Jesus Himself were praying it. Jesus minis-
tered in the Father's name (John 10:25); we minister in His name.

If you are in Christ, ask the Father to honor your prayers *in
the name of Jesus.*

CLOUDS IN THE EASTERN SKY

*This same Jesus, who was taken up from you into heaven, will
so come in like manner as you saw Him go into heaven.*

ACTS 1:11

When Jesus led His disciples to the Mount of Olives and ascended into heaven before their eyes, two angels were standing nearby. The apostles were stunned to see their Lord disappear into the clouds, but the angels reassured them that Jesus would return one day "in like manner as you saw Him go into heaven." What does that mean?

It means: (1) Jesus will descend to the earth just as He ascended. (2) The location will be the same. According to Zechariah 14:4, "His feet will stand on the Mount of Olives." (3) His return will be physical, visible, and observable. (4) His coming will be in the clouds. Just as a cloud hid Jesus from view in Acts 1:9, so He will come in the clouds of glory (Mark 13:26). (5) His coming will be in the presence of angels (Matthew 25:31).

Are you ready for that day? He will come physically, visibly, in the clouds of glory, to the Mount of Olives east of Jerusalem. And we shall behold Him, face-to-face, in all of His glory. Think of *that* the next time you see a cloud in the eastern sky.

OCTOBER

*Now I saw heaven opened, and behold, a white horse.
And He who sat on him was called Faithful and True,
and in righteousness He judges and makes war.*

REVELATION 19:11

October 1

NO HAPPY MEDIUM

So Saul died for his unfaithfulness which he had committed against the LORD, because he did not keep the word of the LORD, and also because he consulted a medium for guidance.

1 CHRONICLES 10:13

ing Saul is a tragic example of a promising leader whose life ended in failure. One of his final mistakes was consulting a medium for guidance. It's remarkable how many people still do that. Bible teachers rightly warn us to avoid anything remotely connected with the occult, such as Ouija boards, séances, fortune-tellers, and so forth. Don't call the psychic hotline or consult the horoscopes in the newspapers. Avoid entertainment that majors on these elements.

We should even go a step further and ignore superstitions. Don't worry about black cats, broken mirrors, four-leaf clovers, or spilled salt. Don't follow old wives' tales.

Be a student instead of the Scriptures. Isaiah 8:19–20 says, "And when they say to you, 'Seek those who are mediums and wizards, who whisper and mutter,' should not a people seek their God? Should they seek the dead on behalf of the living? To the law and to the testimony!"

Make sure you're covered with the blood of Christ and trusting the Word of God. "Greater is He who is in you than he who is in the world" (1 John 4:4).

The Honest Answer

Come now, you who say, "Today or tomorrow we will go to such
and such a city, spend a year there, buy and sell, and make a profit";
whereas you do not know what will happen tomorrow. . . . Instead you
ought to say, "If the Lord wills, we shall live and do this or that."

JAMES 4:13–15

The small boy wandered the aisles of a store, carefully looking down each one. He was scared, but when he saw an employee, he remembered what he was supposed to do. He timidly approached and said, "I lost my mommy." Within moments an announcement was made, and mother and son were reunited.

As a child it is easy to ask for help, but as we grow older, it becomes harder for us to ask for help or direction. We place a high value on independence and self-sufficiency. Oftentimes we put up a front of self-assured confidence, making grand plans for the future, even if we are struggling. These verses from James remind us that God welcomes humility and warns against false pride. When we are honest about our limitations, we can experience a deep connection to God because He is eager to help us. We don't have to hide our needs or pretend we have it all together. When we run into difficulties or are uncertain about the future, we can rely on Him as the highest authority. He has promised to remain with us through every circumstance and challenge, so we can confidently go to Him and ask for His direction and help.

SOMETHING ABOUT THAT NAME

You shall call His name JESUS, for He will save His people from their sins.
MATTHEW 1:21

n biblical times the name *Jesus* was common, which speaks to His humanity. He was called Jesus of Nazareth, a real man from an ordinary town. But there was nothing ordinary about His mission. The name *Jesus* is the New Testament version of the Old Testament *Joshua,* which means "Jehovah saves." His name thus embodies His mission—"to seek and to save that which was lost" (Luke 19:10).

Many of us are immediate thinkers instead of ultimate thinkers. As long as everything's going all right today, we're satisfied. We don't bother to think of ultimate consequences. But the Bible warns that sooner or later, those without Christ must stand before God and give an account of their thoughts and actions and moral behavior. Jesus came to save us from the consequences of our own sins and from the wrath of God. That's the significance of the name *Jesus.* He has the power to deliver us from any habit, from any sin, from any chaos. And He has the power to deliver us from death, judgment, and hell.

Praise Him for His name—Jesus, for He saves His people from their sins.

THE UNLIKELY CANDIDATE

"For the Son of Man has come to seek and to save that which was lost."

LUKE 19:10

He was a traitor. As the chief tax collector for the Romans, he represented greed and extortion. He was short in stature. Who was he? Luke 19 tells his story—how he sought to see Jesus, so he climbed a sycamore tree to see Jesus as He passed by. When Jesus came to the place, He looked up and called him by name—"Zacchaeus." The people were incredulous, "Doesn't Jesus know who he is?" They were so focused on the flaws of Zacchaeus, they failed to remember Who was in their presence—the One who called Zacchaeus by name.

Instead of seeing the generosity and love of Jesus in that moment, the crowd clung to their list of reasons why Zacchaeus should be disqualified from the attention and affection of God. It's easy to relate to that crowd. But when we focus on the failures of others, we miss seeing God's grace and love. God delights in drawing unlikely candidates to Him and transforming them through His powerful presence.

Through his encounter with Jesus, greedy Zacchaeus became generous Zacchaeus. The once-despised chief tax collector became a provider and helper to those in need. Are there unlikely candidates in your neighborhood who need to see Jesus? Help them come and meet the Savior.

October 5

RENEWABLE ENERGY

But those who wait on the LORD shall renew their strength;
they shall mount up with wings like eagles, they shall run
and not be weary, they shall walk and not faint.

ISAIAH 40:31

When we pump a barrel of oil or extract a ton of coal from the ground, it comes from a finite supply. The world's underground deposits—though vast—are reduced by that barrel or ton. When we capture the same amount of energy in a solar panel, a wind turbine, or a waterfall, it doesn't reduce the sun or the wind or the river one bit. That's why it's called renewable. But the politics and economics of it are another story, and political campaigns are won or lost on issues of energy policy.

On a personal level, we have a constant source of renewable energy to keep the lights burning in our hearts. Isaiah 40:31 says, "Those who wait on the LORD shall renew their strength; they shall mount up with wings like eagles."

When you face a problem that drains your energy, get alone with the Lord and give it to Him. Entrust it to Him in a conscious act of faith. Wait on His resolution in hopeful faith. You'll be amazed at how you're inwardly strengthened by the process. That's renewable energy that works!

HOW TO RECOGNIZE
A CHRISTIAN

By this we know love, because He laid down His life for us.
And we also ought to lay down our lives for the brethren.

I JOHN 3:16

onsider how easy it is to tell the religion of many people in the world by their dress or actions. One religion's members shave their heads, wear saffron-colored robes, play musical instruments, and chant and sing in public. The faithful of another religion stop and kneel for prayers, wherever they are, five times a day. Another religion's orthodox members wear black coats and hats, white shirts, and have long, curly locks of hair or beards.

What about Christians? Can you look at the crowd in a mall or an airport and tell who is a born-again follower of Jesus? There is only one mark Jesus asked His followers to display to the world: the mark of love. He told His disciples, "By this all will know that you are My disciples, if you have love for one another" (John 13:35)—not if we dress or speak a certain way or act religious, but if we have love for others. Loving people the way Jesus loves people is the true mark of His followers. Love is the highest kingdom value (see Romans 14:17; 1 Corinthians 13:13).

Let your love and service for Christ be translated today into love and service for others.

GREAT DAY IN THE MORNING

Now in the morning, having risen a long while before daylight, He went out and departed to a solitary place; and there He prayed.

MARK 1:35

es, we can pray without ceasing and practice the presence of the Lord all day long (1 Thessalonians 5:17). But there's something about the morning hours that are perfectly primed for prayer, and it's a shame to start the day without a specific, regular prayer time with the Lord.

The psalmist said, "My voice You shall hear in the morning, O LORD; in the morning I will direct it to You, and I will look up" (Psalm 5:3). When the tabernacle was set up, Aaron was told to burn fragrant incense on the altar every morning when he tended the lamps (Exodus 30:7). The priests were to begin each day with morning sacrifices (Leviticus 6:12). The patriarch Job began each day by offering sacrifices early in the morning for his family (Job 1:5). Mary Magdalene rose early in the morning to tend to the Master's tomb, but instead she came face-to-face with the Master (John 20).

Everyone's schedule is different. But as much as possible, start the day face-to-face with the Master. Begin every day in fellowship with the Lord. You'll find it's a great day in the morning.

THE REAL PROBLEM

He said to the man who was paralyzed, "I say to you, arise, take up your bed, and go to your house." . . . And they were all amazed, and they glorified God and were filled with fear, saying, "We have seen strange things today!"

LUKE 5:24, 26

hysicians know a patient's presenting problem is not necessarily the most urgent issue. To diagnose a problem, the medical professional will ask a series of questions and have tests performed. But the paralytic man who was lowered into the house where Jesus taught had a seemingly easy problem to diagnose. He was lame, so the assumption was that he needed to be healed. When we see visibly broken people, many times we think we have the solution to their problem—forgetting that everyone has a deeper underlying need: to be forgiven.

Forgiveness restores our relationship with our Creator, allows us to find meaning and purpose, and lifts the heavy weight of guilt and shame. When the lame man's friends lowered him through the roof to Jesus, they took a risk. What would Jesus do?

Jesus saw past the man's physical infirmity and recognized his deepest need, "You are forgiven." To illustrate and prove His authority, Jesus then told the man to get up and walk (see Luke 5:17–26). God has power over our visible *and* invisible needs—you can trust Him to resolve your real problem.

October 9

At Home with the Lord

We are confident, yes, well pleased rather to be absent from the body and to be present with the Lord.

2 Corinthians 5:8

The apostle Paul had an unusually optimistic view about death. He wrote, "To die is gain . . . [I have] a desire to depart and be with Christ, which is far better" (Philippians 1:21–23). In 2 Corinthians 5, he said, "How weary we grow of our present bodies. That is why we look forward eagerly to the day when we shall have heavenly bodies. . . . We look forward with confidence to our heavenly bodies, realizing that every moment we spend in these earthly bodies is time spent away from our eternal home in heaven with Jesus. . . . We are not afraid, but quite content to die, for then we will be at home with the Lord" (verses 2–8 TLB). Perhaps Paul's anticipation was heightened by the time he was "caught up to the third heaven . . . into Paradise and heard inexpressible words . . ." (See 2 Corinthians 12:1–6).

While we don't want to leave this planet before God's purposes for us are finished here, it's healthy to cultivate the mind-set of the biblical writers, not fearing death but being "confident, yes, well pleased rather to be absent from the body and . . . present with the Lord."

LIVING FREE

*And He said, "Woe to you also, lawyers! For you load
men with burdens hard to bear, and you yourselves do
not touch the burdens with one of your fingers."*

In *The Pilgrim's Progress*, the burden Pilgrim carries is central to the story. The burden is his sin, and it slows his every step. His primary goal as he travels to the Celestial City is to somehow be relieved of his burden. He is almost tempted to allow Mr. Legality (the Law) and his son, Civility, to remove his burden. Fortunately, Evangelist shows Pilgrim that his burden can only be removed by Christ, not by slavery to the Law.

John Bunyan's story is the story of the Gospel. It is the story of Christ taking upon Himself the burden of the Law so we do not have to carry that burden any longer. Religious leaders in Jesus' day loved to increase the burden of broken laws upon the people without showing them how to be free. But Jesus came and said, "And you shall know the truth, and the truth shall make you free" (John 8:32). The truth is, "by the deeds [burden] of the law no flesh will be justified in His sight" (Romans 3:20).

The gift of salvation is not a burden! Christ removed the burden of broken laws at the Cross!

BETTER TO GIVE

And remember the words of the Lord Jesus, that He said, "It is more blessed to give than to receive."

ACTS 20:35

here is one teaching of Jesus that is not recorded in any of the four Gospels—and it is an important one that can be applied every day: It is more blessed to give than to receive. Giving is a God kind of act, a *godly* act. It is nowhere demonstrated more clearly than in John 3:16: "For God so loved the world that He *gave* His only begotten Son" (emphasis added).

Giving involves loss. When we give something to another person, we forfeit the right to keep it for ourselves. We place the need or want of another person ahead of our own (Philippians 2:4). When the Father *gave* His Son to humanity as a Savior, He gave up the privilege of fellowship with the Son in heaven for our sake; He put our needs above His own desires. Giving is a daily way to imitate God. We can give a gift; we can give our time; we can give up our place in line to someone who is in a hurry; we can give a personal possession to someone in need; we can give a room in our home to someone in need of temporary shelter; we can give a meal; we can give a hug, a smile, or a kind word. There is no end to the ways we can imitate God by giving.

Watch for a time and place today to do the "better" thing—to give as God gives. And if someone gives to you, receive the gift with thanksgiving and humility.

RIGHT PLACE, RIGHT TIME

Then it came to pass, when Pharaoh had let the people go, that
God did not lead them by way of the land of the Philistines,
although that was near; for God said, "Lest perhaps the people
change their minds when they see war, and return to Egypt."

EXODUS 13:17

Think of what the Hebrew slaves had been through in Egypt: four hundred years of bondage, weeks of plagues all around them, and a near-death experience at the Red Sea. Finally, they are gathered in the wilderness between Egypt and Canaan. All they have to do is head north around the shore of the Mediterranean Sea, and they will enter the land flowing with milk and honey. Instead, Moses turned the people due south, straight onto the searing sands of the Sinai Desert—and away from the promised land.

But there was a reason. God showed Moses that the people would be attacked by the Philistines if they followed the normal route to Canaan. And once attacked, the Hebrews would flee for safety back to Egypt. There is no record that Moses explained this to the Hebrews. They simply had to trust that the God of their fathers was at work in their midst.

We must do the same. God puts us where we need to be, when we need to be there to accomplish His purposes. His timing is perfect—He does it for our good and His glory.

October 13

CALLED BUT SCARED

So the LORD said to [Moses], "Who has made man's mouth? Or who makes the mute, the deaf, the seeing, or the blind? Have not I, the LORD?"
EXODUS 4:11

ometimes we get asked to do things that are clearly beyond our ability: donate a million dollars, sing a solo, or run a marathon for charity. Some people can do those things, but most cannot. More often, God puts opportunities in front of us for which we are, in fact, qualified—but we are afraid of failure; we are afraid the challenge is beyond our ability. And sometimes it is. But it is in those moments of life that we recognize our dependence on God.

Moses was brilliant, highly educated, seemingly a born leader, experienced—and scared. When God called him to confront Egypt's Pharaoh and lead the Hebrew slaves to the promised land, Moses dug in his heels. One of the objections this highly literate man gave was his lack of eloquence—his inability as a public speaker. God had to remind Moses that it was He who created man's ability to speak: "Now therefore, go, and I will be with your mouth and teach you what you shall say" (Exodus 4:12).

If you believe God has called you to your current place in life (spouse, parent, employee, volunteer), but you feel inadequate, remember: "He who calls you is faithful, who also will do it" (1 Thessalonians 5:24).

SET APART

The sons of Amram: Aaron and Moses; and Aaron was set
apart, he and his sons forever, that he should sanctify the
most holy things, to burn incense before the Lord, to minister
to Him, and to give the blessing in His name forever.

1 CHRONICLES 23:13

It's Saturday, and you're going to paint the bedroom. You choose your oldest pair of shorts, most faded T-shirt, and rattiest sneakers and dedicate them to painting; you set them apart forever, never to be nice clothes again. In biblical terms, you have made those clothes holy.

That's what the biblical word *holy* means; it means set apart for a special purpose. Aaron and his sons would always be priests—they were set apart as priests forever, just as the vessels used in the tabernacle and temple to serve the Lord would never again be used for common tasks. Things change when something is set apart as holy. And the same is true for "holy matrimony." When we commit ourselves to our spouse, we set ourselves apart for that person. We don't live with one foot in marriage and one foot out. We are set aside as holy unto God and our spouse.

Being set apart means burning the bridges; there is no going back. Rededicate yourself today to be "set apart" in your marriage and in devotion to your spouse.

October 15

SO CLOSE, YET SO FAR

*The Lord God planted a garden eastward in Eden, and
there He put the man whom He had formed.*
GENESIS 2:8

A remarkable photograph appeared in California newspapers. It showed a humpback whale and her calf surfacing beside a small sailboat. The whales were playing and eating fish. Just behind the whales sat a man on the cab of his boat in the open air. He was so close he could have almost touched the creatures. But he didn't even notice them. He was too busy looking at the screen of his phone, apparently absorbed in texting.

We inhabit a beautiful universe, and we shouldn't miss it. The garden of Eden is gone, but much of the original beauty of God's creation shines through. Beneath our feet are remarkable blades of grass. Before our eyes are trees, each unique, filled with birds of many sizes and songs. Above our heads are endless formations of clouds. Every morning and evening we're greeted with a fresh sunrise and sunset.

Let's get our noses out of our busyness long enough to smell the roses, spot the whales, and rejoice in God's creation. Enjoy the world today, and sing the mighty power of God that made the mountains rise.

PERFECTION

The law of the LORD *is perfect, converting the soul; the*
testimony of the LORD *is sure, making wise the simple.*

PSALM 19:7

discriminating diner might taste a chef's dish and
exclaim, "Perfection!" An art critic might stare at
a famous painting for hours and conclude, "It's perfect!" Or a
young bride-to-be might stare at her engagement ring and whisper, "Oh, it's perfect!"

Really? Are meals, paintings, and diamonds actually perfect?
Not really, but we fully understand what "perfection" means in
those situations. Perfection is in the eye of the beholder. So is anything in this world actually perfect? The Bible says one thing is:
"The law of the LORD." And what does that mean? It means that
God's words to man, found in Scripture, are complete, lacking for
nothing; they cannot be improved upon. There is nothing missing,
nothing God forgot to include that we need for faith and practice
in the Christian life. Paul wrote that Scripture is sufficient for
doctrine, reproof, correction, and instruction in righteousness
(2 Timothy 3:16). If it weren't, it wouldn't be perfect.

God's Word should be our first stop and the last word on
anything about which it speaks. A "perfect" way to begin every
day is with the prayerful consideration of God's perfect Word.

How Big Is God?

Now to Him who is able to do exceedingly abundantly above all that
we ask or think, according to the power that works in us . . .

Ephesians 3:20

f for some reason it was your job to design the universe,
how big would you make it? You probably would not
design the universe to look like the one God created. Consider
this: The distance from planet Earth to the observable "edge" of
the universe is 46 billion light-years—and one light-year is about
6 *trillion* miles. So the distance from Earth to the edge of the universe is 46 billion times 6 trillion miles. It is thought there are
more than 100 billion galaxies containing anywhere from 10 million to one trillion stars each.

God doesn't think small. We don't know why God created
such a huge universe—we only know that He did. If the creation
is BIG, that means the Creator is BIGGER. When it comes to us
and our needs, God is always bigger—not just big, but *bigger.* God
is able to do "exceedingly abundantly above all that we ask or
think." Whatever you think would represent a blessing in your
life, God is able to do more. Our challenge is to allow our faith to
see God for who He really is.

If you have a need today that seems bigger than anyone's ability, remember what God did when creating the universe. God is
bigger than all our needs—bigger than we could ask or think.

MATCHLESS DESIGN

. . . from whom the whole body, joined and knit together by what every joint supplies, according to the effective working by which every part does its share, causes growth of the body for the edifying of itself in love.

EPHESIANS 4:16

Adult humans have 206 bones, 640 muscles, 78 internal organs (12 organ systems), 900 ligaments, thousands of tendons, and 100 trillion cells. Humans also have four major appendages (arms and legs), each of which has five separate digits (fingers and toes). And they are all connected to form *one* human body. There is one body with a vast number of parts. All the parts are separate and unique, yet all are connected and unified.

Is it any wonder the apostle Paul used the human body as an example of the Church, the body of Christ (Ephesians 4:12; 1 Corinthians 12:27)? Being a Christian is like being one of the parts of the human body—unique and purposeful. Yet every Christian has the privilege of being part of something larger than himself—the body of Christ.

Consider your two dimensions in Christ: *uniqueness* in Christ contributing to *unity* in Christ. Are you enjoying and fulfilling both? Just as every part of the human body is important, so is every part of Christ's spiritual body.

October 19

LIKE A TREE

He shall be like a tree planted by the rivers of water, that brings forth its fruit in its season, whose leaf also shall not wither; and whatever he does shall prosper.

PSALM 1:3

he Holy Land was never completely forested, like portions of Europe and North America, but there were more trees there in biblical days than there are today. One of the most useful was the date palm, which grew in the Jordan River valley—a tall, branchless tree with clusters of sweet dates at its crown. Jericho was known as "the city of palm trees" (2 Chronicles 28:15). Was this the tree the psalmist referred to in Psalm 1:3?

The tree the psalmist pictured is planted by a river, is fruitful in its season, and never withers because its roots run deep. That is the image of a person the psalmist was describing—and who would not want to be such a person? There are two requirements: Such a person must distance himself from the ways, words, and walk of the sinful and scornful, and must delight "in the law of the LORD," meditating on it "day and night" (verse 2). In New Testament terms, Jesus put it this way: abide in Him (not the world) and let His Word abide in us (John 15:7).

Develop these goals for every day: flee from sin; and cling to the Savior and His Word.

MAN OR GOD?

Some trust in chariots, and some in horses; but we will
remember the name of the LORD our God.

PSALM 20:7

*H*as there ever been a more turbulent era in American history? The two political parties seem hopelessly divided, our role in the flammable Middle East seems indefinable, the value of the unborn and marriage drift further from God's ideal, and our fiscal indebtedness grows by the hour. Yet God remains uninvited into our situation. A nation that proclaims "In God We Trust" seems to put trust in everything but Him.

The Old Testament prophets warned about trusting in man and man's methods instead of in God. When Israel was tempted to appeal to Egypt for help against her enemies, the prophet Isaiah warned the leaders, "Now the Egyptians are men, and not God; and their horses are flesh, and not spirit" (Isaiah 31:3). Could there be any plainer distinction? When man finds himself in desperate situations, why would he call on others who are no greater than himself? Should we not call on the One who is God rather than relying on the abilities of man?

But isn't it also true of us as individuals? When you find yourself in a quandary, don't rely on your own devices. Remember the name of the Lord our God—and trust in Him!

October 21

DON'T BE A SKEPTIC

Then Zechariah said to the angel, "How shall I know this?
For I am an old man, and my wife is advanced in years."

LUKE 1:18 NABRE

he *Oxford English Dictionary* says the phrase "too good to be true" was used as early as 1580. Since then, the phrase has been changed to a warning: "If it sounds too good to be true, it probably is." Regardless of when the phrase was first written down, humans have always been a skeptical lot—even when talking to God.

Zechariah, the priest who became the father of John the Baptist, should have known better than to question the angel Gabriel, who had just announced that Zechariah and Elizabeth would have a baby boy. Zechariah's skepticism was based on the same reasoning as father Abraham's: "We're much too old!" (Genesis 17:17, paraphrase). But what about us? We have read the stories of Abraham, Moses, Gideon, Zechariah, and others— how God was faithful to fulfill His promises—and yet we still sometimes wonder if God will be faithful to keep His Word. We are skeptical about God's goodness, His ability, His timing, His intention, His forgiveness, and more. We have been given great and precious promises, which we have every reason to believe (2 Peter 1:4).

If you are trying to decide whether to trust God today, don't be skeptical. Take Him at His Word and rest in His promise.

GOD'S ITINERARY

And in Your book they all were written, the days fashioned
for me, when as yet there were none of them.

PSALM 139:16

*I*f a vacationer can afford it, concierge-type travel services can plan and provide for every day—actually,
every hour—of an itinerary. From the moment you are picked
up at your door until the moment you return, your trip has been
planned and executed in detail. For some, eliminating the seren-
dipitous, unplanned moments from a trip removes all the fun.
For others, security and not worrying about details is worth the
price.

Life as a child of God provides that kind of security. Psalm
139:16 says that God has written down all the days created for us
before a single day has come to pass. And Philippians 4:19 says
that "my God shall supply all your need according to His riches in
glory by Christ Jesus." That covers the big picture and the details
of our trip to heaven. God has arranged the itinerary—the order
of our days—and has planned to meet all our needs along the
way. So what is there to fear about the future?

Do you know what the future holds? Do you have everything
today that you will need in the future? No to both questions. But
God has already answered yes to both in His Word. We must have
faith and courage.

A Transformed Life

[The man healed of blindness] answered and said,
"Whether He is a sinner or not I do not know. One thing
I know: that though I was blind, now I see."

JOHN 9:25

magine a person who has an encounter with Jesus Christ whose life is radically changed—but who knows almost nothing of the Bible and very little theology as a brand-new Christian. And imagine that new believer is challenged by a committee of famous theologians who quiz him on the validity of his belief in Christ. How should an unschooled new believer respond to the investigating committee?

Perhaps the example of the man healed by Jesus of blindness is worth noting (John 9:1–41). People who knew the man Jesus healed took him to the Pharisees, who promptly declared the healing invalid—that is, not from God because Jesus had been known to break Sabbath laws and traditions. A thorough investigation followed. The Pharisees questioned the man and his parents, trying to convince them that Jesus was a sinner. Exasperated, the once-blind man said, "All I know is that once I was blind, but now I can see!" (paraphrase). That is the answer that no critic can take away: Jesus Christ changed my life.

You don't need to be a theologian to tell friends what Christ has done for you and can do for them. A transformed life says it all.

October 24

HARVEST TIME

*Do not be deceived, God is not mocked; for whatever
a man sows, that he will also reap.*

GALATIANS 6:7

griculture has been an important factor in the devel-
opment of civilization for thousands of years. In
Genesis, we read of Cain, who was a "tiller of the ground," while
his brother Abel, tended sheep (4:2). As people planted and then
harvested crops, a foundational principle of God's creation was
shown: God gives more than is given. We plant one kernel of
grain and harvest hundreds of new kernels. Some are eaten, some
are saved for next year's planting, some are sold, and some are
shared with those in need.

That principle of abundance is illustrated throughout Scripture,
most generally in Galatians 6:7: We reap as we sow. Paul expanded
the idea in 2 Corinthians 9:6, saying, "If we sow abundantly, we
will reap in abundance; if we sow sparingly, we will reap sparingly" (paraphrased). The principle of abundant harvest makes it
possible to give generously and glorify God (verse 11). It is part of
God's blessing on creation. Our part is to sow generously; God's
part is to bless generously in return.

Look for ways to be generous with your time, talent, and
treasure. Instead of an instinctive no, learn to say yes more often.
God always returns more than we give.

October 25

THE RIGHT TRACKS

"Be strong and very courageous. Be careful to obey all the instructions Moses gave you. Do not deviate from them, turning either to the right or to the left. Then you will be successful in everything you do."
JOSHUA 1:7 NLT

A subway operator in New York pulled onto the wrong tracks as he left the Canal Street Station. He headed uptown on the downtown rails. The dispatcher frantically tried to radio the train, but the crew didn't hear the emergency broadcasts. The driver continued for several stops until he saw the headlights of a southbound train coming toward him. Both trains managed to stop in time or it would have been a disaster. Interestingly, the passengers had no idea they were on the wrong tracks. They sat there napping or reading their newspapers or listening to music on their earphones, oblivious to the potentially fatal mistake.

God has a specific strategy for your life and for mine. He saw us before we were born and scheduled each day of our lives before we began to breathe (see Psalm 139:16). How sad that so many people never get on the right tracks.

Commit yourself to Jesus Christ and determine to do His will each day. Seek Him in His Word and obey it. Live for Him so that when your train pulls into the heavenly terminal, you'll hear Him say, "Well done, good and faithful servant" (Matthew 25:21).

STRENGTH IN SMALL NUMBERS

When the three hundred blew the trumpets, the Lord set every man's sword against his companion throughout the whole camp; and the army fled.

JUDGES 7:22

oday's world is run by numbers. Television shows are produced or canceled depending on ratings. Politicians rise or fall depending on polls. If we're not careful, we can evaluate God's work the same way. Numbers, in their proper place, aren't wrong. After all, an entire book of the Bible is named Numbers.

Yet we mustn't despise the day of small things (Zechariah 4:10). Gideon started with thirty-two thousand soldiers, but God said, "The people who are with you are too many for Me to give the Midianites into their hands, lest Israel claim glory for itself" (Judges 7:2). The Lord whittled his army down to three hundred men who were willing to shatter the jars, hold the torches, and cry, "The sword of the LORD and of Gideon!" (7:18).

The victory was claimed.

The Lord specializes in using people with small numbers, meager resources, and insufficient strength. If you feel disappointed today because of some statistic in your life, remember—there's strength even in small numbers when God is the mathematician.

October 27

FREE FROM PAIN

I acknowledged my sin to You, and my iniquity I have
not hidden. I said, "I will confess my transgressions to the
LORD," and You forgave the iniquity of my sin.

PSALM 32:5

ll of us can testify to the "before and after" of relief
from physical pain. It might happen quickly—an
aspirin and a good night's sleep relieves a headache—or it might
be a long-term process—a painful broken bone gradually heals.
However long the transition takes, we know how good it feels to
be relieved of pain.

Guilt can be as painful spiritually as an ailment can be physically. The guilt of sin, whether by omission or commission, can
be removed. And when guilt is removed, the accompanying pain
of fear, stress, despair, or shame is removed as well. The psalmist
David described the pain of his unconfessed sin (Psalm 32:3–4)
and implied the removal of that pain when he "[confessed his]
transgressions to the LORD" (verse 5). We don't know if this psalm
was written in the aftermath of his adultery and conspiracy to
murder (2 Samuel 11–12); but if it was, he had lived almost a year
with the pain of his guilt. He saw confession to God as the path to
the restoration of his joy (Psalm 51:12).

If you are living with an unconfessed sin, ask God to cleanse
you and deliver you from pain to relief (1 John 1:9).

"It Is Good"

*It is good to give thanks to the L*ORD*, and to sing*
praises to Your name, O Most High.

PSALM 92:1

$\mathcal{I}$n our busy lives today, there is no shortage of good
things to do. It's good to exercise, to eat a healthy diet,
to brush our teeth, to call our parents, to spend time with our
children, to be on time for work, to be involved in our church, to
pray and study the Bible, and the list goes on. There are so many
good things to do that we can hardly do them all, so it becomes a
matter of prioritizing and scheduling.

The psalmist mentioned something to do that might not
make the list of many Christians: "It is good to give thanks to the
LORD." With every "good" thing we do in life, we expect a benefit
(eat right = good health). So why is it good to give thanks to God?
What is the benefit that comes back to us? Psalm 92 is a psalm
for the Sabbath, a song to be sung by the faithful. The thanks and
praise are the evidence of a life lived in fellowship with God. And
the result of that life is that "the righteous shall flourish like a
palm tree . . . [They] shall grow" (Psalm 92:12–13). So the person
who gives thanks to God—as a result of walking with God—will
flourish and be fruitful.

Do you want to thrive and grow and bear fruit? It begins with
choosing to give thanks to the Lord each day—"it is good."

October 29

PROGRESS?

*And the LORD said, "Indeed the people are one and they all have
one language, and this is what they begin to do; now nothing
that they propose to do will be withheld from them."*
GENESIS 11:6

In Genesis 11, the Babelites began building a tower to
reach the heavens, wanting to make a name for themselves and act as their own gods. The Lord acknowledged the
potential of human enterprise when He said, "After this, nothing
they set out to do will be impossible for them!" (NLT). The Lord
created us in His image, with incredible creativity and capacity
to advance. But our vast achievements in the column of human
progress are dangerous, unless under the lordship of Christ.

There's a story of four brothers with special abilities. One
could take a bone and create flesh around it. The next could cover
the flesh with beautiful hair or fur. The third could fashion it into
an upright form. The fourth could give it life. Going into the forest, they found the bone of a lion. Each brother did his part. They
were soon killed and eaten by the lion they had created.

That's the danger of our technologies and advancements
unless we approach all of life with the attitude of Colossians 1:18:
"in all things He may have the preeminence."

ALL-SUFFICIENT

"Fear not, for I am with you; be not dismayed, for I am your God. I will strengthen you, yes, I will help you, I will uphold you with My righteous right hand."

ISAIAH 41:10

The neck of a guitar with steel strings has a natural tendency to bend in on itself because of the strong tension of the strings, stressing the instrument over time. Similarly, our natural tendency when faced with challenges and tension is to fold in on ourselves. Challenging situations often make us mentally weary and physically exhausted, and in our frustration we find ourselves spiraling into worry and fear.

The solution for a guitar is a truss rod, which is a metal rod that runs along the neck of the guitar. The truss rod protects the guitar from being destroyed by tension. When difficulties test and threaten our faith, we have a truss rod of our own: Jesus Christ. He never changes. He remains sufficient for every problem—strong and secure.

Jesus invites us to hand Him all of the burdens and difficulties we are encountering. He is not threatened by the tensions that tower over us. Just as a truss rod allows a guitar to create music despite and because of the tension, Christ promises to heal our brokenness, carry our burdens, and give us a future and a hope. Turn whatever you are contending with today over to the One who will "uphold you with [His] righteous right hand."

October 31

LOVE AND FRAGRANCE

Thus says the LORD of hosts: "In those days ten men from every
language of the nations shall grasp the sleeve of a Jewish man, saying,
'Let us go with you, for we have heard that God is with you.'"
ZECHARIAH 8:23

cripture is filled with the working out of redemption:
Noah and his family beginning again after the Flood;
Abraham being the father of a nation through whom all the world
would be blessed; rulers from other nations flocking to Jerusalem
during Solomon's reign; and the prophet Zechariah foretelling a
day when Gentiles will follow Jews into Jerusalem because they
have heard that God is there.

In the New Testament, there are markers of this plan as well:
Jews from the Mediterranean nations witness the coming of the
Spirit at Pentecost; Jesus sends His apostles into the world to
preach the Gospel of reconciliation and redemption. But there
are other ways the knowledge of God will be spread. Jesus said
His followers' love for one another would be a sign to the world;
Paul said Christians will be "the fragrance of Christ among
those who are being saved and among those who are perishing"
(2 Corinthians 2:14–15).

Ask God to give you the kind of love and fragrance that will
signal the presence of God to those who do not yet know Him.

November

But the Lord is faithful, who will establish
you and guard you from the evil one.

2 Thessalonians 3:3

THE MASTER'S PLAN

Then the king said to [Nehemiah], "What do you request?"
So [Nehemiah] prayed to the God of heaven. And [he]
said to the king, "If it pleases the king . . ."
NEHEMIAH 2:4–5

Stewards are in constant touch with their masters regarding the master's plans. When it comes to Christian leadership, the same stewardship principle applies—constant communication. Therefore, prayer is the foundational principle for Christian leaders. Prayer is how Christian stewards stay in touch with the Master about His plans.

One instance in Nehemiah's life is a good example. When Nehemiah wanted permission from the Persian king to return to Jerusalem, he was afraid. When the king asked what Nehemiah wanted, he sent a silent prayer heavenward before he spoke (Nehemiah 2:4–5). Nehemiah knew God wanted the wall rebuilt, but he didn't know if the king would grant permission. So, in the spirit of 1 Thessalonians 5:17—"pray without ceasing"—Nehemiah prayed for the king's positive response.

All Christians are trailblazers in the sense of carrying out God's will in the various arenas of life we find ourselves in. To be about the Master's plan, prayer is the ceaseless channel to know the Father's will and gain His provision.

LET HIM LEAD

The LORD is my shepherd; I shall not want. He makes me to lie down in green pastures; He leads me beside the still waters. He restores my soul.

PSALM 23:1–3

When we consider how to stay calm and peaceful in our chaotic world, we might think of David, the psalmist and king of Israel. He didn't write Psalm 23 as an idyllic picture of his life. After all, this was a man who had faced a giant, done battle with the Philistines, dodged the spear and sword of Saul, been betrayed by his own son, and brought serious trouble upon his own head by his own sinful actions. David led anything but an idyllic life.

The key to reconciling Psalm 23 with David's tumultuous life—and ours—is in the words he chose. To be led into green pastures suggests that some pastures aren't always so green. To reference still waters is to say that sometimes the waters of life are not so still. To describe his soul as being restored implies that his soul *needed* restoring, that it had been in turmoil and needed quieting. Every shepherd wants the best for his sheep, but the best isn't always available. When life is challenging, our Shepherd can be counted on to lead us into a place and time of restoration and healing.

If you are in need of such refreshment today, let your first thought be to seek it from the Good Shepherd. He knows what you need (John 10:14).

November 3

WAITING

*But those who wait on the L*ORD *shall renew their strength;*
they shall mount up with wings like eagles, they shall run
and not be weary, they shall walk and not faint.

ISAIAH 40:31

e live in a "can't wait" world. Our ancestors waited weeks for mail that crossed the Atlantic on ships. Now we send messages to almost anywhere in the world and receive an immediate reply. We can purchase almost anything over the Internet and receive it the next day. We are being taught to assume that not waiting is better than waiting.

To the extent we embrace that mentality, we lose touch with one of God's greatest character-building tools: waiting on Him. Most of the people God used in a significant way went through periods of waiting. The Old Testament has many references to waiting on the Lord, especially during trials. Waiting on the Lord in marriage may be one of the most challenging tests. If we think our spouses need to change, we are tempted to want that change now and to say so. The alternative is to commit that need to the Lord and wait upon Him. It sometimes escapes us that the waiting might be for *our* benefit; God's best work may be in us, not our spouses.

Instead of saying, "I can't wait," get in the habit of saying, "I *can* wait—on the Lord."

N o v e m b e r 4

WORTH REPEATING

"Are not two sparrows sold for a copper coin? And not one of them falls to the ground apart from your Father's will. But the very hairs of your head are all numbered. Do not fear therefore; you are of more value than many sparrows."

MATTHEW 10:29–31

We say that time heals everything because time often dims our memory. This is why parents and trainers know that important principles need to be taught and repeated often. If people were computers, a concept could be entered once and saved, but people forget.

Throughout Scripture, the people of God are reminded, "Do not be afraid." When they come face-to-face with God and His glory: "Do not be afraid." When Peter walks on water: "Do not be afraid." When loved ones die: "Do not be afraid." When all you have is five loaves and two fish: "Do not be afraid."

This simple phrase is God's comfort and invitation to us. We may not have the confidence, skills, or resources needed for our situation, but God does. Jesus invites us to rest, knowing He is God. His peace is ever present. He delights in our requests for more of Him. It is not about ignoring feelings of fear, but about focusing on God's love, power, and provision. As we do, our faith grows as we see God working in the midst of our circumstances. It is worth repeating: "Do not be afraid."

November 5

GOD'S JOB DESCRIPTION

If we are faithless, He remains faithful; He cannot deny Himself.
2 TIMOTHY 2:13

A young man was in an outpatient drug rehab program, meeting with a counselor weekly. Some weeks he had to report that he had succumbed to drug use since their last meeting. "Do you want to get off drugs?" his counselor would ask. Hearing yes as an answer, the counselor would respond, "Then I will be here for you until you succeed." When he asked why she didn't give up on him, the counselor would reply, "My job doesn't depend on your faithfulness. It's my job to be faithful regardless."

It is in God's "job description"—His character—to be faithful. God is loyal, never changing, and committed to His purposes. His purpose for His children is to see them conformed to the image of Christ (Romans 8:28–29). Our reaching that goal is a sign of God's faithfulness, not ours. Yes, God wants us to be faithful and is glad when we are. But whether we are faithful or not, God always is.

"God is faithful, who has called you into fellowship with his Son, Jesus Christ our Lord" (1 Corinthians 1:9 NIV). All day today, even at this very moment, God will be faithful to you. Let that truth be a comfort and a shield, come what may. Let God's faithfulness to you be an inspiration for your own faithfulness to Him.

SURVIVAL AND REVIVAL

Keep his decrees and commands, which I am giving you today, so that it may go well with you and your children after you and that you may live long in the land the Lord your God gives you for all time.

DEUTERONOMY 4:40 NIV

When George Washington was inaugurated as America's first president, his inaugural address included these words: "The [favorable] smiles of Heaven can never be expected on a nation that disregards the eternal rules of order and right which Heaven itself has ordained."

That sounds suspiciously like what Moses told the people of Israel as they prepared to enter the promised land. He reminded them that God's laws—God's "eternal rules of order and right"— would be the foundation of the long life they were promised in that land. Live by God's words and you will live long. Ignore God's words and you will not. America is not Israel, so we cannot apply Moses' words directly to this nation. But we can apply them the way George Washington did. God's principles of "order and right" cannot be ignored individually or nationally. National survival and revival depend on individuals ordering their lives according to God's Word.

Let that revival begin with you. Order your life today according to God's revealed Word and will.

November 7

THE IMPORTANCE
OF OBEDIENCE

Go and wash in the Jordan seven times.

2 KINGS 5:10

The story of Naaman teaches the importance of detailed obedience. Though he was a mighty Syrian commander, Naaman was a leper. When a Jewish girl suggested he consult the prophet Elisha, he was desperate enough to try it. Elisha told him to wash seven times in the Jordan River, but Naaman resisted at first. Afterward, urged by his men, he went to the Jordan and humbly dipped into its muddy waters seven times. He came up the seventh time healed.

God could have cleansed Naaman instantly at Elisha's house, but the Lord wanted to test the commander's obedience down to the details. Suppose Naaman had dipped himself in the Jordan only six times. He would have remained a leper. God gave specific instructions, and the healing came by obeying down to the exact number.

Obedience isn't general; it's specific. Let's obey God down to the details of what He tells us. Is there an area in your life that's not under His complete control? Are you content with obeying six times when God wants seven? Let's obey with precision and diligence.

TAKE IT BY FAITH

"I am the vine, you are the branches. He who abides in Me, and I
in him, bears much fruit; for without Me you can do nothing."

JOHN 15:5

The world's largest furniture retailer, a company founded in Sweden, is known for selling furniture that has to be assembled by the purchaser. The instruction books that accompany their products are precise—woe to any who ignore the steps or skip ahead. Having to start over is all it takes to learn: Trust the instructions; take it by faith even if you think you can do it yourself.

That principle applies to the spiritual life as well. In John 15:5, Jesus makes an amazing statement: "Without Me you can do nothing." The image of the vine and branches lends support—we know a branch can't bear fruit without staying connected to the vine. But how far should we take Jesus' agricultural analogy? Is it really true that we can do nothing in life apart from Him? Conversely, are you prepared to doubt what Jesus has said? The problem is, once we live or act apart from Christ, the deed is done. We will never know how it might have been different had we relied on, and remained connected to, Him in all things.

Even though it looks like you can live your life apart from Christ, it is better to take Jesus' words by faith and follow His instructions. There are no do overs; once done, life is done.

November 9

OPEN YOUR HOME

Do not forget to entertain strangers, for by so doing
some have unwittingly entertained angels.

HEBREWS 13:2

There's no indication that Abraham knew who they were, but he served lunch to two angels one day (Genesis 18:1–6). Three men approached Abraham's camp, the purpose being to tell Abraham that he and Sarah would be having a son about a year from that day. Abraham's and Sarah's response to the news is another story—the point here is the hospitality Abraham demonstrated to strangers. He selected some choice food for his servants to prepare and stood apart while the three men ate. Only after the meal did they reveal the news about the son who would be born. The reader is told that one of the men was "the Lord" (verse 13), and later it is revealed that the other two were angels (Genesis 19:1).

It could be asked, What if Abraham had not received the men hospitably? Would the news of the forthcoming birth of Isaac have been withheld? We don't know. But we can wonder if it is this encounter that led the writer to the Hebrews to remind his readers about being hospitable to strangers (Hebrews 13:2). We never know what blessings may arrive with those we welcome to our home.

As you make your Thanksgiving plans, consider opening your home to others. You never know who the Lord might send and for what unexpected reason—especially through someone you've never met.

REMEMBER WHEN YOU PRAY

*But without faith it is impossible to please Him, for he
who comes to God must believe that He is, and that He
is a rewarder of those who diligently seek Him.*

HEBREWS 11:6

*H*oney, would you have time after work to pick up the
dry cleaning on your way home?"

"Bob, are you heading to the break room? Could you bring
me a bottled water on your way back?"

We make many requests of others during the day, most of
which we already know the answers to. We hardly think about
asking for others' help. In fact, faith rarely enters the equation,
and we don't make our requests "diligently."

But does that casual approach influence the way we seek
God and ask for His help? Most of the time, what we are asking
from God is not something we automatically know the answer
to. Such requests are made as a matter of trust in Him and His
will. For that reason, the writer to the Hebrews says we must
ask in faith. We must seek God, believing He is the God of the
Bible. We must seek Him diligently—that is, with strong faith.
That faith is demonstrated by our coming "boldly to the throne of
grace" (Hebrews 4:16). Not boldly as in arrogantly, but boldly as
in expectantly; boldly as in full of faith in God and His goodness.

Before you pray today, remember who God is; remember to
pray in faith, believing; remember to pray diligently.

333

LET THERE BE LIGHT

For we do not preach ourselves, but Christ Jesus the Lord,
and ourselves your bondservants for Jesus' sake.

2 CORINTHIANS 4:5

We can affirm our faith with intellectual confidence. Biblical theology and the facts of the Bible are logical and reasonable as well as philosophically consistent, historically accurate, emotionally satisfying, and morally exemplary. They produce benevolence, good works, and human kindness. They provide the basis of hope and optimism. They have underpinned every generation of healthy and happy people for the last four thousand years. Christianity offers the one belief system that meets all our needs from birth to death and beyond.

Yet it is ridiculed, rejected, reviled, and railed against. Why is that? It's because Satan has blinded the eyes of unbelievers. Second Corinthians 4:3–4 says, "If our gospel is veiled, it is veiled to those who are perishing, whose minds the god of this age has blinded, who do not believe, lest the light of the gospel of the glory of Christ, who is the image of God, should shine on them."

If you know those who are spiritually blind, offer this prayer adapted from verse 6: "May God, who commanded light to shine out of darkness, shine in their hearts to give them the light of the knowledge of the glory of God in the face of Jesus Christ."

BEING IMMOVABLE

Those who trust in the LORD are like Mount Zion,
which cannot be moved, but abides forever.

PSALM 125:1

ount Zion ("citadel") was one of the hills upon which Jerusalem was built. The Jebusites who originally occupied that hill swore to David that it was impregnable, that David's men would not be able to conquer it. But David did conquer it and established his throne upon it and the slightly higher hill to the north, Mount Moriah, where Solomon eventually built the temple.

Later in Israel's monarchy, we find the psalmist saying the same thing about Mount Zion that the Jebusites said, that it would never be shaken or conquered. The permanence of Mount Zion became an image of the faithful Israelite who trusts in God: "Those who trust in the LORD are like Mount Zion." It wasn't so much that Mount Zion itself might never be shaken (see Zechariah 14:4), but that the God whose kingdom is established on Mount Zion can never be shaken. It is the presence of God that makes the image of Zion an enduring one.

It is the presence of God in our life that makes us as strong as Mount Zion, that makes us unshakable in the face of trouble or attack. If the ground around you is trembling, if spiritual enemies are on the horizon, trust in the Lord and you will not be moved.

THANK YOU FOR THE GIFT

Oh, give thanks to the Lord, for He is good!
For His mercy endures forever.

PSALM 118:1

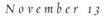arents of young children invest time in teaching their little ones to say thank you when they are on the receiving end of a gift or gracious gesture: "And what do you say to David for this nice birthday gift?" *"Thank you for the gift."* It's a little bit forced, to be sure, but hopefully over time gratitude will become a natural response at the personal level.

Parents don't always require their children to express thanks, of course, but if they did there would be a precedent. When the psalmist said to the congregation of Israelite worshipers, "Give thanks to the Lord," he used an imperative verb. He didn't say, "Let us give thanks"; he said, "Give thanks." Without making the psalmist and the choirmaster into legalists, we can see their point. We need to be reminded that gratitude is the proper response to the goodness and mercy of God. That is true in worship services, for sure. But it is also true at the individual level. Think how many reasons there are each day to stop and give thanks to God: for food, for salary, for health, for recovery from sickness, for a car—and a car repair that was less expensive than you feared.

There is no end to the reasons we have to be thankful, not only in November, but all year long. Take the psalmist's words to heart and give thanks to the Lord.

CALLED TO FAITHFULNESS

And let us not grow weary while doing good, for in due
season we shall reap if we do not lose heart.

GALATIANS 6:9

ven though many people in our world strive for greatness in life, as a Christian our calling is not to greatness,
but to faithfulness. Often our work in life is unheralded, and at
times it may include thankless tasks known only to God. No one
sees when we wrestle in prayer for a grandchild, when we place
our tithes and offerings in the basket at church, when we rake the
leaves for an elderly neighbor, or when we leave a New Testament
at the bedside of a hospitalized friend. Even when we stand before
others, the group we're addressing has no idea how much time
and prayer went into our preparation.

Sometimes we labor quietly and faithfully, only to later wonder if we were helpful or if our work was in vain.

Galatians 6 tells us to keep on—quietly, faithfully, optimis-
tically. Don't quit. Don't grow weary in doing good. Don't lose
heart. God will send the harvest, and those who are faithful now
will be blessed in the end. "So, my dear brothers and sisters, be
strong and immovable. Always work enthusiastically for the
Lord, for you know that nothing you do for the Lord is ever use-
less" (1 Corinthians 15:58 NLT).

FIRST IN LINE

*"For whoever exalts himself will be humbled, and
he who humbles himself will be exalted."*

LUKE 14:11

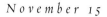t has become a ritual among consumers in the United States: camping out in front of stores days before the announced delivery of the latest tech device, running the risk of being trampled when the doors are opened at midnight for post-Thanksgiving "Black Friday" sales, even hurrying down the aisle to get the best seats at a Christian conference or concert.

Jesus used the human tendency to be "first in line" to make a point about humility—and about pride of place. He was invited to a meal at the home of a prominent Pharisee and noticed the guests scrambling to get the best seats for themselves. So He told a story: Say you're invited to a wedding feast. You get there early to get a prime place at the table only to be embarrassed when the host asks you to move—you took the seat of a preferred guest. How humiliating! Instead, Jesus said, take the lowest seat. If you belong in a better seat, the host will invite you to move up in front of all the guests (Luke 14). Better to be honored than to be humiliated. And better to be humble than to be humbled.

Look for opportunities to be humble, and let God advance you to a higher place in His time. He gives grace to the humble (James 4:6).

YOUR VERY BEST

Let us therefore be diligent to enter that rest, lest anyone
fall according to the same example of disobedience.

HEBREWS 4:11

hristians can sometimes be confused about the idea of "work" in a religion that is based on "grace." Paul wrote that we are saved by grace, not by works (Ephesians 2:8–9). Yet there is work—diligent work—to be done by those who are saved (Ephesians 2:10). And the New Testament writers spared no words in saying the Christian life requires hard, diligent work—our very best efforts for the sake of Christ and His kingdom.

The New Testament word for "be diligent" (*spoudazo*) means to make haste, to make every effort, to be eager, to do your very best. And that is the attitude and approach we are to have in our service for Christ. We are not saved by doing our best, but we express our gratitude for our salvation by being diligent in our service. Think of the apostles. We know more of Paul's labors than anyone else's, but none of them could be accused of being lazy or careless.

How about your service for Christ? How would those around you describe your approach? Diligent, giving your very best, eager, making haste—or not? Make today a day of diligence for the Lord, giving your best to Him who gave His all for you.

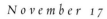

November 17

TODAY IS GRATITUDE DAY

Thanks be to God for His indescribable gift!

2 CORINTHIANS 9:15

We often say, "God bless you!" to others without thinking about what it actually means. When God blesses us, He speaks a word of care or favor over us (Psalm 29:11). And when we bless God, we do the same—we speak a good word about God's many attributes that benefit (bless) us (Psalm 26:12). So when the psalmist said, "I will bless the LORD at all times" (Psalm 34:1), he was saying, "I will continually speak of God's goodness, kindness, generosity, and other traits." That is, I will continually manifest an attitude of gratitude toward God for who He is and what He has done.

Do you see this background of blessing in Paul's words, "In everything give thanks" (1 Thessalonians 5:18)? Not just on Thanksgiving Day, but on every day, we should give thanks to God and bless His holy name for His many gifts of grace to us. Even on challenging days, we can be grateful for the fact that God is with us, causing all things to work together for good for those who love Him (Romans 8:28).

Let Thanksgiving Day, whenever it falls each year, be a day of thanksgiving, for sure. But let every day be one in which you live with an attitude of gratitude toward Him.

ACTIONS STILL MATTER

LORD, who may abide in Your tabernacle?
Who may dwell in Your holy hill?

PSALM 15:1

salm 15:1 and other, similar Old Testament verses could be interpreted as asking, "Who can be saved?" The reference to the tabernacle and God's "holy hill" (Mount Zion, or Jerusalem) helps us interpret the verse more correctly: "Lord, what must I do to merit Your approval and blessing?" Under the Old Covenant, adherence to the Law was the measure—and the psalmist David listed characteristics of the person qualified to stand before God.

Walk blamelessly, act righteously, speak the truth, do not slander others, do no harm to a neighbor, don't speak poorly of others, detest wickedness, honor those who fear the Lord, keep your word, lend money without interest, and accept no bribes (Psalm 15:2–5). How do we interpret these requirements in the New Testament? Jesus boiled all the Law and Prophets down to two: love God and love your neighbor (Matthew 22:37–40), remembering that by the works of the law "no flesh shall be justified" (Galatians 2:16). In the New Testament, keeping God's commands is not the basis of salvation but the fruit of it.

With an emphasis on grace, it is easy to forget that our behavior and actions do matter in God's sight. Live conscious of that truth today.

THE RIGHT CHOICE

And let the peace of God rule in your hearts, to which
also you were called in one body; and be thankful.
COLOSSIANS 3:15

obody plans for it to happen, but sometimes it does: stress at a holiday gathering like Thanksgiving. At the very least, getting food bought, a huge meal prepared, and a house cleaned is challenging enough. Then, the larger the crowd, complete with out-of-town guests or relatives, the larger the possibility for tension at the very moment we are trying to be most thankful.

The apostle Paul wrote a basic rule of thumb, not only for Thanksgiving, but for all of life: "and be thankful." Or we could slightly amend his words and say, "Just be thankful." Be thankful, be thankful, be thankful. Even if the turkey takes an hour longer to cook than anticipated. Even if some arriving guests are late, or others have to cancel. Even if a small child accidentally knocks over a costly vase, and the flowers, to the floor. Even when you are promising yourself that next year you'll plan better . . . just be thankful. Paul wrote those words in the context of a discussion on unity in the church at Colossae. Be at peace, he wrote, and be thankful. When we are thankful, it's easier to "put on love . . . and let the peace of God rule" in our hearts (Colossians 3:14–15).

There are always more reasons *to* be thankful than *not* to be thankful—that is the right choice as a child of God.

EVERYWHERE IN BETWEEN

*You shall teach them diligently to your children, and shall
talk of them when you sit in your house, when you walk by
the way, when you lie down, and when you rise up.*

DEUTERONOMY 6:7

Someone coined a phrase to describe how the early church in Jerusalem went about spreading the Gospel. It was called "gossiping the Gospel"—integrating the Gospel into everyday conversation. There were no tracts, books, or Bibles to hand out. Rather, witnessing was a matter of word of mouth wherever people went.

That idea is found in Deuteronomy 6:4–9 where Moses instructed parents on how to pass on the requirements of the covenant, the details of God's law, to their children. He said to talk to the children in the house and in the street, when you're going to bed and when you rise up—and everywhere in between. It was a common Hebrew way of expressing the idea of totality— the two ends of the spectrum included everything in between. But it doesn't mean simply to teach children the contents of the covenant. It meant to illustrate how the covenant applied to daily life—in the home, in the street, in the market, and "everywhere in between."

How often in a day do you grasp the opportunity to integrate God's truth into your daily conversations—especially with those who are not believers?

BE PURPOSEFUL

At midnight I will rise to give thanks to You,
because of your righteous judgments.

PSALM 119:62

hy would you get out of bed at midnight? Perhaps an infant needs to be fed, or an older child has had a bad dream. Maybe you want to see a lunar eclipse or a meteor shower. Or perhaps you rise at midnight to catch a *very* early flight for a business trip. To say the least, rising at midnight is not normal. Rising at midnight is intentional, something we do on purpose.

The psalmist said he rose at midnight "to give thanks to [God]." Monks in monasteries and nuns in abbeys would not be surprised at such a midnight rendezvous with God. They are known for rising in the early hours to pray and worship; they keep an intentional schedule of devotion. But we don't have to be a monk or nun, or rise at midnight, in order to give thanks intentionally, to be thankful on purpose. We can plan to meet with God at any hour to express our thanks to Him. Not to ask for anything, just to say, "Thank You, Lord." The psalmist rose to thank God for His "righteous judgments." Something different might motivate us to purposefully thank Him.

It's good to be spontaneously thankful too—that's how we normally say "Thank you" to people during the day. But it's good to be intentional as well. Practice setting aside moments to thank God for His blessings—on purpose.

WISDOM AND HOPE

And in the days of these kings the God of heaven will set up a
kingdom which shall never be destroyed . . . it shall break in pieces
and consume all these kingdoms, and it shall stand forever.

DANIEL 2:44

One of the mysteries of the New Testament is that we know so little about Jesus' youth and education. We have one glimpse of a preteen Jesus astounding religious scholars with His knowledge and wisdom in the temple at age twelve (Luke 2:47). He gained wisdom the same way we can—by pursuing it through God and His Word (Proverbs 2:1–10).

For example, when Jesus came preaching "the gospel of the kingdom" (Matthew 4:23; 9:35), He was using language set forth by Daniel the prophet, who recognized this coming kingdom of God in the dream of Nebuchadnezzar, king of Babylon (Daniel 2). Through a pagan king, God revealed that His kingdom would one day replace all earthly kingdoms and "stand forever" (Daniel 2:44). Jesus came announcing that kingdom, taught His disciples to pray for its arrival (Matthew 6:10), and said the promise of its coming would be preached to all the world (Matthew 24:14) before it would be finally established.

There are two lessons: First, study God's Word as diligently as Jesus did to gain wisdom and understanding. Second, don't despair at the state of the world; the kingdom of God is coming.

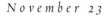

November 23

AGREEING WITH GOD

If we confess our sins, He is faithful and just to forgive us our sins and to cleanse us from all unrighteousness.

1 JOHN 1:9

onfession of sin is multifaceted, but there is a core principle. It is not sorrow, guilt, or shame. It is agreement. The Greek translation for "confess" is made of two words: *homos*, meaning "same," and *lego*, meaning "say or speak." So to confess means "to say the same thing as." As who? As God! We don't inform God of our sins by confessing them. He already knows what we have done. Our greatest need is to humbly agree with Him: "Father, You call what I did 'sin' and I agree with You."

Consider these words from the General Confession in the Book of Common Prayer: "Almighty God, we acknowledge and bewail our manifold sins and wickedness." The key word there is *acknowledge*. It suggests that we are simply agreeing with God about our "sins and wickedness." We aren't hiding our sins or hiding from God. We enter God's presence ready to acknowledge (agree with) what God already knows. Such acknowledgement means we humbly accept God's definition of our actions. We don't try to call our sins "mistakes."

If you have sins to confess today, start by agreeing with God. Only what is rightly confessed can be rightly forgiven.

THE SACRIFICE OF PRAISE

Let them sacrifice the sacrifices of thanksgiving,
and declare His works with rejoicing.

PSALM 107:22

*Y*ou have probably received an unexpected gift on occasion and have likely been the giver of such a gift. What motivates people to give surprise gifts to others? Perhaps we could generalize and say that gifts, be they large or small, are a way to express thanks: "Thank you for loving me." "Thank you for what you did for me." "Thank you for being you!" Gifts are a human way to express thanksgiving.

It is not surprising that a whole class of sacrifices was outlined in the Old Testament as a way to express thanks to God. Thank offerings were categorized as fellowship offerings or peace offerings. They were voluntary gifts, given by worshipers who were enjoying fellowship or peace with God, as an expression of thanks for blessings or favor (Leviticus 3; 7:11–34). While Christ's sacrifice has done away with the need to offer grain or animal sacrifices to God, there is still a sacrifice we can offer as a way of saying "Thank You" to Him: "Therefore by Him let us continually offer the sacrifice of praise to God, that is, the fruit of our lips, giving thanks to His name" (Hebrews 13:15).

November 25

GOD WITH US

But immediately Jesus spoke to them, saying, "Be of good cheer! It is I; do not be afraid."
MATTHEW 14:27

In the classic book *The Lion, the Witch and the Wardrobe* by C. S. Lewis, there's a scene in which the children show up at the beavers' house distraught because their brother, Edmund, has fallen under the spell of the wicked witch. The children want to race off and rescue Edmund, but the beavers have a better plan. The first thing, they tell the children, is to find Aslan (who, in the book, represents Christ). Mr. Beaver explains it with these simple words: "Once he's with us, then we can begin doing things."

We *can* do great things when God is with us! In Matthew 14, we read the account of Jesus feeding the five thousand with two fish and five loaves of bread. After the multitude was fed and sent away, Jesus made His disciples go before Him to the other side of the sea while He remained to pray. During the voyage, the water and winds rose, tossing the disciples about in the middle of the sea. At the fourth watch of the night, Jesus walked out to them. Some feared He was a ghost until He calmed their fears with these words: "Be of good cheer! It is I; do not be afraid" (Matthew 14:27). Just as He was present there on the water, God is always present in our lives. We do not need to fear rough seas or stormy situations in life. He is with us always, even to the end of the world (Matthew 28:20).

JUST ASK

You lust and do not have. You murder and covet and cannot obtain.
You fight and war. Yet you do not have because you do not ask.

JAMES 4:2

*Y*ou spend hours tinkering with a plumbing fixture, trying to figure out how to make a repair. Finally, you take a picture of the broken fixture with your smartphone, go to the hardware store, show it to the clerk, and hear this: "No problem— you just need to replace that with one of these." In other words, all you had to do was ask.

We've all had that experience. After investing hours or days searching for a solution to a problem, we finally discover that an expert could have helped us quickly and easily if we had only asked. James reprimanded his readers for using carnal means to accomplish their goals instead of turning to God first. In fact, it's likely that our modern saying, "All you have to do is ask," came from James's words: "You do not have because you do not ask." Instead of seeing God as our first choice, we often make Him our last resort. And we wonder why we don't have the comfort, guidance, or provision we so desperately need and seek.

If you have a need today, make God your first choice. He is a Father who loves to meet His children's needs—if they will just ask.

MAJESTY

The LORD *reigns, He is clothed with majesty.*
PSALM 93:1

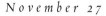isitors to one of our many national parks often speak of the grandeur of the canyons, arches, valleys, mountains, and more, that they have been allowed to view and experience on a special vacation or outing. Whether it is Yellowstone, the Great Smoky Mountains, the Grand Canyon, or another unique national park, you will find visitors armed with cameras and backpacks pausing to admire the beauty and majesty of the scene before them. God's creation often fills our hearts with awe, and seeing these sites personally reminds us of His workmanship.

But if you genuinely want to experience the majesty of God, try worship. Job 37:22 says, "With God is awesome majesty." And in 1 Chronicles 29:11, we read, "Yours, O LORD, is the greatness, the power and the glory, the victory and the majesty." Psalm 29:4 declares, "The voice of the LORD is full of majesty." Jude verse 25 adds, "To God our Savior, who alone is wise, be glory and majesty."

Locations on Earth may convey magnificent aspects; but when we worship God, we enter into the true splendor of Him who reigns and is clothed with majesty. As you worship Him, recollect the sense of wonder and awe that befits the One who created all things.

INFINITE FORGIVENESS

*In Him we have redemption through His blood, the
forgiveness of sins, according to the riches of His grace.*

EPHESIANS 1:7

*M*ost of us would call this symbol—∞—a figure 8
turned sideways, but math majors know it as the
symbol for infinity. Our English word *infinite* comes from the
Latin *infinitus*, a combination of *in* (not) and *finitus* (finished).
Therefore, *infinity* means "not finished" or never-ending.

Infinity isn't easy to grasp, but it is biblical. For instance,
Psalm 147:5 says, "Great is our Lord and mighty in power; His
understanding is infinite"—meaning His understanding is limitless. The infinite grace of God is able to reach far beyond what
we ask or think in any situation. There are limits to our capacity
to reason or understand, and God's thoughts and ways are far
above our understanding. Consider the matter of forgiveness. If
we think there are limits to God's forgiveness of our sins, we need
to remember that God is able to exceed our limits in terms of
what we ask or think. The psalmist made this heartfelt cry: "If
You, LORD, should mark iniquities, O Lord, who could stand? But
there is forgiveness with You" (Psalm 130:3–4).

If you despair of asking God to forgive you "yet again" for your
sins, remember that His understanding—and His forgiveness—
are infinite.

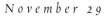

November 29

CONSTANCY

But you are a chosen people, a royal priesthood, a holy nation,
God's special possession, that you may declare the praises of him
who called you out of darkness into his wonderful light.

1 PETER 2:9 NIV

The German car company Volkswagen introduced its Type 1 car in 1938. The Type 1 became affectionately known as the VW Beetle or the VW Bug because of its iconic shape that has changed little over the decades. While other car companies have continued to revise the exterior of their cars, the Beetle's upgrades have been internal. The never-changing shape of the Beetle became its marketing charm.

There is something to be said about staying the same while everything around you changes. That is what God wanted for His people. He created a unique and distinct people, a nation that was to walk according to His never-changing statutes. Israel's constancy was to set the nation apart from the always-changing nations of the world. The constancy of holiness—set-apartness, uniqueness—is to characterize the church of Jesus Christ as well.

Does your life change with the ebb and flow of the world's standards? Or does it remain the same? Ask God to make you content with His original design.

AMAZING!

*When Jesus heard these things, He marveled at him, and turned
around and said to the crowd that followed Him, "I say to you,
I have not found such great faith, not even in Israel!"*

LUKE 7:9

hese days it is easy to be amazed. With access to videos
from all over the world via the Internet, we see things we
have never seen before in all realms of life: science, sports, nature,
even dogs riding skateboards and surfboards. "Wow, that's amazing!" has become a cliché—but only because it's most often true.
We do live in an amazing world.

What do you think amazed Jesus? While there are many
instances in the four Gospels of people being amazed at Jesus'
words and works, there are only two times when we read of Jesus
being amazed at something (or "marveling" at something). Both
times He was amazed at faith: once when He found it where He
least expected it (Luke 7:9) and once when He didn't find it where
He most expected it (Mark 6:6). Faith, or its absence, is apparently
a subject of amazement to Jesus. He works in its presence (Luke 7)
and doesn't work in its absence (Mark 6).

If you want to amaze Jesus and commend yourself to Him,
pray with great faith. After all, without faith, it is impossible to
please God (Hebrews 11:6).

DECEMBER

Through the Lord's mercies we are not consumed,
Because His compassions fail not.
They are new every morning;
Great is Your faithfulness.

LAMENTATIONS 3:22–23

Counselor and King

For unto us a Child is born, unto us a Son is given; and the government will be upon His shoulder. And His name will be called Wonderful, Counselor, Mighty God, Everlasting Father, Prince of Peace.

Isaiah 9:6

O ne of the embarrassing facts about King David's affair with Bathsheba was that she was the granddaughter of Ahithophel the Gilonite, one of David's most trusted counselors (2 Samuel 15:12). Seeking counsel from Ahithophel was "as if one had inquired at the oracle of God" (16:23).

Kings had counselors, even if they didn't always follow their advice. The sage—the wise man—was an important part of God's economy in Israel, along with prophet, priest, and king. But counselors were fallible; their advice was not perfect, so kings had more than one. But the prophet Isaiah foresaw a day when One would come who was both king *and* counselor, One who would be a counselor to those He ruled. That person was the Messiah, Jesus of Nazareth. After giving Israel counsel for three years on earth, He returned to heaven and sent the Holy Spirit to continue His ministry of Counselor to His people (John 14:16, 26; 15:26; 16:7 HCSB).

If you need counsel, start with the One who is both Counselor and King—the One who is the source of both wisdom and power.

In the Fullness of Time

But when the fullness of the time had come, God sent forth
His Son, born of a woman, born under the law.

GALATIANS 4:4

God often does the most extraordinary things in the most ordinary ways. Sometimes His acts are clearly extraordinary—like the burning bush where Moses encountered Him (Exodus 3:1–6). But other times, they are so ordinary their significance is only gradually realized—like the birth of a child in a stable in Bethlehem (Luke 2:1–7).

There is no exact reason given in Scripture for the timing of Jesus' birth. The apostle Paul said it happened "when the fullness of the time had come." As for location, it seems a comparison was at work: King David had been born in Bethlehem, and Jesus would be the "Son of David." And a contrast: Bethlehem's small stature in Judah would be contrasted with Jesus becoming the "Ruler in Israel" (Micah 5:2). In hindsight, we might have picked a different time and place for the Son of God to enter the world—just as we often question the times and ways God works in our life.

One of the many messages of Christmas is God's timing. Just as God sent His Son into the world in a seemingly "ordinary" way, so He works in our lives with the same purposefulness. As you celebrate Christ's birth, remember that every work of God is extraordinary—including the times and ways He acts in your life.

December 3

WHAT GIFTS SAY

And when [the wise men] had come into the house, they saw the young
Child with Mary His mother, and fell down and worshiped Him.
And when they had opened their treasures, they presented gifts to Him:
gold, frankincense, and myrrh.

MATTHEW 2:11

hurch Christmas pageants always feature three wise
men bearing gifts of gold, frankincense, and myrrh.
The Bible notes the gifts they brought, but the tradition that there
were three wise men is based on there being three gifts. But the
tradition is reasonable: three gifts, three gift-givers.

What we must not speculate about, though, is what the Magi's
gifts said. Their gifts were very valuable: Frankincense and myrrh
were both costly ingredients used in making incense and perfume. And gold was gold—valuable in its own right. But why did
the wise men bring such valuable gifts? The answer is found in
their own words: "Where is He who has been born King of the
Jews? For we . . . have come to worship Him" (Matthew 2:2). Do
you see why they brought valuable gifts—gifts fit for a king? Their
gift giving was an act of worship. They knew Jesus was more than
just a king; He was a King come from God.

Gifts say a lot. They say something about us and they say
something about how we esteem the recipients. As you choose
and give gifts this Christmas, let them speak of love, honor,
worth, and sacrifice.

That About Wraps It Up

For all seek their own, not the things which are of Christ Jesus.

PHILIPPIANS 2:21

*G*ift wrapping is an art. Some people create packages so beautiful that recipients hate to tear off the paper, but many of us are slightly embarrassed by our gift-wrapping skills. Our presents suffer from jagged edges, crumpled corners, and patches of tape.

As a person, how are you wrapped? John Ruskin quipped, "A person all wrapped up in himself makes a very small package." If we're others centered, we'll be a blessing; but if we're clothed in selfishness, we'll be of limited value to others.

Writing to the Philippians, Paul said of Timothy, "I have nobody else with a genuine interest in your well-being. All the others seem to be wrapped up in their own affairs and do not really care for the business of Jesus Christ. But you know how Timothy has proved his worth, working with me for the Gospel like a son with his father" (Philippians 2:20–22 PHILLIPS).

When we're wrapped up in our own affairs, it's a sign we're not as Spirit filled as we should be, and we're not being the blessing we could be. Let's not be like "all the others." Let's be Timothys—all wrapped up in Christ!

December 5

JOURNEY OF THE MAGI

*Now after Jesus was born in Bethlehem of Judea in the days of
Herod the king, behold, wise men from the East came to Jerusalem,
saying, "Where is He who has been born King of the Jews? For we
have seen His star in the East and have come to worship Him."*

MATTHEW 2:1–2

*I*f you're traveling during the holidays, you're partici-
pating in one of the oldest Christmas traditions. Two
thousand years ago, the Magi gave a parting glance at home and
trekked westward, where they found and worshiped the Savior.

Who were these strange travelers? In the days of the Old
Testament, the prophet Daniel, a young Jewish exile in Babylon,
interpreted the dream of King Nebuchadnezzar and was appointed chief of the wise men of Babylon (Daniel 2:48). Daniel
wrote extensively about the coming of Christ, so we suppose he
passed along a keen sense of anticipation for the coming Messiah.
Perhaps the wise men in Matthew 2 were from a sect among the
Eastern Magi devoted to the writings or oral traditions of Daniel.

If so, Daniel cast a long shadow. So do we. Future generations
will be influenced by how we live, what we believe, and how we
pass on our faith. Should Christ tarry, you can still be influencing
the world a hundred years from now by your devotion to Christ
today.

THE YULE LOG

Your wife shall be like a fruitful vine in the very heart of your house, your children like olive plants all around your table.

PSALM 128:3

Yule was an Old English word for Christmas Day, possibly derived from a Viking word, *jól*, referring to a twelve-day festival. Somewhere, the tradition of cutting a large, hard log to burn in the family fireplace during Christmas—a yule log—became a tradition. And while fewer houses today are built with wood-burning fireplaces, the notion of the family hearth at Christmas is a well-established one. Families gravitate to the warmth and light of the fireplace at Christmas as a place to bind hearts together.

The Bible, of course, doesn't speak of fireplaces or yule logs, but it does speak of family. Just as the fireplace in the center of the house is a gathering place for families, so should godliness, the Word of God, and the love of Christ be the center of every family—especially at Christmas. While a yule log is temporary and generated by man, the Spirit of God provides permanent warmth and light wherever He is welcomed.

Around a fireplace or in some other way, gather your family and loved ones together this Christmas to bask in the glow of Christmas love that only Christ can give.

December 7

GOD KNOWS THE FUTURE

"But you, Bethlehem, in the land of Judah, are not the
least among the rulers of Judah; for out of you shall come
a Ruler who will shepherd My people Israel."

MATTHEW 2:6

*A*ll of us have ideas about the future, ideas that range from a hunch to extremely confident depending on the situation. But nobody knows the future with 100 percent certainty. In fact, Scripture warns against predicting the future with certainty that borders on arrogance (James 4:13–17).

But when Herod asked the Jewish priests and teachers where the Christ child would be born, they didn't hesitate or equivocate: "In Bethlehem of Judea, for thus it is written by the prophet" (Matthew 2:5). They were certain He would be born in Bethlehem. And why were they so certain? Because God had told the prophet Micah. They believed that God knows the future and could reveal that knowledge to His prophets. To quote the old saying, "God said it, we believe it, and that settles it!" The priests and teachers were right, of course. Jesus was indeed born in Bethlehem, just as the prophet had written hundreds of years before it happened.

The Christmas lesson from this event is simple, and yet too often we tend to forget its message: God knows the future. If you are anxious about something in your future, don't be. God knows what you don't know and will reveal it in good time. And you can trust Him.

THE PERFECT GIFT

. . . looking unto Jesus, the author and finisher of our faith, who for the joy that was set before Him endured the cross, despising the shame, and has sat down at the right hand of the throne of God.

HEBREWS 12:2

When we care about someone, we're willing to put time and money into finding that person the perfect gift. Whether it is a special occasion, a birthday, or Christmas, we try to communicate how important our loved ones are to us through the words and gifts we give. Think of a gift you received and how much it meant to you, or think of a gift you gave.

When we were living apart from God in our brokenness, Jesus carefully prepared a gift for us. This gift would replace our failings and brokenness with His righteousness, and allow us to commune with God and enter His kingdom. This was a gift people desperately sought to obtain on their own, but no amount of good works could purchase it.

Jesus gave all of Himself to obtain this costly gift; He held nothing back. Allow the value and love of His gift to fill your heart. Meditate on the preparation, the cost, and the impact of His gift. Because of Christ's perfect sacrifice, we are free, accepted, and loved.

GOD IN THE FLESH

And the Word became flesh and dwelt among us, and we beheld His glory, the glory as of the only begotten of the Father, full of grace and truth.

JOHN 1:14

hen Daniel was a captive in Babylon, Nebuchadnezzar the king had a dream. He demanded that the wise men of his court not only tell him the *interpretation* of the dream but the dream itself! How else would he know if they truly had access to "the divine"? His courtiers recoiled at the very idea: "It is a difficult thing that the king requests, and there is no other who can tell it to the king except the gods, whose dwelling is not with flesh" (Daniel 2:11).

Therein lies the human dilemma: We are "here," and God is "there." While God dwelt with man in the Holy of Holies, He was not "with flesh." It was not until the first Christmas that God "became flesh and dwelt among us" so that we might know Him and behold God's glory (John 1:14). At the first Christmas, the gap between God and man was bridged in a way never before imagined in history—God becoming a man! Jesus of Nazareth came to live a life acceptable unto God so that we could be forgiven for our unacceptable (sinful) lives.

As you celebrate Christmas this year, don't lose sight of what Christmas means: God became a man and dwelt among us. Not just in spirit, but in bodily form so that humanity and deity might be reunited forever through faith in Him.

WHY THERE IS CHRISTMAS

He humbled Himself.

PHILIPPIANS 2:8

The trappings of Christmas are wonderful—the colors, lights, bows, and wreaths. But it is possible to become trapped in the trappings and miss the truth. And the truth of Christmas is far better than its trappings. The truth of Christmas is Christ.

In a sense, of course, Christmas is about *us.* God loved *us,* became flesh for *us,* died to forgive *our* sins, and rose to give *us* everlasting life. Christmas is the celebration of what Jesus did for us. But in return, we should make it all about *Him*: loving *Him,* serving *Him,* praising *Him*, and emulating His attitude of humility.

He humbled Himself to become human; in turn, Joseph and Mary put His interests before their own. The shepherds, too, put Him first. They left their flocks and bowed before Him. The Magi worshiped Him and presented Him with their gifts. In the temple, the aged Anna and the venerable Simeon praised God because of Him. They gladly let Him be the central focus.

Let's have ourselves a humble Christmas. Turn your thoughts toward Him and others. What a great time to rededicate the remainder of your days on earth to serving Christ with a humility that transcends the holidays.

EXPECT THE UNEXPECTED

When [Joseph] arose, he took the young Child and His mother by night and departed for Egypt, and was there until the death of Herod.
MATTHEW 2:14–15

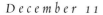nplanned expenses can appear at any moment; we often find ourselves rearranging things to pay the bills. We may have savings or a short-term credit card available, but many people have no such resources.

Mary and Joseph were like that. Joseph was a humble carpenter of modest means. He and Mary had enough money to make the round trip from Nazareth to Bethlehem to register for the census (Luke 2:1–5). Unexpectedly, their plans changed. God showed Joseph in a dream that he and Mary should take baby Jesus to Egypt for safekeeping to avoid the evil aim of King Herod. How could they afford this expensive change of plans? We don't know exactly, but consider this: They had just received three valuable gifts from the Magi. The gold they could have spent, and the frankincense and myrrh they could have sold in the market since they would have had little use for aromatic spices. We don't know what they did, of course. But consider this: just before an unplanned expense occurred, God made provision for them.

Christmas is about the ultimate provision of God—His Son Jesus Christ. This example of His provision offers confidence that we can trust Him during the unexpected moments in our lives.

D e c e m b e r   1 2

CHRISTMAS STOCKINGS

*So He called His disciples to Himself and said to them,
"Assuredly, I say to you that this poor widow has put in
more than all those who have given to the treasury."*

MARK 12:43

poor man, the father of three beautiful daughters, had no money to provide for their marriages or their futures. Hearing this, Saint Nicholas secretly put a bag of gold in the daughters' stockings, which were hanging by the fireplace to dry overnight. Upon rising, the family was overjoyed. Ever since, children have hung up stockings on Christmas Eve in hopes of a visit from Saint Nicholas.

That's the closest we can come to the origin of Christmas stockings. Regardless of the origin of the practice, one thing is evident: Christmas stockings can only hold small gifts. Indeed, what would fit in a child's stocking was the extent of the earliest Christmas gifts from parents to children. And therein is the lesson: it's the little things that matter most at Christmas. Jesus Himself revealed the true meaning of value when He commended a widow in Jerusalem for putting two pennies into the temple treasury.

As you plan your Christmas giving this year, keep "value" in mind. Gifts wrapped in Christmas love are the most valuable of all.

SAVIOR OR EXAMPLE?

"Behold, the virgin shall be with child, and bear a Son, and they shall call His name Immanuel," which is translated, "God with us."
MATTHEW 1:23

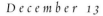

he popular Internet "encyclopedia" *Wikipedia* has an article listing books written about Jesus Christ, divided by century. While it lists hundreds of titles, the article makes no claim to the list being exhaustive—nor could it. No doubt Jesus is the most written-about person in history. And with that interest come opinions: Who exactly was Jesus?

Perhaps opinions can be grouped into two camps: human example and divine Savior. Jesus certainly was a good example for humanity; but if He wasn't God, He couldn't be a Savior. And the Bible is clear that He was God. The prophet Isaiah saw Him coming as Immanuel ("God with us"—Isaiah 7:14), which was confirmed in the New Testament (Matthew 1:23). John the apostle understood Jesus to be the divine Word and said that He had come to earth to dwell with humanity (John 1:14). If Jesus was just a good example, He could have died on a cross. But it was His Resurrection that demonstrated that God had accepted His death as divine payment for sin.

This Christmas, rejoice that the Child born in Bethlehem came as God incarnate to rescue you from your sins.

A BIBLICAL REMINDER

For unto us a Child is born, unto us a Son is given; and the government will be upon His shoulder. And His name will be called Wonderful, Counselor, Mighty God, Everlasting Father, Prince of Peace.

ISAIAH 9:6

*B*efore digital tools beeped at us and sent us messages, people used all manner of methods as reminders: a string around a finger; a rubber band around a wrist, a note on the refrigerator, mirror, or steering wheel; setting an alarm clock. Part of our human frailty is that our memory is not perfect. We need reminders in all parts of life.

The apostle Paul understood this. He pointed out that our regular observance of the Lord's Table is a way to "proclaim the Lord's death till He comes" (1 Corinthians 11:26). Every time we consume the cup and the bread, we are reminded of the broken body and shed blood of the Savior. We need that reminder "till He comes." Christmas is a reminder as well—a reminder that one day Jesus Christ will rule the world as He is destined to do. A Child was born and a Son was given at the first Christmas. And He deserves the names Isaiah gave Him: "Wonderful, Counselor, Mighty God, Everlasting Father, Prince of Peace." Although the government has not yet rested upon His shoulders, it will when He comes again.

His ultimate purpose was not defeated; it was simply postponed. Let this Christmas remind you of what God has in store for this world.

THE EMPTY CHRISTMAS

But this Man, after He had offered one sacrifice for
sins forever, sat down at the right hand of God.
HEBREWS 10:12

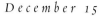ost people don't understand Christmas. They never
think beyond the Babe in the manger. But Christmas
is actually about emptiness—an empty throne, an empty manger,
an empty cross, and an empty tomb, all of which fill our empty
hearts. It's a circuit. When Jesus traveled from heaven to earth,
He used a round-trip ticket with stops along the way. He left the
throne for the manger, the manger for the cross, the cross for the
tomb, and the tomb for the throne. He left blessings behind at
every stop. He emptied Himself so we might be filled. That's the
true story of Christmas.[1]

That means Jesus came into the world with the cross in mind.
Since God cannot die, the Second Person of the Trinity entered
into the human race through the virgin womb of Mary, taking on flesh and becoming a man. He did this to offer Himself
as a sacrifice for our sins. He was born to die, and He died to
rise again. Because of His death, we can live forgiven; because
of His Resurrection, we can live forever. That's why an "empty"
Christmas is so fulfilling.

THE NATIVITY

And they came with haste and found Mary and
Joseph, and the Babe lying in a manger.

LUKE 2:16

our family may have one—it may have even been passed
down from prior generations: a nativity set that finds
its honored place on a mantel or side table every Christmas season. The English *nativity* comes from the Latin *nativus*—"arisen
by birth." Francis of Assisi gets credit for the first nativity scene
in 1223, a live scene such as many churches host for several nights
preceding December 25. But by far the most popular nativity
scenes are those we use in our homes—especially the beautiful
sets carved from olive wood by craftsmen in Bethlehem.

A complete nativity set reminds us of all the elements of the
first Christmas: Mary and Joseph, the humble shepherds, the
wealthy Magi, even the animals whose manger (feeding trough)
served as the bassinet for the baby Jesus. Each element of the
nativity is important: Joseph from the House of David, Mary an
obedient servant, shepherds and Magi representing the full spectrum of humanity, and lowly animals representing all creation.

A nativity scene is a wonderful teaching tool for children and
for Christmas family devotions—bringing the first Christmas
into the present.

They Came with Haste

Let us now go to Bethlehem and see this thing that has come to pass, which the Lord has made known to us.

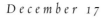

LUKE 2:15

he angelic chorus could have appeared to everyone in Bethlehem. They could have materialized above Jerusalem. They could have hovered over the skies of Rome or Athens or Corinth or any of the great cities of antiquity. But they appeared just to the shepherds—lowly, lonely shepherds keeping watch over their flocks by night.

Why? Perhaps there are reasons known only to God. But certainly in His omniscience God knew the shepherds would act on the revelation He gave. For as soon as the angels departed, the shepherds rushed to see the Babe wrapped in swaddling clothes and sleeping in a manger.

Faith isn't just knowing something, but doing something about it. The Lord speaks to us every day as we study His Word. Whenever God speaks to us, we must respond. If He tells us to stop worrying, that's what we are to do. If He tells us to tame our tempers, that's what we must do. If He tells us to go to the ends of the earth with His message, we pack our bags. Christ is worthy of our faith, and faith always leads to obedience.

Search for the message God has in His Word for you today, and then act on it.

TIME TO CELEBRATE!

And suddenly there was with the angel a multitude of the heavenly host praising God and saying: "Glory to God in the highest, and on earth peace, goodwill toward men!"

LUKE 2:13–14

Think of all the ways we celebrate: birthdays, a Super Bowl victory, the Fourth of July, anniversaries, graduations, and more. Those celebrations are carried out in different ways by different people, but they have one thing in common: There is a personal as well as a corporate dimension. The best celebrations are when we make sure the personal reason isn't overshadowed by the corporate reason. For instance, it's fine to celebrate the Fourth of July nationally, but what do freedom and liberty mean to you personally?

The same is true of Christmas. It has become such a cultural event that it's easy to lose sight of the personal reasons to celebrate. When the angels from heaven appeared to the shepherds outside Bethlehem to announce the birth of Jesus, it wasn't just an announcement. They were celebrating! They were praising God! It wasn't because *they* needed a Savior. They were celebrating because they knew that God coming to earth was the next step in redeeming a cursed creation. They were happy for us, those who *do* need a Savior.

As you celebrate Christmas this year, join in the corporate aspects for sure. But don't forget to celebrate what Christmas means to *you*. Jesus came to save you!

THE IMPOSSIBLE MADE POSSIBLE

For with God nothing will be impossible.

LUKE 1:37

ow many times, maybe even lately, have you said or thought to yourself, "This is impossible!" Even if we don't say it, we certainly find ourselves in situations that seem utterly without solution or remedy. It's human nature, even for those who have deep faith in God. The Bible makes the point clearly that nothing is impossible for God (Genesis 18:14; Jeremiah 32:17; Matthew 19:26).

Surprisingly, the first Christmas in Bethlehem was pretty impossible. But it happened because nothing is impossible for God. That's what Gabriel said to Mary when he announced the Christ's birth to her. So something must have seemed impossible to Mary. There were actually two things: First, Mary was a teenage virgin who was just told she would be quickened by God to give birth to Jesus. That would have seemed impossible enough. But second, Gabriel also said that Mary's cousin, Elizabeth, who was well past childbearing age, was six months pregnant. So a virgin and a supposedly barren woman would bring into the world the Son of God and His forerunner, John the Baptist. Gabriel explained this simply: "For with God nothing will be impossible."

This Christmas, if you are facing a seemingly impossible situation, remember that Christmas itself was the impossible made possible. The same can be true for you.

THE NEVER-ENDING WONDER

Where is He who has been born King of the Jews?

MATTHEW 2:2

he *Baptist Press* reported about a missionary who saw a collection of nativity sets in an open-air market in a staunchly Buddhist area of Southeast Asia. This region had no knowledge of Christianity. The missionary tracked down the family making the nativities and learned they had started selling them after a French tourist suggested it. The family had no idea what the nativity sets meant. They just started making the figures for business based on the tourist's description. This missionary had the joy of taking up the various characters of the set, one at a time, and telling the family the story of the Lord Jesus. Now the whole village is responding.[2]

Imagine hearing about Christmas for the first time! Imagine first learning about the One born King of the Jews! The wonder of the Christmas message is that God revealed Himself and His love to us by becoming a man.

Keep Christmas fresh in your heart. Our Lord is a Savior worth worshiping, and His Gospel is a message worth sharing.

MARY AND JOSEPH

*Joseph also went up from Galilee, out of the city of
Nazareth, into Judea, to the city of David, which is called
Bethlehem . . . with Mary, his betrothed wife.*

LUKE 2:4–5

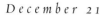

here's much we don't know about Joseph and Mary. We assume Mary was quite young. Somehow we think Joseph was a bit older, for he was a carpenter. In a land of few trees and unlimited rocks, where houses were built of stone, that may indicate he was more of a stonemason than a woodcrafter. But still, there's so much we don't know. For example, how did the couple feel when they left Nazareth for Bethlehem? Did they cast a parting glance at their little hometown on the hillside?

Here's what we do know. Joseph and Mary were devoted to caring for their baby. Jesus came first. They searched for the best spot for His birth, dedicated Him to God in infancy, and undertook a rigorous trip to Egypt when He was endangered. The most important thing about Joseph and Mary was their devotion to Christ.

The same should be true for us. People don't need to know everything about us, but one thing should be clear to all—our absolute devotion to Jesus Christ. He comes first. He alone has the preeminence.

THE TRUE SPIRIT OF CHRISTMAS

For He has regarded the lowly state of His maidservant; for behold, henceforth all generations will call me blessed.

LUKE 1:48

he three most prominent women in the Gospels were all named Mary. The first was Mary of Nazareth. God chose her to raise Jesus because of her servant's heart. "He has regarded the lowly state of His maidservant," she said.

The second was Mary of Bethany. She was His student. Whenever she appeared in the Gospels, she was at the feet of Jesus. In Luke 10:42, the Lord said of her habit of sitting at His feet hearing His words: "One thing is needed, and Mary has chosen that good part."

The third was Mary of Magdala. Though successful in business, she had deep spiritual needs in her life. Jesus freed her from demons, saved her, and she became His zealous supporter. She supported His ministry from her own resources, according to Luke 8:1–3.

Three Marys—a servant, a student, a supporter.

That's the true spirit of Christmas. Jesus came to earth to die for us and rise again. He meets our deepest needs. Today, let's rededicate ourselves to being His faithful servants, students, and supporters. That's the way to have a *Mary* Christmas!

GOD SENDING HIS SON

Therefore the Lord Himself will give you a sign: Behold the virgin shall conceive and bear a Son, and shall call His name Immanuel.
ISAIAH 7:14

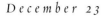t's a wonderful experience to gather with our loved ones for Christmas, but the real meaning of Christmas is the opposite. It's goodbye. When Jesus came to earth, He cast a parting glance at the glories of heaven and left home, traveling here to live among us for a while. In John's Gospel, Jesus reminded His listeners that He had come down from heaven. He told Nicodemus, "[I] came down from heaven" (John 3:13). He told His disciples, "For I have come down from heaven, not to do My own will, but the will of Him who sent Me" (John 6:38).

Perhaps you're away from home this month and unable to be near those you love. Perhaps you're serving in the armed forces. You're reading this devotion with some sadness in your soul, trying not to feel homesick as you remember past holidays with their sights, sounds, and smells. You may be a missionary, unable to return home for Christmas. Like Jesus, you've left home to give the world the Gospel.

Whatever the reason, remember—Jesus was away from home at Christmas too. He understands, and He loves you wherever you are in the world.

DIVINE INTERVENTION

*Now in the sixth month the angel Gabriel was sent by God to a city of
Galilee named Nazareth, to a virgin betrothed to a man whose name
was Joseph, of the house of David. The virgin's name was Mary.*

LUKE 1:26–27

How many times have you prayed for divine intervention? Sometimes we know that only the hand of God
will be adequate for the need that exists. Is that an appropriate
prayer? Does God intervene when He is needed? If the biblical
record is to be trusted (and it is), the answer is *yes*! God has inter-
vened throughout history to meet the needs of the world and His
people.

Christmas is the best example of divine intervention we
have—in more than one way. For starters, God sent the angel
Gabriel to intervene in the life of Mary and Joseph, her fiancé.
This was not to meet a need that *they* had, but to explain their role
in meeting the need the *world* had. Sometimes God's intervention
in our life is for our benefit; sometimes it is for the benefit of
others. The greatest intervention at that first Christmas was the
Word of God becoming flesh and dwelling among us. When we
celebrate Christmas, we are reminded that God takes the initia-
tive and intervenes in life to accomplish His purposes.

Christmas (and many other examples) reminds us that God
is active. He is an "interventionist." He breaks into the affairs of
our lives for our good (Romans 8:28–29).

IT'S OKAY TO BE LITTLE

"But you, Bethlehem Ephrathah, though you are little among the thousands of Judah, yet out of you shall come forth to Me the One to be Ruler in Israel, whose goings forth are from of old, from everlasting."
MICAH 5:2

As of today, there are more than 7.4 billion people in the world. It is easy to think of ourselves as Bethlehem thought of herself—as "little among the thousands." We often wonder what difference one person can make among the billions.

God delights in doing significant things from small things. In nature, a mighty tree grows from a tiny seed. In spiritual matters, Jesus compared the kingdom of God to a mustard seed, one of the tiniest of seeds. God created a mighty nation unto Himself through the union of Abram and Sarai, an elderly couple. God even said through the prophet Zechariah, "For who has despised the day of small things?" (Zechariah 4:10). That was when the Jews had returned from captivity and were faced with rebuilding the temple—one stone at a time. Christmas reminds us of what God does through small things: a tiny baby, born in a tiny Judean village, would become King of kings and Lord of lords.

This Christmas season, if you are doubting your significance in the world or in God's plan . . . don't. God delights in using one person or one small thing to do significant things. Kingdom significance is not determined by size, but by eternal worth.

PARTING GLANCES

*Forgetting those things which are behind and reaching forward
to those things which are ahead, I press toward the goal for
the prize of the upward call of God in Christ Jesus.*

PHILIPPIANS 3:13–14

*D*uring our devotions this month, we've considered the goodbyes of Christmas. For some, Christmas means separation rather than reunion. It means a parting glance: Jesus leaving heaven, Joseph and Mary leaving Nazareth, the Magi leaving Babylonia, and maybe you being away from your loved ones.

But now it's time for us to say goodbye to Christmas as we haul off the tree, throw away the leftover candy, box up the decorations, help the guests out the front door, and try to get our routine back to normal.

Here's the great thing. The incarnation of Christ—the truth of His entering the world for us—is a reality we never leave behind. His abiding presence is a constant reality. We never say goodbye to Him. We're never separated from Him, not today, not ever. The Bible says, "Neither death nor life, nor angels nor principalities nor powers, nor things present nor things to come, nor height nor depth, nor any other created thing, shall be able to separate us from the love of God which is in Christ Jesus our Lord" (Romans 8:38–39). Take a parting glance at Christmas and then press onward into a new year with Christ!

THE EYES HAVE IT

The commandment of the LORD is pure, enlightening the eyes.
PSALM 19:8

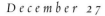thers can tell a lot about us by our eyes. If we have dark circles, we're probably fatigued or struggling with a thyroid problem. Bloodshot eyes can indicate eyestrain or even glaucoma. If our eyes are yellowish, we may have liver disease. Puffy eyes indicate too much salt. Our moods and emotions also show up in our eyes, which are the mirrors of our souls.

The best way to keep our spiritual eyes healthy is by directing them to God's Word. When we read and ponder the Scripture, it enlightens our eyes. To have a vibrant life in Christ is to know and obey God's Word. The psalmist taught us to pray, "Open my eyes, that I may see wondrous things from Your law" (Psalm 119:18).

It may seem hard at first to find time for daily Bible study. But once we decide to do it, make it a firm choice, and begin to work it into our schedule, it becomes a habit. Experts warn it may take several months for a new habit to become engrained, but don't give up. Start at once, and in this coming year, feast your eyes on God's Word every day.

LIVING LIKE JESUS

*. . . how God anointed Jesus of Nazareth with the Holy Spirit
and with power, who went about doing good and healing all
who were oppressed by the devil, for God was with Him.*

ACTS 10:38

Sometime this week you will likely be asked, "How was your day?" or "What did you do today?" The answers to those questions range from A to Z; our lives are filled with busyness and activity leading often to a collapse at the end of the day.

Have you considered what Jesus did all day while on earth? The closest description we have is found in Acts 10:38: He went about "doing good" and freeing those who were oppressed by the devil. That is, He preached and demonstrated the reality of the kingdom of God (Mark 1:14–15; Luke 8:1). He went about bringing light into a spiritually dark world (John 1:5–9). He went about destroying the works of the devil (1 John 3:8). When we are asked to describe our day, are we able to describe it in similar terms? We are not called to work miracles and confront the devil in the same way Jesus did, but we are called to let our light so shine before men that they might know the reality of God (Matthew 5:14–16). We are called to manifest the presence and power of the kingdom of God as we share the Gospel in word and deed.

Ask God to help you manifest the kingdom of God in whatever you do and say today.

100 Percent Prepared

"I will give you a new heart and put a new spirit within you; I will take the heart of stone out of your flesh and give you a heart of flesh."
Ezekiel 36:26

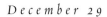As parents, we cannot foresee all the circumstances our children will face. If we could, we would be tempted to focus on and prepare them only for those specific situations. Since we cannot see the future, our best investment is helping develop the person our child is becoming. For example, if a child develops into a person who is compassionate and courageous, he will bring these characteristics into every circumstance he encounters.

Christ was clear in His invitation to us. While He does not promise health, wealth, or ease, He has promised to transform us from the inside out. God is intensely interested in the persons we are becoming. God equips us for the future by transforming who we are. His Word brings clarity, wisdom, and guidance. While God is the One who transforms, we can embrace the process through setting aside time to reflect upon His Word. While our outward circumstances may not change, our trusting and transformed heart will find hope in Him. Make preparations to become more like Him.

A HAPPY COUNTENANCE

Be of good cheer. Rise, He is calling you.

MARK 10:49

Our English word *cheer* comes from a Latin word, *cara*, meaning "face" or "head." By the late fourteenth century, the word was coming to refer to a positive mood as reflected on the face. Cheerfulness is joy showing up on the face. That's biblical, for Proverbs 15:13 says, "A merry heart makes a cheerful countenance."

Jesus is the one who brings cheerfulness into our hearts and onto our faces. In Matthew 9:2, He told the paralytic who had been lowered from the roof: "Son, be of good cheer; your sins are forgiven." In Matthew 9:22, He said to the woman with the issue of blood: "Be of good cheer, daughter; your faith has made you well." When the disciples were in the storm, Jesus walked across the water to them, saying, "Be of good cheer! It is I; do not be afraid" (Matthew 14:27). In the Upper Room, He told His disciples, "Be of good cheer, I have overcome the world" (John 16:33).

Let *cheer* be your word for the day from the Bible; work on a happy countenance. It's the best cosmetic available.

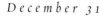

December 31

AS YOUR DAYS . . .

As your days, so shall your strength be.

DEUTERONOMY 33:25

nly one man is listed twice among the presidents—Grover Cleveland. He served two nonconsecutive terms, so he's listed as the twenty-second and the twenty-fourth president. Cleveland was a Presbyterian preacher's kid who was trained in Christian truth. He faced a lot of troubles in office, but was considered honest. His dying words seem to have summed up his life: "I have tried so hard to do right."

Cleveland had a motto he lived by, and it hung directly over his bed, where he would see it every night on retiring and every morning when awakening. He once said, "If I have any coat of arms and emblem, it is that." It was a verse of Scripture— Deuteronomy 33:25: "As your days, so shall your strength be."

That's a verse for you too. As we face a new year, none of us knows the challenges ahead. But as a believer, you have the strength of God in you just waiting to be made manifest in your life.

He gives strength for each new day. "The God of Israel is He who gives strength and power to His people. Blessed be God!" (Psalm 68:35). In Him, you will find strength for today and hope for tomorrow.

About the Author

David Jeremiah is the founder of Turning Point, an international ministry committed to providing Christians with sound Bible teaching through radio and television, the Internet, live events, and resource materials and books. He is the author of more than fifty books including *Is This the End? The Spiritual Warfare Answer Book*, *The David Jeremiah Morning and Evening Devotional*, and *Airship Genesis Kids Study Bible*.

David serves as the senior pastor of Shadow Mountain Community Church in San Diego, California, where he resides with his wife, Donna. They have four grown children and twelve grandchildren.

NOTES

JANUARY

1. Lee Roberson, *Touching Heaven* (Murfreesboro, TN: Sword of the Lord, 1994), 116–17.
2. John Piper, *Desiring God* (Colorado Springs: Multnomah WaterBrook, 2003), 170.

FEBRUARY

1. Joel A. Carpenter, *Revive Us Again* (New York: Oxford University Press, 1997), 82.
2. *A Dictionary of American Proverbs* (New York: Oxford University Press, 1992).
3. The Gideons International, "From the Inside Out," Gideons. org, September 12, 2014, http://blog.gideons.org/2014/09/ from-the-inside-out/.
4. Stewart M. Green and Ian Spencer-Green, *Rock Climbing* (Augusta, GA: Morris, 2010), 7.

MARCH

1. Cath Martin, "Evangelicals Admit Struggling to Find Time for Daily Bible Reading and Prayer," *Christianity Today*, April 14, 2014, https://www.christiantoday.com/article/daily.bible.reading. and.prayer.is.a.struggle.for.many.evangelicals/36765.htm.
2. Tony Evans, *The Grace of God* (Chicago: Moody, 2004), 12.

APRIL

1. Quoted by Lillian Eichler Watson in *Light from Many Lamps* (New York: Simon & Schuster, 1951), 24–32.

JUNE

1. Margaret J. Wheatley, *Finding Our Way* (San Francisco: Berrett-Koehler, 2007), 275.
2. Kay Warren, *Choose Joy* (Grand Rapids: Revell, 2012).
3. "Girl Scouts Help Catch Supermarket Thieves," *NewDay* (CNN blog), March 14, 2014, http://newday.blogs.cnn.com/2014/03/14/girl-scouts-help-catch-supermarket-thieves/.

JULY

1. Reuben Gold Thwaites, *Daniel Boone* (New York: Appleton, 1903), 237.

AUGUST

1. *(Toronto) Daily Mail and Empire,* December 28, 1900, 1.
2. T. Herbert Bindley, *St. Cyprian on the Lord's Prayer: An English Translation with Introduction* (London: Society for Promoting Christian Knowledge, 1904), 25.

SEPTEMBER

1. Elahe Izadi, "The Powerful Words of Forgiveness Delivered to Dylann Roof by Victims' Relatives," *Washington Post*, June 19, 2015, https://www.washingtonpost.com/news/post-nation/wp/2015/06/19/hate-wont-win-the-powerful-words-delivered-to-dylann-roof-by-victims-relatives/?utm_term=.7f620fb65766.

December

1. Robert J. Morgan, "A Blue Danube Christmas," in *12 Stories of Christmas* (Nashville: Thomas Nelson, 2014), 171.
2. Evelyn Adamson, "Nativity Set Maker in Asia Begins Learning the Real Story," *Baptist Press*, November 1, 2013.

Notes

NOTES

NOTES

NOTES

NOTES

NOTES

NOTES

NOTES